IN SEARCH OF
THE HISTORICAL JESUS

In Search of
the Historical Jesus

◇◇◇◇ EDITED BY HARVEY K. McARTHUR

CHARLES SCRIBNER'S SONS · NEW YORK

5791113151719 **V/C** 201816141210864

Printed in the United States of America

SBN 684-41360-4

Library of Congress Catalog Card Number 69-11956

Scribner Source Books in Religion

FOR every topic worthy of consideration there are generally several alternative positions possible, each with its
own conviction and its own ramifications. Through the examination of various views this series presents significant
scholarship to engage the reader, inform him of the problem, and suggest various viewpoints by which he may
come to a clearer understanding of his own position. The
individual editors are authorities in their field. The topics
are of importance not only to students of theology, but
to those in other disciplines as well. Theological considerations are not isolated from the examination of the total man.
Hopefully these books will be useful in the innumerable
segments of man's intellectual endeavors.

The individual selections have not been altered for the
sake of stylistic conformity such as in spelling or punctua-
tion. This was prompted by a desire to maintain the feeling and style of the authors.

PREFACE

JESUS of Nazareth is the focal point of faith for the Christian community, and for western culture generally he remains a figure of central significance. With the rise of new forms of historiography in the nineteenth century, however, the "historical Jesus" became a problem both for the believing community and for secular historians. During the past few generations whole libraries of books dealing with this problem could have been amassed.

The purpose of this anthology is to provide an introduction to the current discussion concerning the historical Jesus. Why is there a problem? What are the various views concerning the sources and the methods for using those sources? What are the results of the research? How are the results of technical research related to the faith-affirmations of the Christian community?

It should be noted that the primary concern of this anthology is with the *historical* question. In theological circles today there is a further question which is the source of much controversy, namely, the question of "demythologizing," i.e., the translation of first-century stories about supernatural beings and events into modern categories. Is such translation necessary, and, if so, how is it to be carried out? This is essentially a theological and philosophical problem rather than the strictly historical question with which this study is concerned. The distinction may be illustrated rather easily. The Gospels imply that Jesus identified himself by the use of the somewhat mysterious title "Son of Man." We are in the strictly historical area when we ask: what was the first-century meaning of the title "Son of Man"? Was the term as used by Jesus a self-designation or did it originally refer to someone else? On the other hand, after these historical questions have been answered (if they can be answered) it is still necessary to ask the philosophical-theological question: can or must the phrase be translated into other categories in order to be meaningful to a twentieth-century man? If so, what are the possible alternatives? While these two levels of discourse are separable they are seldom wholly distinct. Thus it is possible to insist that a researcher has not really understood what "Son of Man" meant in the first century until he has discovered a twentieth-century equivalent. Without some such equivalent, it may be argued, he knows the term "Son of Man" only from the outside, i.e., he does not yet appreciate what it really meant to a first-century audience. In view of the necessary limitations of space this anthology centers on the logically prior question, the strictly historical. Yet there will be occasional reference to the more ultimate question, particularly in part two, "The New Historiography," and part four, "Historical Uncertainty and Christian Faith."

Certain principles have guided the editor in the frustrating task of selecting and eliminating items. *First,* an effort has been made to include a representatively broad spectrum of views. Two extremes have been omitted on the ground that they are not serious participants in the current conversations: the extreme "left" which has denied that there ever was a historical Jesus; and the extreme "right" which continues to reject the methods of historiography which have emerged in the last two centuries. Otherwise a wide diversity is presented and the editor has attempted to ignore his own predilections. *Second,* every effort has been made to introduce the reader to major figures in the midtwentieth-century discussion. Fortunately most of the leading European scholars have been translated into English, and so samples of their work and views are available. (Excerpts have been taken only from materials available in English.) *Third,* it has been necessary to select statements which are complete within a relatively brief number of pages. Sometimes the most important author on a given problem has written nothing which lends itself to brief quotation; then it has been necessary to quote some other representative of that position.

The limitations of this anthology which are most obvious to the editor are chiefly those which plague all anthologies, namely, the number of the selections must be limited, and the selections themselves are too fragmentary. It is hoped that they may, nevertheless, serve to introduce the novice to contemporary thinking concerning the historical Jesus. In addition to a bibliography of the materials from which the quotations are made there is, on pages 285–286 a list of comparatively recent "Lives" of Jesus. This will assist the reader who wishes to go beyond the samples provided in the anthology. The herculean task of listing monographs or special studies on details of the question has not been attempted.

A warning must be given to any who use this study without having had previous orientation in the field. The Introduction is intended to provide the necessary, minimal background for the individual passages. Without reading the relevant section of the Introduction the novice may fail to grasp the significance of a particular selection, or, what is worse, he may misunderstand its significance.

It only remains for the editor to express his appreciation to Father Raymond E. Brown of St. Mary's Seminary, Baltimore, for his comments about Catholic scholarship in this field. He is, of course, in no way responsible for the selections made or for the opinions expressed concerning them. It has not been possible to include as many extracts from Catholic or Jewish scholars as might have been desired. The Appendix to the Introduction (pp. 19f.), "Jewish and Roman Catholic Scholarship," provides a little further information.

CONTENTS

Preface   vii

INTRODUCTION   3

  A. A Brief Sketch of Earlier Scholarship   3

  B. The Synoptic Gospels as Sources: Three Options   7

  C. The Fourth Gospel as a Source   9

  D. The Chronology of the Gospels   10

  E. Non-Canonical Materials as Controls for the Gospels   11

  F. Criteria of Authenticity   13

  G. The Emergence of a New Historiography   14

  H. The Results of Research: "Lives" of Jesus   15

  I. Historical Uncertainty and Christian Faith   16

  J. Appendix: Jewish and Roman Catholic Scholarship   19

PART I / THE GOSPELS AS SOURCES

VARIOUS VIEWS ON THE SYNOPTICS

SUBSTANTIAL EYEWITNESS MATERIAL

1. Thomas W. Manson, *Studies in the Gospels and Epistles*   23

PROFESSIONALLY TRANSMITTED ORAL TRADITION

2. Birger Gerhardsson, *Memory and Manuscript*   33

ANONYMOUS ORAL TRADITION REFLECTING
THE COMMUNITY'S FAITH

3. Gunther Bornkamm, *Faith and History in the Gospels*   41

OTHER COMMENTS

4. X. Leon-Dufour, *The Synoptic Gospels*   54

5. A. Wikenhauser, *Assessment of Form Criticism*   68

6. Vincent Taylor, *The Historical Value of the Gospel Tradition*   74

THE FOURTH GOSPEL AS A SOURCE

7. C. H. Dodd, *Some Considerations upon the Historical Aspect of the Fourth Gospel*   82

8.   Charles K. Barrett, *The Gospel According to St. John*   93

9.   Reginald H. Fuller, *The New Testament in Current Study*   97

10. Raymond E. Brown, *The Value of John in Reconstructing Jesus' Ministry*   103

     THE CHRONOLOGY OF THE GOSPELS

11. C. H. Dodd, *The Framework of the Gospel Narrative*   109

     NON-CANONICAL MATERIALS AS CONTROLS FOR THE GOSPELS

12. Ethelbert Stauffer, *Jesus and His Story*   119

13. Joachim Jeremias, *The Problem of the Historical Jesus*   125

     CRITERIA OF AUTHENTICITY

14. N. A. Dahl, *The Problem of the Historical Jesus*   131

15. Harvey K. McArthur, *Basic Issues, A Survey of Recent Gospel Research*   139

PART II / THE NEW HISTORIOGRAPHY

16. Rudolf Bultmann, *View-Point and Method*   147

17. James M. Robinson, *A New Concept of History and the Self*   153

PART III / THE RESULTS OF RESEARCH, "LIVES" OF JESUS

     MINIMAL "LIVES"

18. Rudolf Bultmann, *The Primitive Christian Kerygma and the Historical Jesus*   161

19. Gunther Bornkamm, *Jesus of Nazareth*   164

20. Reginald H. Fuller, *The New Testament in Current Study*   174

21. Samuel Sandmel, *We Jews and Jesus*   184

     MAXIMAL "LIVES"

22. Vincent Taylor, *The Mission of the Twelve*   194

23. Ethelbert Stauffer, *Jesus and His Story*   201

PART IV / HISTORICAL UNCERTAINTY AND
              CHRISTIAN FAITH

HISTORICAL UNCERTAINTY ACCEPTED

24. Rudolf Bultmann, *Jesus and the Word*   209

25. Van A. Harvey, *Symbol, Event, and Once-for-Allness*   211

26. Paul Tillich, *The Reality of the Christ*   219

HISTORICAL UNCERTAINTY REJECTED

27. Joachim Jeremias, *The Good News of Jesus and the
     Proclamation of the Early Church*   229

28. John Knox, *The Church and the Reality of Christ*   232

29. James S. Stewart, *The Christ of Faith*   245

30. Oscar Cullmann, *Out of Season Remarks on the "His-
     torical Jesus" of The Bultmann School*   259

Bibliography

A. MATERIALS USED IN THE ANTHOLOGY   281

B. ADDITIONAL RECENT FULL SCALE STUDIES OF JESUS   283

IN SEARCH OF
THE HISTORICAL JESUS

INTRODUCTION

A. A BRIEF SKETCH OF EARLIER SCHOLARSHIP

The four Gospels were probably written during the second half of the first century of the Christian era. During this same period other works were produced which purported to portray aspects of the life of Jesus, and this type of literature has continued to emerge through the centuries. By the end of the second century, however, the major centers of the Christian Church were in agreement that the four Gospels now in the New Testament should be regarded as the normative presentations of the life of Jesus. It was assumed by the Church that two of the Evangelists (Matthew and John) had themselves been among the original disciples of Jesus and thus were eyewitnesses of the ministry, while the other two were regarded as close associates of the earliest disciples. Mark was regarded as an aide of the Apostle Peter whose preaching he reproduced; Luke was identified with Paul's one-time companion, "the beloved physician," who would have had contact with the original eyewitnesses in his travels. It was also assumed that the four Gospels had been written independently of one another, and thus their agreements corroborated their general accuracy. Granting these assumptions there was little reason to expect any serious difficulty in reconstructing the historical life of Jesus. There was recognition of the need to harmonize the four Gospel accounts (see Tatian's *Diatessaron* from about 170 A.D.); and some Church Fathers dealt extensively with the minor differences in the Gospel narratives (see Origen, *Commentary on John,* Bk.X; and Augustine, *The Harmonization of the Gospels*). But historical questions were subordinated to theological and devotional interests, and they were further blurred by the emergence of the four-fold view of Scripture, i.e., the belief that any given passage might have four meanings: the literal or historical plus the three symbolic meanings (tropological or moral, allegorical, anagogical).

With the beginning of the modern period, however, historical questions reasserted themselves as is indicated, for example, by the sudden flood of Catholic and Protestant Gospel Harmonies in the sixteenth century. Yet the modern quest of the historical Jesus did not really begin until the end of the eighteenth century. It was

3

assisted in its birth by the growing specialization of knowledge, by the emergence of new and stricter forms of historiography, and by the widespread rebellion of the academic disciplines against the theological control exercised by the Church.

The eighteenth century, with its Rationalism, raised a host of questions about the historical Jesus and his relation to the theological systems which had emerged. But it was not until the nineteenth century that intense preoccupation with the problems of historiography developed. It was recognized that the key issue in all historical research is the evaluation of the available sources. It was recognized, further, that the Gospels, and not the Epistles of the New Testament or the Creeds, should be used as the sources for the reconstruction of the life of Jesus. There followed then a narrowing down of the sources which were to be accepted as primary for this task. First, the four Gospels. Then the four were reduced to three as John was set aside on the grounds that it was theological interpretation presented as history. After attention had focussed on the Synoptic Gospels (Matthew, Mark, and Luke) for a time it was agreed that they were not independent of one another as had previously been assumed. By the end of the nineteenth century there was a general concensus that Mark was the earliest of the three and that it had been used as a source both by Matthew and by Luke. It was widely agreed, also, that Matthew and Luke had in addition each used a source containing a collection of the sayings of Jesus. This hypothetical source acquired the name "Q" (presumably from the German word *Quelle*, i.e., "source"). Since Matthew and Luke contained materials which had no parallels in the other Gospels the terms "M" and "L" were used to designate the material distinctive of Matthew and Luke respectively. (It should be noted that some scholars used these same symbols to denote not all of the unique *material* in Matthew or Luke but rather certain hypothetical *documents* which were thought to stand behind a portion of this special material in each Gospel.)

Thus at the beginning of the twentieth century there was widespread agreement that Mark provided the basic source for an outline of Jesus' ministry, while "Q" was the earliest version of his teaching. The other sources were generally regarded as later and less reliable. "Q" was dated about 50 A.D., Mark just before or after 70 A.D., with "M" and "L" reflecting later traditions. There was a minority of scholars who doubted the existence of "Q," arguing that Luke had used Mark and Matthew. This view continues to be held by some scholars and, of recent years, even the priority of Mark has been challenged. But the priority of Mark and the existence of "Q" continue to be the basic presuppositions for most work on the Gospels today.

It was on the basis of the above analysis of the sources that Protestant scholars wrote their "Lives" of Jesus at the turn of the century. It is true that there was a very conservative group of scholars who wrote as if nineteenth century scholarship did not exist. This latter group was determined to demonstrate that the historical Jesus was identical with the ecclesiastical image of the Christ, while some in the mainstream of Protestant scholarship seemed determined to demonstrate that he had been totally other than that image. In retrospect it is evident that the scholars, whether conservative or radical, tended to portray Jesus in colors drawn from their own theological palettes. Thus the "liberals" tended to eliminate the miraculous elements in the Gospels regardless of the sources in which they appeared. It should be noted, also, that there were considerable differences between the individual "Lives" produced by scholars even of the same general tradition—a fact which suggests either that the sources were not adequate or that the scholars added too much of their own imaginings. Broadly speaking the liberal tradition, using Mark as a base, portrayed the ministry of Jesus as falling into two parts: a successful ministry in Galilee ("the Galilean springtime"), then a somber ministry in Jerusalem leading to the final confrontation and crucifixion.

Developments in the twentieth century may be summarized under three headings. *First,* there emerged the conviction (Wrede) that even the earliest Gospel (Mark) was not a simple historical narrative but was impregnated with the theological interpretation of the Christian community. This conviction led in two directions: it led to the affirmation of the inadequacy of Mark as a source for the actual career of Jesus; and it led, more positively, to the affirmation that from the beginning the believing community was concerned to proclaim its *kerygma* (i.e., message), and that this *kerygma* revealed the significance of the ministry of Jesus for that community even though not primarily concerned with "facts" in the ordinary sense of that term.

Second, there was the rediscovery of the eschatological element in the Gospel tradition, i.e., that the message of Jesus was closely linked with his views about the coming of the Kingdom and the end of history (Weiss, Schweitzer, Dodd). The stress on eschatology created a gulf between the historical Jesus and the modern man since the latter does not easily think in terms of a catastrophic and imminent end of the world (although events of the mid-twentieth century have made such expectations more intelligible). The past generation has been marked by various reevaluations of the eschatological element in the Gospel tradition, though it is not always clear whether these reevaluations are primarily attempts to comprehend the historical Jesus or attempts to make eschatological concepts palatable to moderns.

Third, there was the emergence of the movement known as Form Criticism (Schmidt, Dibelius, Bultmann). This approach to the Synoptic Gospels accepted the previously established conclusions about them but attempted to deal with the so-called "tunnel period," the period before the emergence of the written tradition. At the risk of vast over-simplification the following four statements may be made about the Form Critics. The Form Critics agree

a. that during the first Christian generation the stories about Jesus circulated in oral form,
b. that during this period there was no continuous narrative but instead single, isolated stories (the Passion Narrative was the earliest portion of the tradition to acquire consecutive form),
c. that the stories were repeated in response to the various needs of the community, e.g., preaching, teaching, controversy, ethical guidance,
d. that as the stories were told they tended to fall into certain stereotyped patterns, or forms, characteristic of oral tradition.

While the name of the movement is derived from item "d" above, this may be the least important aspect of Form Criticism as far as the question of the historical Jesus is concerned. A careful consideration of the first three items indicates that if they are correct the material in the Gospels is the written precipitate of an anonymous, oral tradition, in which each item was repeated many times by unknown persons and *may* have been profoundly modified in response to the diverse needs of the various communities that repeated it. The radical possibility raised by this line of thought is that most of the material in the tradition may have been modified during the period of oral transmission and much of it may even have been created by the communities through which the tradition passed.

This radical possibility prepares the way for a consideration of the various ways in which the Synoptic Gospels are viewed today as sources for the reconstruction of the ministry of Jesus.

B. THE SYNOPTIC GOSPELS AS SOURCES: THREE OPTIONS
   (SEE CHAPTERS 1–6)

As previously stated, modern historiography recognizes that the question of the sources is determinative for historical research. A revolution in the understanding of the Gospels as sources occurred in the nineteenth century when it was concluded that the three Synoptic Gospels were not independent of each other. While this was a real revolution, it did not prevent historians from continuing to write "Lives" of Jesus once they had come to terms with the priority of Mark, the existence of "Q," etc. The more radical among the Form Critics, however, propose a further revolution which, if successful, would destroy the possibility of writing any full scale life of Jesus. They propose that behind the written tradition there is an anonymous, oral tradition which has passed through various Christian communities, being shaped, modified, and transformed by the situations through which it passed. There is a wide diversity of response to this radical skepticism but, with a little arbitrariness, this diversity may be described under three groupings.

First, there are those who purport to refute the more radical versions of Form Criticism by contending that the Synoptics can be shown to contain substantial amounts of basically eyewitness material. If this is correct then the skepticism of the more radical Form Critics is unjustified since that skepticism is based on the assumption of a wide gulf between the eyewitnesses and our present Gospels. According to the ecclesiastical tradition the Gospel of Matthew was the only one of the Synoptics by an actual eyewitness. Today very few scholars accept this tradition (although some Catholic scholars defend a modified version of it, namely, that our Greek Matthew is a version of an original Aramaic Gospel actually written by the Apostle Matthew). The earliest tradition about Mark's Gospel, however, asserts that Mark was an assistant of the Apostle Peter and that he repeated the reminiscences of Peter in this Gospel. (See

Eusebius *Ecclesiastical History*, III, 39:15, for the quotation from Papias who wrote about 140 A.D.) In so far as Mark contains the reminiscences of Peter it may be said to contain substantial, eyewitness material. The excerpt from Professor Thomas W. Manson in chapter 1 presents his argument that it is possible to identify the Petrine material in Mark. He also argues that the Apostle Matthew, while he was not the author of the Gospel which bears his name, was the author of the "Q" document which was later incorporated both into Matthew and Luke. If Manson's argument is valid then there is substantial eyewitness material both in Mark and in "Q," and this would be sufficient to provide a solid base for a relatively detailed reconstruction of the ministry of Jesus.

Second, there are those who accept the contention of the Form Critics that the Gospel tradition passed through a period of oral transmission. They insist, however, that the Christian community exercised careful control over the development of this oral tradition. They understand developments in the Christian community to have paralleled those in the Jewish Rabbinic community where the handing on of an oral tradition was a professional, carefully controlled operation. This stress has been characteristic of the Scandinavian scholars (see Gerghardsson, chapter 2), but it is supported at least in part by those who insist that the eyewitnesses who were alive during the generation of the oral tradition must have had a sobering effect on the transmittors of the tradition. Thus, they argue, radical modification or free invention would not have been a possibility. Those who reject this approach reply that the Rabbinic techniques for handing on oral tradition were at an early stage in the first century, and that the Christian movement was essentially a lay movement as against the more professional, scholastic pattern of the Rabbinic tradition. They say, furthermore, the divergences between John and the Synoptics make it clear that there was no effective control of the oral tradition.

Third, there are those who accept the contention of the Form Critics that the Gospels contain the products of an anonymous, oral tradition. There are differences of opinion within this group as to the extent to which this presupposition undermines confidence in the factual accuracy of the incidents and conversations reported in the tradition. Bultmann represents a radical position, while Bornkamm (see chapter 3) is typical of the moderate Form Critics. Most of those in this group would want to stress that while oral tradition is notoriously inaccurate about bare facts it does tend to reflect, in its own way, the central significance of the person around whom it has been gathered.

In view of the importance of the Synoptics as sources, excerpts are included from three other scholars, two of them Catholics (see chapters 4 and 5), and the third a British scholar (see chapter 6) who utilizes Form Criticism but rejects the skepticism which characterizes some of its proponents.

C. THE FOURTH GOSPEL AS A SOURCE (SEE CHAPTERS 7–10)

For over a century, i.e., since Strauss, the advance guard of New Testament scholarship has taken for granted that the Gospel of John could be ignored as a source for the ministry of Jesus. This conclusion was based on the radical differences between John and the earlier Synoptics, and also on the conviction that John's Gospel reflected the Hellenistic world. It was generally held that the Gospel was not by John the Apostle and that it might not have been written until after the turn of the century. During the past generation the alleged gulf between John and the Synoptics has narrowed, partly because the Synoptics are now believed to contain theological interpretation as well as John. The discoveries at Qumran have convinced some scholars that the Fourth Gospel is predominantly "Jewish" in tone and not Hellenistic. Unanimity on this subject is not likely in the near future, yet there is need for a clear decision by anyone who attempts to reconstruct the ministry of Jesus since John differs too radically from the Synoptics for a compromise to be satisfactory. It may be helpful to chart some of the more obvious differences.

	Synoptics	*John*
1. Beginning of Ministry	After the arrest of John the Baptist, Mark 1:14	During John's Ministry, John 1–4
2. Length of Ministry	Only 1 Passover, i.e., only 1 year, Mk.14:1ff.	3 Passovers explicitly, John 2:13, 6:4, 12:1
3. Locale of Ministry	Chiefly Galilee and north, except for final "week"	Back and forth between Judea and Galilee

	Synoptics	*John*
4. End of Ministry	Last Supper was Passover, Mark 14	Last Supper *before* the Passover, John 13:1, 18:28
5. Focus of Ministry	Kingdom of God	Eternal life as present result of response to Jesus
6. Controversies	Interpretation of the Law	Attitude toward Jesus
7. Messianic Question	Messianic secret—not generally discussed	Public Messianic claim from John 1 onward
8. Manner of Teaching	Parables, brief aphorisms	Allegories, extended discourses
9. Temple Cleansing	At end of ministry, Mark 11:15ff.	At beginning of ministry, John 2:13ff.
10. Role of Jesus	Proclaimer of the Kingdom of God's will	The Son sent by the Father

Some of the differences indicated above are incidental and external. This is not true, however, of items 5, 6, 7, and 10. Thus, for example, two radically different views of the ministry emerge depending on whether one denies or affirms that throughout his ministry Jesus was proclaimed as the Messiah and claimed a unique relationship with God. Perhaps the current trend is to insist that there is more history in John than was believed a generation ago, but scholars continue to be cautious about determining precisely which elements are historical. The scholars quoted in chapters 7 to 10 are typical of the mainstream today.

D. THE CHRONOLOGY OF THE GOSPELS (SEE CHAPTER 11)

Of the four Gospels it is Luke that displays the most interest in chronology. Thus there are important chronological notes in Luke 1:5, 2:1f., 3:1f., and 3:23. Even if these are accepted as strictly accurate they still do not allow us to do more than to state that the birth of Jesus occurred before 4 B.C. and that his ministry must have begun about 28 A.D. If the Gospels agreed as to the day of the week on which the final Passover occurred, and if it could be assumed that the date of the Passover was set by astronomical calculation rather than by observation, and if there were no question of an occasional intercalary month in the Jewish calendar, it would be possible to determine year and date of the crucifixion. But these variables make all such calculations highly speculative. It is equally difficult to determine the length of the ministry since the Synoptics refer to one Passover only (suggesting a ministry of less than one year), while John mentions three explicitly (John 2:13, 6:4, 12:1) and there is a possible allusion to a fourth (John 5:1). In fact there is considerable question as to the seriousness of the Evangelists' interest in such chronological matters.

But what about the sequence of events within the ministry? If the Form Critics are correct the original units of the tradition were circulated without chronological links and it could be that the ostensibly chronological arrangement in the Gospels is wholly artificial, or has been developed on principles other than that of historicity. For example, it has been argued that liturgical considerations influenced the sequence in which the narratives were arranged in Mark and in John. Perhaps the most famous attempt to reassert the validity of the basic Marcan sequence (which presumably was utilized by Matthew and possibly Luke) appeared in an article by C. H. Dodd (see chapter 11). A critique of his view is cited in the introduction to that article.

Our understanding of the historical Jesus would not be greatly affected by the discovery that his ministry centered around 33 A.D. instead of 30 or 28, or that it lasted less than a year instead of the traditional three years. But the question of the sequence of events within the ministry is significant for modern historiography since it assumes that a knowledge of such sequence is essential to the understanding of the development of a movement or a personality. Something may be known of a person by isolated, impressionistic images, but the full story, it is alleged, requires a knowledge of the historical development.

E. NON-CANONICAL MATERIALS AS CONTROLS FOR THE GOSPELS (SEE CHAPTERS 12–13)

There are three possible sources of direct information about Jesus outside of the canonical writings. *First,* there are the classical Greek and Roman historians. Unfortunately they ignored the Christian movement as unworthy of consideration and, in their writings, there are only a few passing references to Jesus (cf. Pliny the Younger,

Epistle 10; Tacitus, *Annals* XV, 44; Suetonius, *Claudius* 25; Josephus, *Antiquities* XVIII, 3:3; XX, 9:1). These scattered references are useful in the discussion with those eccentrics who deny even the existence of Jesus but they provide no real information concerning his career. *Second,* there are a larger number of references in Jewish literature. These have been carefully examined and it is probable that most of them are responses to the Christian community rather than expressions of an independent historical memory of Jesus (cf. J. Klausner, *Jesus of Nazareth,* pp. 18–54; M. Goguel, *The Life of Jesus,* pp. 70–74). Those that may be early provide some information about his death, his gathering of disciples, and the accusation of sorcery brought against him. *Third,* there is the extensive literature of the apocryphal Gospels, i.e., those Gospels which deal with the life of Jesus, or some aspect of that life, but which did not win general approval in the Church. Some of these may even have been from the first century, but, unfortunately, it is precisely these earliest apocryphal Gospels which we know only through fragments quoted by later writers. A more extensive literature of this type developed during the second and third centuries and, as a matter of fact, has continued down to the present time. In general these are products of popular piety and imagination lacking any serious historical base. A few, such as the recently discovered Coptic *Gospel of Thomas,* may well contain some early traditions about Jesus but it is even more difficult to separate these elements from later accretions than in the case of the Synoptics. So it remains true that the Synoptic Gospels, and possibly John, are the most important sources for the life of Jesus.

The previous paragraph has dealt with materials which refer *directly* to Jesus. Materials from outside the New Testament which contain no explicit reference to Jesus may, however, also be useful in so far as they provide a picture of the general situation in Palestine about 30 A.D. The more complete our knowledge is of this period the more easily we may determine which narratives in the Gospel tradition "fit" into that pattern and which, on the contrary, reflect a somewhat different cultural or historical situation. Stories in the latter category are, presumably, not strictly historical—at least not in their present form. On the other hand stories which "fit" the original milieu are not necessarily authentic. They could be the products of the earliest Palestinian Christian community. Yet clearly the non-canonical materials may serve as one norm for testing the authenticity of incidents recorded in the Gospels. By way of warning it should be added that while it is easy to talk about materials that reflect the situation in Palestine about 30 A.D., in actual fact we are to a considerable extent dependent on sources which took written form at a somewhat later date, e.g., the Rabbinic literature. The peculiar importance of the Dead Sea Scrolls is that they are probably from the time of Jesus and the immediately preceding generations. Experts in first century Judaism and Aramaic studies differ in the ways in which they utilize these sources. Ethelbert Stauffer has used them with great boldness and appears confident that he can authenticate much in the Gospels by demonstrating the conformity of the material with patterns which he regards as characteristic of the Palestinian situation (chapters 12 and 23). Many other New Testament scholars feel that Stauffer's position is extreme and that the non-canonical materials cannot demonstrate so definitely the historicity of Gospel narratives. Joachim Jeremias has made more cautious claims for the use of non-canonical materials and his approach is illustrated also (chapter 13). His discussions of *abba* (Father) and *amen* are particularly instructive.

F. CRITERIA OF AUTHENTICITY (SEE CHAPTERS 14–15)

Historical criticism, whether applied to the Gospels or to some other body of literature, is an art and not a science. Nevertheless among those who have engaged in the historical study of the Gospels there is some agreement concerning criteria which assist in determining authenticity. Unfortunately these criteria are not absolutes but represent tendencies, that is, one can say that other things being equal the application of this criterion indicates that item A is more apt to be authentic than item B. While all those involved in Gospel research use criteria of authenticity it is a regrettable fact that they seldom collect these into a single brief article, perhaps because a brief statement necessarily involves oversimplification. It is for this reason that the editor has included an extract from one of his writings (chapter 15) as well as the selection from N. A. Dahl (chapter 14). The reader's attention is also called to a selection relevant to this topic which has not been included here, Norman Perrin's *Rediscovering the Teaching of Jesus* (New York, 1967).

The novice must be warned that while it is relatively easy to draw up a list of criteria, only long practise makes possible the intelligent use of these same criteria. The cynic may suggest that in actual fact long experience merely inflates one's self-confidence without actually making the use of the tools more expert. Such cynicism is probably exaggerated.

G. THE EMERGENCE OF A NEW HISTORIOGRAPHY (SEE CHAPTERS 16–17)

The historiography which emerged so significantly during the nineteenth century was concerned with facts. According to the often quoted phrase of Leopold von Ranke, it is the historian's business to discover "how it actually happened." In its original setting this phrase was not a boast but rather a limitation of the task of the historian. It was his task to know the actual facts, the literal events; the interpretation of these facts could be left to philosophers, theologians, or others. This methodology tended to equate historiography with the natural sciences and it was remarkably successful in uncovering certain of the dimensions of history.

Despite the manifest success of this form of historiography, by the end of the nineteenth century there were those who raised questions concerning the adequacy of the approach (Dilthey, Collingwood). These questions have continued down to our own generation, and we live in an era of vigorous dispute concerning the method and function of the historian. Perhaps the problem may be summarized most simply by stating that it concerns the role of the subject in the historical process, in historical research, and in historical understanding. One dimension of history is clearly "how it actually happened"; but another dimension is what those happenings meant to those involved with them, what they meant to those who came afterwards, and what they mean, or may mean, today to those who consider them. It is evident that this new emphasis, which was never totally absent from nineteenth century historiography, has a real place in historical understanding, but it is equally evident that it creates a nest of new problems. If one distinguishes between "external history" and "internal history" then, when sufficient evidence is available, it should be possible for all historians to agree on the "external history"; but can there ever be agreement concerning the "internal history"?

In German theological circles two terms for "history" have been differentiated so that one connotes the tangible, external happening, while the other expresses the meaning or significance which the events are alleged to carry. The term for external history is *Historie* (adjective: *historisch*); while the designation for meaning or significance is *Geschichte* (adjective: *geschichtlich*). The distinction is a useful one, but it is not yet clear what the precise relation is between *Historie* and *Geschichte* or what the rules are for determining *Geschichte*.

While these problems are of significance for all historical research they are of particular interest to those concerned with discovering the historical Jesus. If the sources do not provide a solid base for research into the *Historie* is it possible that they may nevertheless provide what is needed for *Geschichte*? Since the Evangelists may not have been as much concerned with "how it actually happened" as with "what it really meant" is it possible that their message will come through more clearly when approached from this perspective? Both Rudolf Bultmann and James M. Robinson (chapters 16 and 17) are concerned with this new historiography, Bultmann arguing that we encounter the significance in the *kerygma* and Robinson contending that through the new method it is possible to reach back to the intention of the historical Jesus himself.

H. THE RESULTS OF RESEARCH: "LIVES" OF JESUS (SEE CHAPTERS 18–23)

The evaluation of the Gospels as sources is not an end in itself but only the indispensable preliminary work for the construction of a "Life" of Jesus. The writing of a "Life," however, presupposes the determination of the sequence of events within the life-span of the individual under consideration. Some of the evaluations of the Gospels as sources already considered (the more radical of the Form Critics, for example), exclude the possibility of assuming that the Gospels provide valid information concerning the sequence of events in Jesus' ministry. Furthermore they suggest that only a minimum of the recorded incidents are history in the ordinary sense of that term. This does not eliminate the possibility of a partial portrait of the figure behind the Gospels, but it does exclude the possibility of a true "Life" in the conventional sense. "Lives" of Jesus may be classified in accord with their response to these radical conclusions.

For convenience, the excerpts from various "Lives" are classified under two headings, "Minimal Lives" and "Maximal Lives." In the former group are represented authors who stress the veiled character of the historical Jesus and who produce at best an impressionistic sketch of the one believed to stand behind the Gospel tradition. In the latter group are those who affirm more confidently the possibility of establishing both the general sequence of events and the authenticity of many details. Obviously there are also scholars who stand all along the line between these two extremes. The reader will note that of the scholars excerpted, Bultmann (chapter 18) displays the greatest historical skepticism, while Stauffer (chapter 23) evidences the greatest confidence in the reconstruction of the "Life" of Jesus. There are, of course, other "Lives" which are more conservative than that of Stauffer. Some of them, without the use of any clear historical method, simply rearrange the incidents recorded in the Gospels and tell the story with colors provided either from the historical background or the piety of the writer. Stauffer has been used as an illustration, however, because he utilizes the techniques of historical criticism but arrives at a surprisingly traditional result. Taylor's "Life" (chapter 22) is less conservative than that of Stauffer and represents a typical British middle-of-the-road approach.

An anthology faces an acute problem when excerpting "Lives" of Jesus. It is possible to give a fairly complete picture of what Bultmann (chapter 18) or Bornkamm (chapter 19) would affirm about the historical Jesus—since they do not affirm a great deal! It is impossible, however, to include the entire statement of a Stauffer (chapter 23) or a Taylor (chapter 22). The procedure followed here has been to take one or two incidents out of the total "Life" illustrating the way the particular scholar proceeds. Nothing more can be done within the limits of an anthology.

I. HISTORICAL UNCERTAINTY AND CHRISTIAN FAITH (SEE CHAPTERS 25–30)

Thus far attention has been concentrated on the strictly historical problem, what the historian can affirm about the earthly career of Jesus from Nazareth. In Western culture, however, Jesus has been not simply a historical figure but also a focus for theological faith. While it has long been recognized that history and theology are not identical, the precise relationship between the two has been brought into question in a new way by the radical character of some Gospel research. If the results of historical investigation are ambiguous, or at best probability results, can they serve as the base for theological affirmations? Or, are theological affirmations in some sense independent of historical research? In a certain sense the Chalcedonian definition that Jesus was "truly God and truly man . . . in two natures, without confusion, without change, without division, without separation" (451 A.D.) was an attempt to relate the visible, historical figure, and the theological meaning. But the historical skepticism which permeates a substantial portion of New Testament scholarship today introduces new dimensions into the discussion.

The radical form which this problem has taken in the twentieth century is too new for a generally acceptable conclusion yet to have emerged. For convenience the conflicting views may be classified in two groups: on the one hand there are those who accept historical uncertainty so that, for them, historical research cannot affect the theological affirmations which they make (chapters 24–26); on the other hand there are those who are dissatisfied with historical uncertainty and who insist that affirmations about literal history are inherent in the Christian faith (chapters 27–30). The contrast has here been stated in its bluntest form and may require some modification. Thus even those who are most dubious about historical certainty usually insist that it is theologically important that there actually was a historical Jesus! To use the phrase popularized by Bultmann they insist on the *that* of Jesus but not on the *what;* it is essential, that is, for their theological affirmations that Jesus was not a myth but a person and the one standing behind the Gospel portraits, but the details of his life are no longer crucial, not even the details associated with the "Resurrection." On the opposite side those who insist that specific affirmations about historical aspects of Jesus' life are essential to Christian faith would not usually hold that all the incidents recorded in the Gospels must be regarded as literally true. Most in this group would be content to affirm that the Gospel portrait of Jesus is "substantially historical"—to use a conveniently elastic term!

While the selections in this anthology are divided into these two groups it may be helpful to identify more narrowly the logical possibilities within these groupings and also beyond their limits. The options listed below are intended to suggest the diversity of possibilities; they are not exhaustive since an almost indefinite number of positions and combinations of positions are possible.

1. Total indifference to the question of the historical Jesus. This is the perspective of those who are concerned with the Christ figure solely as a religious or ethical symbol. The symbol serves as a law, norm, guide, or challenge, and it is quite unnecessary that it should be the expression of the life of an actual, historical person.

2. Affirmation of the historical Jesus as source or presupposition of the Christian community and its *kerygma,* but indifference to the determination of the historical details of Jesus' life. The significance of the historical Jesus is carried by the community and the *kerygma* and is independent of the results of historical research into the life which gave rise to the movement.

3. Insistence that certainty about *some* historical details is essential to the Christian faith and that historical research establishes the validity of these details. Should research make these details improbable, or impossible, Christian faith would cease to be possible. The risk of faith includes the risk of being refuted by historical discoveries.

4. Insistence that certainty about *some* historical details is essential to the Christian faith, but this certainty is based on some form of faith affirmation and is finally independent of historical research. (Obviously many things are true which cannot be proved to be true by research.) Such faith affirmations might arise from one or more of several sources:

   a. A particular view of Scripture which would lift it above historical research.

   b. The authority of the Church as witness to historical as well as theological truth.

   c. The nature of the faith experience, i.e., its validity includes the historicity of certain facts.

Perhaps two further points should be made which are related to the problem of the relation between history and theological affirmations. *First,* there is increasingly widespread agreement that historical facts, even if demonstrated with certainty, do not, and of themselves cannot, demonstrate the validity of the Christian theological claims. For example, if it could be demonstrated with certainty that the Virgin Birth actually happened this would not of itself establish the traditional Christian doctrine of the Incarnation. This fact would be classified by the scientist or historian as a biological anomaly, and there would be renewed investigation of the possibility of parthenogenesis among human beings. On the other hand, while the demonstrated historicity of certain events would not establish the validity of theological affirmations, it is possible that the demonstrated non-historicity of such events would disprove the validity of those theological affirmations. Thus most New Testament scholars would agree that historical certainty about a physical resurrection of Jesus would not of itself establish the Christian claim that Jesus was the Christ. On the other hand the scholars are divided as to whether proof of the non-historicity of the physical resurrection would disprove the Christian claim. It is at this point that further clarification is needed.

It should be noted, in the *second* place, that there is inevitably a gap between what the historical Jesus actually did and said and what modern historians can prove about him. This may be expressed by saying there is a gap between the historical Jesus and the Jesus of the historians. Occasionally confusion is created by the fact that the phrase "the historical Jesus" sometimes refers to Jesus "as he actually was" and sometimes to Jesus "as the modern historian can reconstruct him." While this distinction is obvious and important, it may be objected that it serves no practical purpose to talk about Jesus "as he actually was" except in so far as that can be identified by the tools of historical research. Presumably the reply to this is that it is useful to be reminded of the limitations of the historian's craft. Furthermore it is possible that some may want to affirm out of faith what they cannot demonstrate by historical methodology. (See option 4 on page 18.)

J. APPENDIX: JEWISH AND ROMAN CATHOLIC SCHOLARSHIP

The quest for the historical Jesus has been predominantly a preoccupation of Protestant scholarship. Notable contributions, however, have been made by Jewish scholarship, and, especially in recent years, by Roman Catholic scholars.

In this anthology Jewish scholarship is represented only by the selection from Samuel Sandmel's *We Jews and Jesus* (chapter 21). His entire book is a mine of information about Jewish scholarship and Jewish attitudes toward both the historical Jesus and the theological Christ. The particular passage selected was chosen, at least in part, because it includes references to other Jewish scholars who have contributed to this field. Even the briefest list of such scholars should include Israel Abrahams, Joseph Klausner, Claude G. Montefiore, David Daube, Paul Winter, and, of course, Samuel Sandmel. Furthermore there are many Jewish scholars who have contributed indirectly to this question since research into Judaism at the beginning of the Common Era is of assistance in providing the background against which the historical Jesus must be understood.

The situation is somewhat different with respect to Roman Catholic scholarship. It did not participate in the nineteenth century quest for the historical Jesus to any significant extent, despite notable contributions in other areas. But of recent years Catholic New Testament scholarship has entered into the quest with vigor. Significant factors in this development have been the 1943 Encyclical of Pope Pius XII, *Divino Afflante Spiritu,* the competent and creative work of scholars such as Father Marie Joseph Lagrange and the Dominican Biblical School in Jerusalem, and the relaxation of the attitude toward the earlier decrees of The Pontifical Biblical Commission. Despite these promising new beginnings it may still be a few years before full scale "Lives" of Jesus appear which incorporate fully the newer trends in Catholic scholarship. Thus, somewhat surprisingly, Lagrange's *The Gospel of Jesus Christ* (1938) is relatively traditional in form despite the author's distinguished work in Gospel research. The same is true of the similar works by Leónce de Grandmaison, Jules Lebreton, and Ferdinand Prat. The more recent works of Raymond L. Bruckberger and especially Jean Steinmann reflect the increasing dialogue with the techniques of modern historiography. It must be remembered that traditional "Lives" may still be of great value, but that value is in the area of religion and edification rather than of historical research.

The three Catholic selections in this work (chapters 4, 5, 10) are illustrative of the best in current Catholic Gospel research. They represent three different countries: X. Leon-Dufour, France; A. Wikenhauser, Germany; R. E. Brown, the United States. It is not to be expected, or desired, that Catholic scholarship will follow the pattern set by Protestant research, but the interplay of new perspectives and minds on the common problems of historical research should advance our knowledge of the historical Jesus.

PART I

The Gospels as Sources

CHAPTER 1

Studies in the Gospels and Epistles

THOMAS W. MANSON

Dr. Manson, who was Rylands Professor of Biblical Criticism and Exegesis at Manchester University, died in 1958, and the present volume was published posthumously. The first half is appropriately entitled "Materials for a Life of Jesus," and contains lectures which he had given relating to this subject. The two passages quoted below present his argument that Mark contains material which can be identified as coming from the Apostle Peter, and that "Q" was written by an eyewitness of the ministry, the Apostle Matthew. Another scholar who stresses the role of eyewitnesses, though perhaps not as directly as Manson, is Bruce M. Metzger in *The New Testament, Its Background, Growth, and Content,* 1965, pp. 84–88, 96–99. See also Manson's *The Teaching of Jesus,* 2nd ed. 1935. For a critique of this stress on the role of eyewitnesses see D. E. Nineham, "Eyewitness Testimony and the Gospel Tradition" in *The Journal of Theological Studies,* new series, IX (1958), pp. 13–25, 243–252; and XI (1960), pp. 253–264.

THE upshot of all this is that Mark, from the early days of the Jerusalem community, was in touch with the Christian tradition, and had ample opportunity of learning facts about the Ministry quite apart from his association with Peter. There does not seem to be any reason why he should not have used this information in the composition of his Gospel, along with that derived from Peter, especially since, as we have already seen, the Petrine information was not a dictated continuous story, but only separate pieces or small groups gathered probably over a considerable period and recalled

From *Studies in the Gospels and Epistles,* by T. W. Manson, pp. 40–45, 75–83, edited by Matthew Black. The Westminster Press. © 1962 Mrs. Nora Manson. Used by permission.

at a later date. We should, *prima facie*, expect to find in the Gospel matter that can be called without hesitation 'Petrine'; other material which *may* be Petrine; and, again, other which there is no good reason to assign to Peter at all. That expectation is borne out when we examine the text.

In his valuable and stimulating commentary on Mark,[1] C. H. Turner drew attention to a frequently recurring phenomenon in the Gospel. He describes it thus (p. 48):

> In strong contrast to Matthew and Luke, Mark's Gospel may be called autobiographical. They write Lives of Christ, he records the experience of an eye-witness and companion. It is crucial in this respect to note the predominant use of the plural in the narrative of Mark. Time after time a sentence commences with the plural, for it is an experience which is being related, and passes into the singular, for the experience is that of discipleship to a Master. So in i. 21 'they enter Capernaum; and at once he taught on the sabbath in the synagogue'; v. 38, 'they come to Jairus's house; and he sees the tumult . . .'; ix. 33, 'and they came to Capernaum: and when he was in the house he asked them . . .'; x. 32, 'and they were on the road going up to Jerusalem, and Jesus was going on ahead of them . . .'; xi. 12, 'and on the morrow, when they had left Bethany, he hungered'; xi. 27, 'and they came again to Jerusalem: and as he was walking in the temple . . .'; xiv. 32, 'and they came to . . . Gethsemane: and he saith to his disciples . . .'. In none of these cases does either Matthew or Luke retain the plural. . . .
>
> If the reader will now take one step further and put back Mark's third person plural into the first person plural of the narrative, he will receive a vivid impression of the testimony that lies behind the Gospel: thus in i. 29, 'we came into our house with James and John: and my wife's mother was ill in bed with a fever, and at once we tell him about her.'

In his note on Mk. i. 21 (p. 54) Turner gives a list of passages in which 'Mark's third person plural may be reasonably understood as representing a first person plural of Peter's discourses.' The list is as follows: i. 21, 29; v. 1, 38; vi. 53, 54; viii. 22; ix. 14, 30, 33; x. 32, 46; xi. 1, 12, 15, 20, 27; xiv. 18, 22, 26, 32. In what follows I

---

[1] In *A New Commentary on Holy Scripture*, Pt. III, pp. 42–124.

shall refer to the phenomenon appearing in these passages as 'Turner's mark.'

Now if we take the passages that have Turner's mark and examine them in their context, it becomes clear that in some cases the adjoining passages belong naturally to the passages with the mark. For example, in the first chapter, verses 21-28, the account of the visit of Jesus and his disciples to the Capernaum Synagogue has the Turner mark; and it presupposes verses 16-20 which do not have the mark, but which describe the call of the first four Apostles. Further, in verses 29-31, the cure of Peter's mother-in-law, Turner's mark is present; and again verses 32-39 are the sequel. Now it is admitted by K. L. Schmidt that verses 23-38 form a pre-Markan unity. Similarly, iv. 35-41, which has not the Turner mark, is bound up with v. 1-20 and 21-43, two passages which have the mark; and again the whole section, iv. 35—v. 43, is recognised as a pre-Markan unity by Dibelius and Schmidt. Pursuing this line of inquiry, it becomes possible to draw up a tentative list of Petrine paragraphs in Mark, consisting of those paragraphs which have the Turner mark along with other paragraphs which seem to attach themselves. The extent of the Petrine matter is as follows: i. 16-39; ii. 1-14; iii. 13-19; iv. 35—v. 43; vi. 7-13, 30-56; viii. 14—ix. 48; x. 32-52; xi. 1-33; xiii. 3-4, 32-37 xiv. 17-50, 53-54, 66-72.

The matter dealt with in these sections are the call of the first disciples, the Synagogue service, the cure of Peter's mother-in-law, travel-preaching in Galilee, the cure of the paralytic at Capernaum, the appointment of the Twelve, the storm on the lake, the cure of the Gerasene demoniac, the Hæmorrhousa and the raising of Jairus' daughter, the Mission of the Twelve, their return and the feeding of the 5000, the walking on the sea and the return to Gennesaret, the warning against the leaven of the Pharisees and of Herod, the healing of the blind man at Bethsaida, Peter's confession and the first prediction of the Passion, the Transfiguration, and healing of the epileptic boy, the second prediction of the Passion, the rebuke to jealousy and self-seeking among the disciples. All these events are set on the Galilean background, with Capernaum as the principal centre.

A second group begins with the third prediction of the Passion, on the road going up to Jerusalem, the request of the sons of Zebedee, the cure of Bartimaeus, the triumphal entry, the story of the barren fig-tree and the cleansing of the Temple, the question about

Jesus' authority, the question about the time of the end, the last supper, the events in Gethsemane, the arrest of Jesus and removal to the High Priest's house, Peter's denials.

Of the material that falls outside this collection it is not possible here to make a detailed examination. For the present it must suffice to notice a few well-defined blocks. Mark i. 1-15 covers the period prior to the call of Peter; and, at the other end of the story, xiv. 55-65 and xv. 1—xvi. 8 describe incidents at which Peter was not present. (Mk. xiv-xvi is regarded as a pre-Markan unity by K. L. Schmidt.)

The account of the death of the Baptist (vi. 17-29) has its peculiar problems. At the same time, it has all the appearance of being a piece of Palestinian (originally Aramaic) tradition. The most attractive solution is perhaps that proposed by J. Thomas,[2] that the Evangelist has here made use of a written document embodying the tradition of the followers of John, what might be called the *Passio Iohannis* as it circulated in the Johannite [3] sect.

The so-called 'Little Apocalypse,' which appears in the non-Petrine collection, is thought by many to have circulated in the Early Church as a separate document; and it is at least possible that the specimen parables, given with comment in iv. 1-34, were extracted from a collection of parables. The passage x. 1-12 is regarded by Dibelius [4] as a pre-Markan unity.

Specially interesting are the two groups of polemical passages in chapters ii-iii and xii. These have been the subject of an illuminating discussion by B. S. Easton.[5] He observes that the former block *ends* at Mk. iii. 6 with the statement that the Pharisees and Herodians plotted to kill Jesus: the latter *begins* at xii. 13 with the statement that the Pharisees and Herodians sent representatives to entrap him in his talk. Apart from a parallel in Mt. xxii. 16 to Mk. xii. 13, these are the only instances of 'Herodian' in the New Testament. The difficulty about the word, according to Easton, is that while in Galilee 'Herodian' could mean any official of Herod, it could hardly mean that in Jerusalem where Herod's writ did not run. Hence it

---

[2] *Le Mouvement Baptiste en Palestine et Syrie,* pp. 110 f.

[3] Following a suggestion made by Thomas, I use Johannite as a convenient means of distinguishing persons and things connected with the Baptist from those connected with the John (or Johns) of the Early Church.

[4] *Formgeschichte des Evangeliums,*[2] p. 233.

[5] *Studies in Early Christianity,* ed. S. J. Case, pp. 85 ff.

must be explained in Jerusalem as being the name for those in Jerusalem who supported Herodian rule, and, since that was not in force in the capital, supported the Roman rule as the next best thing.[6] But it is awkward to have to give two interpretations of the same term. Easton further noted that the plot mentioned in iii. 6 leads to nothing, and indeed comes too early in the story. In xii. 13 however, he argues, the appearance of the Herodians is natural. They were the one class of Jews who favoured the payment of tribute to Rome.

Easton also notes that the matters discussed in these polemical passages would not have any very lively interest for Gentile converts. From that it would presumably follow—though Easton does not argue the case in this way—that they would not be likely to form part of Peter's preaching to the Gentiles.

Easton's solution is that ii. 13—iii. 6 and xii. 13-27 originally formed a single continuous whole; that 'this account was formed in pre-Markan times and belonged to the tradition of the Palestinian Christian community.'[7] Why did Mark split it up? Having begun to incorporate it where he does he had to 'break off at iii. 5, for tribute to Rome, the theme of the next paragraph was paid only in Judæa, while the Sadducees of xii. 18-27 were scarcely to be found in Galilee. But as iii. 5 was too abrupt a conclusion for the first part, Mark wrote iii. 6, forming it out of the next sentence in the tradition (xii. 13), without noticing (or caring) that he had made Galilean characters of the Herodians. The remainder of the tradition he was obliged to postpone until his narrative could treat of Jerusalem events.'[8]

All this seems to be quite possible. The only reservation that needs to be made is in favour of ii. 13-14, the call of Levi.[9] This paragraph seems to me to hang together with the preceding matter.

With this somewhat hasty survey of a large subject the present discussion must close. It is obvious that there are—and probably always will be—many loose ends. But a few things seem to emerge

[6] For a full discussion of the name 'Herodian,' see H. H. Rowley's article, 'The Herodians in the Gospels,' J.T.S. xli. (1940), pp. 14–27.
[7] *Op. cit.* p. 92.
[8] *Ibid.*
[9] I very much doubt whether ii. 15–17 has anything at all to do with ii. 13–14. They could—so far as Mark goes—be treated perfectly well as separate paragraphs.

fairly clearly. First and foremost is the conclusion, suggested by converging lines of argument, that the basis of the Markan story is a good deal broader than we sometimes think. Petrine reminiscence is part of the foundation, perhaps the main part; but other sources have made their contribution. And we need not suppose that 'non-Petrine' necessarily means inferior in historical worth. The further we go back the larger the number of available first-hand witnesses becomes. If the identification of the Evangelist with John Mark of Jerusalem is sound, he was from the beginning in touch with many such witnesses. And, secondly, if our interpretation of the traditions about Peter, Mark and the Gospel is anywhere near the truth, the composition of the Gospel may be put several years earlier than the date commonly accepted.

. . . When, therefore, Papias or his informant says that Matthew compiled τὰ λόγια, the simplest and most natural meaning to be given to the words is that Matthew made a collection of oracles, i.e. sayings analogous to those of the old prophets, uttered by divine inspiration and containing the commandments and promises of God for the new Israel, the Church of Christ.

'Matthew compiled τὰ λόγια in the Hebrew tongue and every man translated them as he was able.' This brief sentence makes four separate assertions:—

(a) That a book of λόγια was composed.
(b) That it was composed in the Hebrew tongue (i.e. probably in the spoken language of the Palestinian Jews—at that time = Aramaic. Parallels to this use of 'Hebrew' where 'Aramaic' is meant in Dalman, *Gramm.* § 1.)
(c) That the composer of this work was named Matthew—presumably the Apostle.
(d) That various people translated it as best they could—doubtless into Greek.

If we try applying these propositions to the Gospel of Matthew we find that they do not fit. As applied to Mt. (a) and (d) are, I think, demonstrably false. One of the really assured results of Synoptic criticism seems to be the priority of Mk.: and, if that is so, Mt. becomes a Greek document from the first and not an Aramaic composition subsequently translated into Greek. It is true that Prof. Torrey in his book, *The Four Gospels,* maintains the view that Mt.

is a translation from Aramaic; but even he has to make allowance for the results of synoptic study by the hypothesis that 'each of the translators, Mt. and Lk., adopts the Greek wording of his predecessor, *wherever a faithful use of his source permits him to do so*' (p. 275). This would imply that the translator of Mt. had before him, not only the Aramaic original of this Gospel but also the Greek version of Mk.; while Luke, who on Torrey's reconstruction both composed and translated his Gospel, had his own Aramaic original, the Greek version of Mk. and the Greek version of Mt. This seems rather too elaborate to be plausible. Further it is worth noting that among the evidences of translation from Aramaic which Torrey finds in Mt., the most convincing in Markan contexts are already to be found in Mk. That is to say they are not really evidence for an Aramaic original of Mt. in those sections at all. More than that: where Matthew does not reproduce Mk.'s supposed mis-rendering of a Semitic original, what he does give looks very like a conjectural improvement on Mark's Greek rather than a correction of it from the Aramaic original. A good example of this is Mk. xiv. 72 = Mt. xxvi. 75. Mk. has καὶ ἐπιβαλὼν ἔκλαιεν. ἐπιβαλών has always been a problem. Torrey says it is a literal but unidiomatic rendering of an Aramaic original which meant 'as he thought upon it'—i.e his denial of the Lord. But Mt. has neither ἐπιβαλών nor anything representing the supposed Aramaic behind 'as he thought upon it.' He has ἐξελθών.

In general it may be said that the notes to Torrey's translation do not prove Aramaic originals for Mt. and Lk. At most they make a case for Aramaic sources behind those Gospels and possibly behind Mk. and Jn. also. Mt. remains a Greek work compiled most probably from Greek sources—of which Mk. in Greek was one. These sources may quite well go back to more primitive Aramaic documents of which they are translations. That the Gospel of Mt. ever existed *as a whole* in Aramaic I do not believe.

That Mt. consists of λόγια is not correct if we take λόγια in the plain and natural sense. It contains λόγια: indeed, it contains five considerable collections of λόγια; but it is not itself τὰ λόγια. It is a book made up partly of collections of λόγια and partly of narrative.

Finally the statement that Mt. as we know it was the work of Matthew the Apostle is, to say the least, improbable.

Suppose then, seeing that the identification of τὰ λόγια with Mt. breaks down, we try again with the other way and see whether the four statements of Papias will fit Q.

(*a*) There was a compilation of the Oracles. This as applied to Q is absolutely correct. Q is a compilation of oracles—sayings of Jesus and nothing else, except a few similar oracles of John the Baptist, and a line or two of narrative in the Temptation story. But it may be objected that Q did contain narrative: that the story of the Centurion's servant stood in the document, and that some at least of the Q sayings have narrative settings. The answer is that there is no evidence that the story of the Centurion's servant stood in Q at all. What did stand there was the account of a conversation between Jesus and a Centurion, the point of which was the saying of Jesus, 'I have not found such faith—no, not in Israel.' Nor is there any evidence that the narrative settings of Q sayings belonged to Q. For, after all, what is the ground for believing that anything is derived from Q? It is verbal agreement between Mt. and Lk. And the narrative settings of Q sayings and conversations is just the place where we do not get this agreement, but wide divergence. In the Centurion passage agreement between Mt. and Lk. begins where the conversation begins and ends where it ends. There is simply nothing to show that Q contained anything except sayings and conversations.

(*b*) and (*c*) This document was composed in Aramaic and everyone translated it as best he could. These two statements can be taken together: and the conditions are met if we can show a probability that (1) Q was written in Aramaic and (2) that Mt. and Lk. represent two versions of this Aramaic original. There are several lines of argument tending towards such a conclusion.

(i) The probabilities of the case. The sayings of Jesus were certainly uttered in Aramaic—perhaps some of them in scholastic Hebrew. If a collection of them were made, it would be most probable that it should be by one of his own circle and naturally in the original language. Jesus was regarded as 'the prophet of Nazareth' and it was in accordance with custom that the oracles of a prophet should be preserved by his disciples.

(ii) The analogy of the O.T. points to the possibility, at least, of several translations of such a document into Greek. There were at least four Greek versions of the O.T. made at various times and for various reasons.

(iii) We can compare the versions of Mt. and Lk. with parallel cases in O.T. For example the book of Daniel possesses two complete Greek versions, the old LXX and the translation of Theodotion. We select a passage at random and compare the two. The Aramaic passage Dan. vii. 9-14 is turned by LXX into 166 Greek words by θ′ into 157. There is complete agreement in 105 of these and partial agreement in 12. The differences amount to about 27 per cent. of the total. We take a passage of about the same extent from Q—the testimony of Jesus to John the Baptist. Mt. gives it in 158 words, Lk. in 170. There is complete agreement about 115 words, partial agreement about 20 and the difference comes to about 19 per cent. of the total. Mt. and Lk. stand rather closer to one another than LXX and θ′; but the general resemblance is very striking.

(iv) The most cogent evidence of translation is mistranslation. And such evidence is not wanting. The most notable instance is in the well-known Q passage about the cleansing of the inside and outside of the dish. Mt. correctly gives 'cleanse the inside of the dish' while Lk. has the absurd text 'give alms of the inside.' Wellhausen showed that Luke's 'give alms' is a mistranslation of the Aramaic verb rightly rendered by Mt. A similar misrendering may underlie 'Wisdom is justified of her children (works)' and 'He who does not take up his cross . . . is not worthy of me' ⎫
                                   cannot be my disciple' ⎭

Fortunately such cases are rare enough to permit us to keep our confidence in the ability of the translators of Q.

(v) There is still another sign of translation in those cases where Mt. and Lk. have different words or phrases either of which is a legitimate rendering of a single Aramaic original. These are more numerous: and I have made a collection of them. All that is required is Hatch and Redpath's concordance to the LXX, Field's *Hexapla*, and unlimited patience. You start with a Q passage in which Mt. and Lk. are agreeing fairly closely. Then there comes a difference: Mt. uses one word, Lk. another. It may be that these are just different ways of rendering the same Semitic original. The matter can be tested. There are four Greek versions of the O.T. Unhappily three of them survive only in fragments, which are collected in Field's *Hexapla* and indexed in Hatch and Redpath. We can soon see whether the same divergence occurs in the Greek versions of the O.T. Now the interesting thing is that it does. In quite a number of cases we have exact parallels for the differences of wording in Mt. and Lk. in Greek texts which are undoubtedly translations of the same Hebrew original.

. . . I do not maintain that the facts which we have been considering *prove* that Q is the Aramaic document called the λόγια in the

Papias fragment. But I do maintain that the phenomena presented by Mt. and Lk., in the passages where we may suppose them to have used Q, are consistent with that hypothesis. Three out of the four propositions contained in the Papias testimony fit Q like a glove.

(*d*) There remains the fourth—that the author of this document was Matthew—presumably Matthew the Apostle. This, of course, cannot be tested in the same way as the others. There is, however, this much to be said for it:

> (i) On the supposition that the Papias tradition does refer to Q, we can see that three of its four statements are reliable. There is therefore a presumption that the fourth will also hold good.
>
> (ii) If the Papias statements really refer to Q then they must be much older than the time of Papias. That is, the tradition is thrown back to the end of the first century or the very beginning of the second. It is thus brought very close to the events which it reports.
>
> (iii) An Aramaic original of Q implies a Palestinian authorship and that means a Palestinian Christian. Nobody else in Jewish circles would have the inclination to compile such a record and of those who would be inclined, those would be best qualified for the task who had been—in Lk.'s words—eyewitnesses and ministers of the word from the beginning. There was a Matthew among those who were in close contact with Jesus during his ministry. And there we are. The bits of the puzzle fit in satisfactorily enough. The whole thing is consistent on the supposition, not hard to make, that Papias had his older tradition about Q, and, misled by the mention of Matthew, supposed it to refer to the Gospel current in his day under Matthew's name.

Our conclusion is that the statement reported by Papias refers not to Mt., but to one of the sources of Mt., the document Q.

CHAPTER 2

Memory and Manuscript

BIRGER GERHARDSSON

In 1957 Professor H. Riesenfeld of Uppsala delivered a
lecture at the Oxford Congress on the Gospels which was
subsequently published as *The Gospel Tradition and Its
Beginnings,* 1957, in which he accepted the general pattern
of the Form Critics, namely, that the Synoptic tradition
passed through a period of oral transmission. He contended,
however, that this oral transmission was carefully controlled
from the very beginning. In 1961 his student, Birger Gerhardsson, published the book cited above which is a detailed argument in support of this thesis. For a critique of
this position see W. D. Davies, "The Gospel Tradition" in
Neotestamentica et Patristica, Essays in Honor of Dr. Oscar
Cullmann, 1962, pp. 14–34.

WE have good reason for believing that Jesus taught both in
word and deed. Some of his works are didactic symbolic actions, and nothing more. In most cases, however, the didactic
symbolism is only one side of the picture: Jesus' works did not only
fill a pedagogical function. At all events, the young Church saw all
Jesus' works—in fact his whole life—as being teaching. This appears
to agree in principle with the Master's intentions.

Turning to Jesus' oral teaching, we must reckon with the fact
that he used a method similar to that of Jewish—and Hellenistic—
teachers: the scheme of text and interpretation. He must have made
his disciples learn certain sayings off by heart; if he taught, he must
have required his disciples to memorize. This statement is not intended to be dogmatic or apologetic but is a consideration based

"Memory and Manuscript. Tradition and Written Transmission in Rabbinic Judaism
and Early Christianity" (Acta seminarii neotestamentici Upsaliensis XXII) by Birger
Gerhardsson, CWK Gleerup, Lund, 1961. Used by permission.

on a comparison with the contemporary situation. It can of course be used for dogmatic purposes, but the task of critical scholarship is only to estimate probability on the basis of the evidence of the source material.

We must now ask, how much of the tradition from Jesus gives us the impression of being made up of condensed memory tests, and how much of chance elements in his teaching as a whole? In the synoptic tradition we also find material which interprets sayings of Jesus, e.g. in the exposition *(talmud)* of parables.[1] Even though these expositions were not stressed by Jesus himself as being memory texts, and were therefore not delivered with a fixed wording, we must reckon with the fact that they derive *in principle* from Jesus' own interpretative exposition of his parables.

If we now turn our attention to the young Church, we must account for the fact that the Torah tradition was still there—and that the young Church recognized at least the written Torah without reservation—and further, that Jesus' disciples were still there. The implication is that the words and works of Jesus were stamped on the memories of these disciples. Remembering the attitude of Jewish disciples to their master, it is unrealistic to suppose that forgetfulness and the exercise of a pious imagination had too much hand in transforming authentic memories beyond all recognition in the course of a few short decades.

The sources show that Jesus' closest disciples had a particularly authoritative position in the young Church. Luke's evidence is supported not only by historical probability (the matter is virtually self-evident, seen against the background of the contemporary situation). Paul confirms it, directly and indirectly, and his evidence is particularly valuable, since it comes from a man who has had himself to fight for recognition as an Apostle of Christ.

"The twelve" do not appear in the sources as particularly well-defined individual figures, but as a *collegium*. It is really only their leader, Peter, and the inner triumvirate of Peter, James and John who stand out as distinctive individuals. Their stay in Jerusalem was not the result of mere chance; important doctrinal considerations also played their part in the course of events.

The *collegium* of Apostles was still in residence in Jerusalem in

---

[1] After a linguistic analysis of the interpretation of the parable of the Sower, Joach. Jeremias concludes: "Die Deutung des Säemannsgleichnisses gehört der Urkirche an," *Die Gleichnisse*, p. 67.

the forties and, to judge from the evidence, even as late as the fifties; they had thus been there between fifteen and twenty years.

We have comparative material from Qumran which shows what an authoritative *collegium* in an eschatologically self-conscious congregation did. Material from other contemporary groups is also extremely telling. It is no longer possible to under-estimate this evidence as the first form-critics did. We cannot find out how authoritative tradition originates if we ignore the tradition's authorities.

There can be no doubt that the twelve proclaimed a burning message about the atoning death and resurrection of Christ. But the poetic picture of ignorant men, suddenly delivering unprepared and unlearned sermons and speeches under the influence of powerful inspiration—and continuing the process for a generation or more— is a peculiar combination, arrived at on the basis of certain distinctly dogmatic tendencies in the sources and a number of romantic ideas in modern research. The historian, without neglecting the evidence for early Christian enthusiasm, must make up his mind on certain other elements in the picture painted for us by the sources.

Against the background of the Jewish milieu, it is evident that the early Christian Apostles were *compelled* to present their message as an eyewitness account, as "that which we have seen and heard," and in connection with the Holy Scriptures—even supported by a convincing exposition of the Scriptures. There is no evidence that these needs were first felt at a later stage in the history of early Christianity. The eyewitnesses and the Scriptures were already there in the kerygma.

In addition, the Apostles' preaching had an essential complement in their *teaching*. The aspect of the "eyewitness account" is also to be found there. They taught in the name of their Master, and bore witness to the words and works of their Teacher in a way which recalled—at least formally—the witness borne by other Jewish disciples to the words and actions of their teachers.

It is unrealistic to try to sum up the varied activities of the young Church under one function, whether this function be identified as preaching or teaching. It is certain that in the life of the rapidly growing congregation there were a great number of varied activities: preaching, teaching, prayer, sacred meals, charitative activity, exorcism, healing, church discipline, jurisdiction, stewardship, and many more. Problems arose, and questions were asked. We may assume that in all these varied activities the members of the congregation "remembered" and made use of authoritative sayings, not only passages from the Holy Scriptures, but sayings of Jesus, and memories of what Jesus did. But the question is, which of these forms of activity provided *the essential Sitz im Leben* for the "actualization," collection and fixing of the tradition about Jesus? In the course of this present investigation we have come to the conclusion that the leading *collegium* in the Jerusalem church carried out a direct work on ὁ λόγος τοῦ κυρίου (i.e. the Holy Scriptures and the tradition from, and about, Christ). From certain points of view this work resembled the labours of Rabbinic Judaism on יהוה דבר (the Holy Scriptures and the oral Torah) and the work carried out in the Qumran congregation on דבר יהוה (the Holy Scriptures and the sect's own tradition, which was partly oral and partly written). This apostolic work on "the word of God" was thus the most important element in the comprehensive concept ἡ διδαχὴ τῶν ἀποστόλων (Acts 2.42) and the concept ἡ διακονία τοῦ λόγου (Acts 6.4).

This work on "the word of the Lord" certainly took varying forms, but two of these forms demand our particular attention.

We must suppose, first, that an intensive study of the Scriptures took place. They "searched the Scriptures" in order to win deeper insight into "the secrets of the Kingdom of God." This study of the Scriptures was, formally speaking, midrash exegesis, similar in principle to that carried out by the Rabbis, the Qumran sect and the Apocalyptic groups. There were variations, but the technique employed was roughly similar. The essential difference between the midrash exegesis of the Jerusalem church and that of the other groups is that the Jerusalem church interpreted the Scriptures in the light of the teaching of Jesus, given in word and deed, and in the light of the distinctive events experienced by the Apostles during and immediately after the first Easter. The early Christian Church had a new point of departure: one which was not shared by Rabbinic Judaism, and one which the Qumran sect possessed only in part. Several of the Scripture quotations which are to be found in Acts and in the synoptic tradition appear to be derived from this midrashic Scripture study in the young Jerusalem church. From these quotations we are able to see the way in which this study functioned.

Secondly, we must take into account the discussions of doctrinal questions[2] raised by members of the *collegium*, by the Apostles'

---

[2] Cf. Bultmann, *Geschichte*, pp. 39 ff.

disciples—for there were certainly such—and by individual members of the congregation, as well as by opponents. When deciding such questions there were two natural authoritative sources from which answers might be drawn: the Scriptures and the tradition from Jesus. We have attempted in an earlier chapter to reconstruct the process followed here.[3]

In the course of this work on "the word of the Lord," sayings of Jesus were "remembered," repeated, expounded and applied. Such was the practice in rabbinic doctrinal debates, using sayings of the great teachers; such was certainly the practice in early Christianity, too. Eloquent witness is borne by the fact that although sayings of Jesus in the Gospels are relatively few in number, they prove to have been used for many different purposes.[4] As in the rabbinic tradition, one and the same "saying" appears in several different contexts. It is often extremely difficult to decide the "original" meaning of a saying of Jesus which has become separated from its situation.

In the course of this work, they also "remembered" how Jesus acted in various situations; narratives about Jesus' actions were formulated as answers to definite questions. This does not mean that these narratives were mere inventions. The rabbinic comparative material does not favour such a view.

Since Jesus was considered to be the Messiah, *the "only" teacher* (Matt. 23.10), his sayings must have been accorded even greater authority and sanctity than that accorded by the Rabbis' disciples to the words of their teachers. A fact which has been pointed out by a number of scholars is that the Jesus-tradition in the early Christian documents is *isolated* from the sayings of other authorities;[5] this shows that it had a distinctive position among early Christian doctrinal authorities, and a peculiar dignity.

This brings us to the question of the groupings of the Jesus-tradition. Its arrangement among the disciples of Jesus is a matter of the psychology of memory, which we cannot consider in this

---

[3] 14 E; cf. 15 E.

[4] See G. Lindeskog, Logiastudien, in *Studia Theol.* 4 (1950, printed 1952), pp. 129 ff.

[5] Thus already G. Kittel, *Die Probleme des palästinischen Spätjudentums und das Urchristentum* (1926), p. 69: "Die Isolierung der Jesustradition ist das Konstitutivum des Evangeliums."—On the fact that *adapted* sayings of Jesus were, together with other maxims, incorporated into tractates which were compiled for various practical reasons, see above [Gerhardsson], pp. 303 f.

context. We can, however, ask: How was this tradition grouped when it was to be taught to disciples? We might expect, on a basis of the Jewish parallel material, two different methods of grouping: the midrashic and the mishnaic. In the former case, the grouping of the Jesus-traditions would have been based on their association with the consecutive text of Scripture: with passages or selections from the text. This method would seem to have been used to some extent in the young Church,[6] but it must have been somewhat unpractical. It is possible that traces of the much-discussed *testimonia* collections might be worth following in this context. Were these texts key-words to certain traditions about Jesus?

In the latter, mishnaic case, sayings of Jesus were grouped in more or less extensive blocks, "tractates," put together for various purposes and arranged on various principles: either factual or mechanical mnemotechnical. It is a well-known fact that we are able to catch glimpses of such "tractates" in the written Gospels. We may for example recall the instruction of the Apostles (or missionaries) in Matt. 10 with par.,[7] the parable tractate in Mk. 4 with par., and "the bread traditions" in Mk. 6.31—8.26 with par.[8] It is probable that relatively comprehensive "tractates" of Jesus-traditions had to be compiled at a fairly early stage for use of missionaries and teachers who went out from Jerusalem. But how early is the enigmatic traditional collection which we usually call "Q"? It is difficult to say whether or not Paul was acquainted with this extensive collection; but there is no doubt that Paul had access to a fairly comprehensive collection of traditions about Jesus, even though it is difficult to reach any definite conclusion as to the extent or the arrangement of this collection.

An intensive work on the logos was also carried on in other churches, but the Jerusalem church was the centre of the early Christianity and the leaders of this congregation were considered as the highest doctrinal authority of the whole Church.[9]

[6] Cf. J. W. Doeve, *Jewish Hermeneutics in the Synoptic Gospels and Acts* (1954), pp. 177 ff., *idem,* Le rôle de la tradition orale dans la composition des Évangiles synoptiques, in *La formation des Évangiles,* pp. 70 ff.

[7] Cf. e.g. L. Cerfaux, Les Unités littéraires, *ibid.,* pp. 24 ff.

[8] L. Cerfaux, La section des pains, in *Recueil* L. Cerfaux I, pp. 471 ff.—On the grouping, see also T. Soiron, *Die Logia Jesu* (1916) and M. Smith, *Tannaitic Parallels to the Gospels* (1951), pp. 115 ff.

[9] On the relation between the leading *collegium* in Jerusalem and the other Christian Apostles and teachers, see my remarks in Ch. 14–15.

We have reason to suppose the Jesus-tradition to have been originally passed on by word of mouth—for ideological as well as for practical reasons. The distinction between written and oral Torah was familiar to the young Church; the Jesus-tradition was a higher equivalent of the oral Torah. Furthermore, according to the prophetic word, God would in the last days write His Torah on the hearts of His Covenant people (Jer. 31.31), i.e. Israel was to memorize the Torah. When we remember the way in which such sayings were interpreted in contemporary Judaism, it is not improbable that such concepts as these were significant for the thought of early Christianity; we cannot however build too much on this assumption.

We must at all events take into account the fact that the actual transmission of such collections of traditions about Jesus was a distinct activity—a direct methodical delivery of the kind we have described in Chapters 9–12 of this work. The traditionist/teacher passed on the tractate, passage or saying to his pupil or pupils by means of continual repetition; he taught the pupil to repeat it, after which he gave the required interpretation. We catch glimpses in the synoptic material—particularly in Matt., "the rabbinic Gospel" [10] —of certain teaching situations which are worthy of our attention in this context, since they certainly reflect teaching practice in the Church in which the tradition in question was formed. But there is little point in stopping at such a statement. It was precisely the teacher's pedagogical measures which were the object of special observation and imitation. Jesus' teaching methods were certainly imitated by his disciples. It ought therefore to be possible, on the basis of the practice of these disciples, to draw certain conclusions as to the methods applied by their Master.

If the gospel tradition was carried in this way, how can there be variations between different parallel traditions? We must take a number of factors into consideration. First and foremost, we must make a very careful attempt to decide when we are actually dealing with variations of one and the same basic saying, and when with sayings of Jesus, delivered by Jesus himself in more than one version. The ease with which many scholars explain all differences between related traditions as being secondary versions of one basic saying, seems most remarkable to anyone who has noted the role played by the category of "theme and variations" in Jewish teaching. Further-

[10] See Stendahl, *The School.*

more, we must take into account the fact that most of the gospel material is haggadic material, and that haggadic material is often transmitted with a somewhat wider margin of variation in wording than halakic material. Nor must we overlook certain adaptations, carried out at an early stage, when the traditional material was gathered. Certain types of variation are due to the material having been translated—not only on one definite occasion, but in a process which was protracted and certainly complicated. Despite careful transmission, the occurrence of certain small alterations as a result of faulty memorization cannot be excluded. Finally, attention must be paid to the principles of redaction used by the different Evangelists.

We must distinguish in principle between this *transmission* in the strict meaning of the word, and the many *uses* to which the transmitted oral texts were put. It is not impossible that the tradition of Jesus, as the special ἱερὸς λόγος of the early Church, was recited in the course of worship; this point of view has been advanced by RIESENFELD.[11] Further, we must take into account a number of other contexts in which the transmitted sayings were *used:* in preaching, in various forms of doctrinal debate and teaching, and others of the manifold activities of the young Church.

When the Evangelists edited their Gospels, however, they did not take their traditions from these forms of activity. They worked on a basis of a fixed, distinct tradition from, and about, Jesus—a tradition which was partly memorized and partly written down in notebooks and private scrolls, but invariably isolated from the teachings of other doctrinal authorities.

We must be content with these suggestions as to the origins and transmission of the gospel tradition. A more detailed picture would require a thorough analysis of both the synoptic and the Johannine material; it has not however been possible to undertake such an analysis within the bounds of this investigation.

[11] *The Gospel Tradition and its Beginnings.*—Cf. above [Gerhardsson], Ch. 5.

CHAPTER 3

Faith and History in the Gospels

GUENTHER BORNKAMM

Professor Bornkamm of Heidelberg University stands in
the Bultmann tradition. He is, however, somewhat more
concerned than Bultmann with the historicity of the events
of the ministry. He is a leader in the new quest for the historical Jesus. (See chapter 19.) The passage quoted indicates
his attitude toward the Synoptic Gospels as sources. See
Rudolf Bultmann, *The History of the Synoptic Tradition*,
1963; also "The Study of the Synoptic Gospels" in *Form
Criticism*, 1962.

FAITH AND HISTORY IN THE GOSPELS

No one is any longer in the position to write a life of Jesus. This
is the scarcely questioned and surprising result today of an
enquiry which for almost two hundred years has devoted prodigious
and by no means fruitless effort to regain and expound the life of
the historical Jesus, freed from all embellishment by dogma and
doctrine. At the end of this research on the life of Jesus stands the
recognition of its own failure. Albert Schweitzer, in his classic work,
The Quest of the Historical Jesus, has erected its memorial, but at
the same time has delivered its funeral oration.

Why have these attempts failed? Perhaps only because it became
alarmingly and terrifyingly evident how inevitably each author
brought the spirit of his own age into his presentation of the figure
of Jesus. In point of fact the changing pictures of the innumerable
"Lives" of Jesus are not very encouraging, confronting us as they

do with now the "enlightened" teacher of God, virtue, and immortality, now the religious genius of the Romantics, now the teacher of ethics in Kant's sense, now the protagonist of social theory. But that could be just an argument for a genuine, historical enquiry, enabled by a sharper criticism even of the presuppositions and ideals provided by its own age, to start afresh on the old task and to better purpose. Has all the life gone out of research? Does it lack today a sympathetic exponent? If that is so we would have reason to speak of a scholarly fade-out, in which research has perhaps found itself the victim of its own hypercriticism. In truth this state of affairs has deeper causes, and compels us to affirm the futility of any renewal of attempts at Lives of Jesus now or in the future.

This judgment is based on the special nature and character of the sources to which we owe almost exclusively our historical knowledge of Jesus. These are the Gospels of the New Testament, mainly the first three (Mark, Matthew, Luke). We call them commonly the synoptic Gospels because they are interconnected and interdependent, a fact which becomes evident as their respective records are looked at "synoptically." The Gospel according to John has so different a character in comparison with the other three, and is to such a degree the product of a developed theological reflection, that we can only treat it as a secondary source. Admittedly the synoptic Gospels themselves are not simply historical sources which the historian, enquiring after Jesus of Nazareth as a figure of the past, could use without examination and criticism. Although their relation to history is a different one from that of John, they none the less unite to a remarkable degree both record of Jesus Christ and witness to him, testimony of the Church's faith in him and narration of his history.

Both should be continually distinguished in the understanding of the Gospels and in each individual part of their tradition; on the other hand, both are so closely interwoven that it is often exceedingly hard to say where one ends and the other begins. Mathematical certainty in the exposition of a bare history of Jesus, unembellished by faith, is unobtainable, in spite of the fact that the critical discernment of older and more recent layers of tradition belongs to the work of research. We possess no single word of Jesus and no single story of Jesus, no matter how incontestably genuine they may be, which do not contain at the same time the confession of the believing congregation or at least are embedded therein. This makes the search after the bare facts of history difficult and to a large extent futile.

It follows that anyone who takes upon himself the aim of this book, to give an historical presentation of Jesus and his message, sees himself, in relation to his readers, in an embarrassing position. Quite understandably the reader wishes to know what actually happened, what took place then and there, what was said then and there. In no case can these questions be set aside. Nevertheless, we must learn to restrain them, and must not grant them the urgency normally accorded them. Under their pressure we already find ourselves far too much in a completely hopeless position. It is to be noted that the insistent question "what actually happened" in no wise brings us to the point. Such questions can actually lead us astray. So much at least is clear: were we to accept uncritically everything handed down to us as historical (in the usual sense), we would be subjecting the Gospels to an investigation alien to them, and forcing upon them an understanding of the history of Jesus quite unsuited to them. But on the other hand, this is also true: should we reduce the tradition critically to that which cannot be doubted on historical grounds, we should be left ultimately with a mere torso which bears no resemblance to the story set forth in the Gospels. In the course of research both paths have been sufficiently trodden. Each movement has resulted in a counter movement. In contrast to a blind and uncritical approach, historical criticism appeared with perfect right on the field, and destroyed the foundation, thought to be so secure, on which the other relied. And then in turn came the constantly renewed efforts of the conservative historians and theologians, who sought with more or less good fortune to restore some of its limbs to that torso; only themselves to be succeeded by an even sharper criticism which removed the limbs still remaining. And so there resulted in the history of research an agonising alternation between critical and conservative tendencies, sad for any who in the spirit of scientific enquiry seek enlightenment, and even more painful for those who as believers seek after the history of Jesus.

No one should think that he can escape the aforementioned difficulties with a violent solution, as with one blow upon the Gordian knot. Without the process of criticism and countercriticism there is no knowledge of historical truth in this field or in any other. Such a process teaches us to examine more strictly, to find better grounds for our arguments, not to rest on mere tradition, nor to succumb to a criticism entirely uncontrolled. Since research has learned to engage in untrammelled historical investigation and no longer to be content with Church dogma and doctrine, such questioning is entrusted to research. Genuine faith is certainly not dependent upon the course of this research. But when anyone, out of a concern for the understanding of history, has embarked upon these questions, he will hardly keep a good conscience if thereafter he is driven in desperation to take refuge from the problem of investigation and its frequently controversial results in what is considered the safe fold of Church tradition.

All the same, it must be our concern to extricate ourselves from this dilemma. We shall be well advised, prior to the historical questions concerning the reconstruction of just exactly how the sequence of events ran, to solve the question as to the understanding of the history and person of Jesus found in the Gospels. It is basically different from that familiar to modern thought. To the original Christian tradition, Jesus is not in the first instance a figure of the past, but rather the risen Lord, present with his will, his power, his word. Jesus Christ—no other than the rabbi from Nazareth, whose earthly history began in Galilee and ended on the cross in Jerusalem: and yet at the same time the Risen One, the author of salvation, and the fulfilment of the divine decree. The interest of the Church and her tradition does not cling to the past, but to today; and this Today is not to be understood as a mere date in the calendar, but as a present appointed by God, and together with it a future made accessible by God. In light of this Now and To Come accomplished and decreed by God and opened up through the crucifixion and resurrection of Jesus, the Church understands the past in the history of Jesus before Good Friday and Easter. This she includes in her message, but always as a history which pertains to the present and opens up the future (cf. for example Acts x. 37-43). This understanding of the history of Jesus is therefore an understanding from the end backward and to the end forward. This understanding is built into all the traditions collected together in the Gospels.

That is already apparent in the oldest brief sermonic and confessional formulae, in which we have before us the original form of the Gospel long before there were Gospels committed to writing. (Acts iii. 13 ff.; iv. 10 ff.; v. 30 ff.; compare especially 1 Cor. xv. 3 ff., etc.) They all speak with extreme concentration simply of the death and resurrection of Jesus Christ and proclaim thereby the end of this old age and the breaking in of the new world of God in salvation and judgment. The primitive Christian proclamation confines itself so exclusively to this history—a history which shatters the horizon of all events confined to this world and shifts the ages, that it can pass over the pre-Easter life and work of Jesus to an extent which seems astounding to us (2 Cor. v. 16). Doubtless Paul and the authors of other New Testament writings knew extremely little of the detail which is known to us from the Gospels.

Neither do the Gospels, which for the first time make the pre-Easter history of Jesus their theme, differ essentially in their understanding of this history from the older formulations of the message of Salvation (the Gospel or Kerygma). They also grow out of the proclamation and are in its service. As an example of this, the description of the few days of the passion occupies so disproportionate a space that one could describe these books, not without reason, as "Passion narratives with extended introduction" (M. Kahler). Whatever of reliable historical recollections may have been preserved in this part of their records (see pages 153 ff.), it is certain that the Gospels in their treatment did not follow out a chronological interest, but wished to proclaim what the Risen Lord said to the disciples at Emmaus: "Was it not necessary that the Christ should suffer these things and enter into his glory?" (Lk. xxiv. 26). In the relating of past history they proclaim who he is, not who he was. What the passion narratives show applies also to the Gospels as a whole: what belongs to the past in the history of Jesus should always be investigated and understood in relation to its significance for the present time today and the coming time of God's future.

Because the earthly Jesus is for the Church at the same time the Risen Lord, his word takes on, in the tradition, the features of the present. From this standpoint are to be explained two apparently conflicting characteristics of the tradition which nearly every page of the Synoptics presents: an incontestable loyalty and adherence to the word of Jesus, and at the same time an astonishing degree of freedom as to the original wording. The word of Jesus is preserved, and yet not with the piety of an archivist, nor is it passed on like the utterances of famous rabbis with expositions attached. In fact, one can go on to say this: the tradition is not really the repetition and transmission of the word he spoke once upon a time, but rather *is* his word today. From this standpoint alone can we grasp the different renderings of his word in the tradition. It is not a sufficient explanation to say that popular, oral tradition always tends to alter, adorn, and omit, as well as to preserve: although, of course, the laws of popular tradition and the forms which it habitually takes are without question to be seen in the Gospels.

For the clarification of this contemporary nature of the word of Jesus, let us here refer to a single obvious example, to which we can find many parallels. When one compares the different versions of Jesus' parable of the Great Supper (Mt. xxii. 1 ff.; Lk. xiv. 16 ff.), one sees that Luke tells it differently from Matthew, and moreover provides the older text. A rich man invites his friends to the feast, but the guests refuse the invitation with plausible though fatuous excuses. The account in Luke remains in the quite natural setting of a parable. In Matthew the telling is strengthened by lurid features. The man of means has become a king. The meal has become the marriage feast for his son. The servants (no longer only one) are maltreated and killed. We read further in Matthew that the infuriated king sends out his armies against the thankless and murderous guests and burns down their city. One sees at once that this is no longer a simple parable. Each special feature demands interpretation and understanding. The king is a standard picture of God. The king's son is the Messiah. The marriage is a picture of the joy of the Messianic age. In the fate of the servants we recognise the martyrdom of God's messengers. In the military campaign we recognise the Jewish war, and in the destruction of the city, the catastrophe of A.D. 70. The old people of God, having become rebellious, will be rejected and a new people will be called. But this new people is still a mixture of good and bad on the way to judgment and the final separation of the unworthy. (Only in Matthew does the parable end with the rejection of the man who came to the wedding without a wedding garment.) In Matthew's version we find clearly worked into the parable of Jesus his own story, a picture of Israel and the picture of the early Church. The word of Jesus long ago has become today's word.

Luke, at least at first, has better preserved the original character of the simple parable, but he also reveals the tendency of the word of Jesus to become contemporary. He makes the servant of the nobleman go out not only twice but three times; after the first refusal he is sent to the poor, lame and crippled *in* the town, and after that once again to those in "the highways and hedges" *outside* the town. There can be no doubt that the evangelist intended to represent thereby the advance of the mission from Israel to the heathen world.

One learns from the example of such a text how strongly the tradition collected in the Gospels has been influenced by the believing interpretation of the history and person of Jesus. The understanding of the "once" of the history of Jesus in its significance for the "today" of his lordship over the Church and for the divine consummation that lies ahead was able to lead to what in our terms would be considered a relativisation, often even to an elimination of the historical boundaries between the period before and after Easter. The history of the tradition shows that frequently not only the words of Jesus spoken while he was here on earth (as in the parable mentioned above) soon took on a post-Easter form. For words spoken by the Risen Christ also became words of the earthly Jesus. In principle this is the same process. We have to reckon with it wherever circumstances and questions of the later Church are presupposed in a saying coming from the tradition. In the course of this book we shall meet frequently with such examples. Such sayings will originally have been declared to the Church by her inspired prophets and preachers, as the Revelation of John shows in its Letters to the Churches (Rev. ii and iii). The extent to which the Church's faith and theology have formed and added to the tradition of the history of Jesus appears most clearly in the legends and in a story's legendary embellishments, as these increase from one evangelist to another. This is especially evident in the infancy narratives of Matthew and Luke, and in the Easter stories of all four evangelists. This tendency is frequently found to have been raised into the realm of phantasy in the later noncanonical Gospels, of which fragments remain in considerable number.

The tradition's lack of historical concern appears in its style of storytelling. The modern historian to whom where and when, cause and effect, inner development and personality are all important questions, receives small satisfaction. As a rule, historical and factual notes serve only to frame and to connect the individual scenes. They confine themselves to indicating time in general terms (thereafter, on that evening, a few days after, etc.). Equally stereotyped are descriptions of place (house, road, field, lake, etc.); descriptions which are used in quite different ways by the different Gospels. Every reader has only to compare the romantic expansion of precisely these exterior features of the history of Jesus in many sermons and children's lessons, and in the literature relating to the life of Jesus, with what is contained in the actual text. With the text, too, let him compare the frequently irreverent and sentimental discussions of what took place in the soul of Jesus. We should learn from this that we would be well advised not to try to help out the "defectiveness" of the text in the interest of a more realistic story, but to stick to the subject which the text has in view.

Only in more recent times have the character and form of the tradition become the subject of more detailed investigation, a task which has been the especial province of so-called form criticism. It has revealed laws of tradition which stem from pre-literary, oral tradition and which are still preserved unchanged in the first three Gospels. Observing these laws is an excellent aid in distinguishing the essential from the non-essential in any passage. But the results reach further. They prove the unique character of the Gospels compared to all other kinds and classes of ancient historiography and literature. Above all these laws of tradition teach us to look for the connection between the entire Jesus tradition and the faith and life of the Church, out of which that tradition arose and for which it was meant. The extent to which the Church was responsible for its formation need not be stated here in detail. It is more important to recognise the existence of its responsibility. The critical exegete and the historian is therefore obliged, in questions concerning the history of tradition, to speak often of "authentic" or "inauthentic" words of Jesus and thus to distinguish words of the historical Jesus from "creations by the Church." Even today he usually incurs the horrified reproach of theologians and laity that he is merely destructive. This critical task should, however, be understood in principle as pointing out a very positive factor, namely the interpretation of the history of Jesus in terms of his resurrection and the experience of his presence. We should not, therefore, dismiss as mere fancy or invention what criticism might term "inauthentic" and "creations by the Church." Such an erroneous conception appears frequently both among supporters and opponents of criticism. While the one declares that under no circumstances is the Church to be credited with such a degree of creative phantasy, the other holds that precisely this assertion is required of us. Meanwhile we should ask ourselves whether the categories employed here really suit the case. Though one should not deny the part played by subjective experience and poetic imagination, the tradition which first grew out of the faith of the Church is not to be dismissed, by reason of its foundation and origin, as the mere product of imagination. It is an answer to Jesus' whole person and mission. It points beyond itself to him whom the Church has encountered in his earthly form and who proves his presence to her as the resurrected and risen Lord. In every layer, therefore, and in each individual part, the tradition is witness of the reality of his history and the reality of his resurrection. Our task, then, is to seek the history *in* the Kerygma of the Gospels, and in this history to seek the Kergyma. If we are asked to differentiate between the two, that is only for the purpose of revealing more clearly their inter-connection and inter-penetration.

A long tradition, whose spell we cannot so easily escape, has alienated us from this understanding of the history of Jesus, and has made it the sole—or at least the first—essential for us to enquire into the historical happenings. This applies to those who cling to the tradition and secretly or openly consider historical-critical research an attack on the foundations of Christian faith. It applies equally to those who draw their weapons for attack on the Christian message from historiography and criticism. It is for this reason that we needed to speak here in such detail, although by no means exhaustively, of the understanding of history implicit in the Gospel tradition, and of its disagreement with our way of thinking. In view of the position we are in today, all these considerations as to method were unavoidable, although they may well have put the patience of the reader to a severe test. Unfortunately we show this patience and freedom too infrequently; some of us because the work of historical-critical theology is regarded as purely destructive, and others of us who defend it, because we have never faced the theological problems posed in such research. In consequence historical criticism and Christian faith have parted company to an almost hopeless degree, and one of our noblest tasks, both exacting and rewarding, has been left unfinished. But in this fashion the recognition of the truth is clouded for us and rendered impossible. This truth does not lie before us as self-evidently and openly as we might think. Perhaps other times have been more fortunate. For us the way lies through precisely that narrow pass of such considerations concerning principle and method as have engaged us.

What has been said so far must in no way discourage us from raising the question of the historical Jesus at all. True, it may appear as if scholarship and faith, from opposite points of view, would wish to dismiss it as an impossible question. Representatives of critical biblical scholarship dismiss it because they consider the entanglement of confession and report, of history and faith in the Gospels so indissolubly close, that they consider every quest of the historical Jesus entirely vain. The supporters of believing tradition dismiss it because from the very start they dispute the suitability of critical historical scholarship for this subject, and consider the unqualified recognition of the tradition in its given form the first requirement of faith. Both offer solutions senseless and forced. There is no need of long discussions in defence of our position that critical research cannot allow itself to be ordered off the field. Such discussions would, in any case, be fruitless in face of dogmatic prejudices. If what we have said about the character of the Gospels is true, it is clear that research is faced with a great number of questions and tasks. The torrent cannot be halted, no matter how much of its water has strayed from its course. We shall have to set about building real dams until these waters subside and the dry land becomes visible again. But it cannot be seriously maintained that the Gospels and their tradition do not allow enquiry after the historical Jesus. Not only do they allow, they demand this effort. For whatever the opinions of historians on matters of detail, none can dispute that the tradition of the Gospels is itself very considerably concerned with the pre-Easter history of Jesus, different though this interest is from that of modern historical science. The Easter aspect in which the primitive Church views the history of Jesus must certainly not be forgotten for one moment; but not less the fact that it is precisely the history of Jesus before Good Friday and Easter which is seen in this aspect. Were it otherwise, the Church would have been lost in a timeless myth, even if for some irrelevant reason or other she had given the bearer of this myth the name of Jesus. The Gospels are the rejection of myth. To whatever extent mythological conceptions from time to time find access to the thought and faith of the early Church, they are given once and for all the function of interpreting the history of Jesus as the history of God with the world. As the language of the New Testament puts it: the "once" of Jesus' history as God's "once and for all," certain to faith.

Nothing could be more mistaken than to trace the origin of the Gospels and the traditions collected therein to a historical interest apart from faith—irrespective of whether that historical interest were to be considered questionable or wholesome. Rather these Gospels voice the confession: Jesus the Christ, the unity of the earthly Jesus and the Christ of faith. By this the Gospels proclaim that faith does not begin with itself but lives from past history. Of this past history we must speak, as do all the Gospels, only in the past tense: and this precisely because of the present in which faith has its being.

In another respect also, faith's interest in pre-Easter history must be made clear. The following question could be posed concerning the post-Easter Church which lived in the assurance of the presence of the risen Christ and in the hope of his speedy return: Did not the Church fall into a strange anachronism? She made herself contemporary with her earthly pre-Easter Lord. She made herself contemporary with the Pharisees and high priests of long ago. She made herself contemporary with the first hearers of Jesus who heard his message of the coming of God's kingdom; with the disciples who followed after him; with the sick whom he healed; with the tax collectors and sinners with whom he sat down at table. But what may appear here as anachronism corresponds exactly with the Church's understanding of herself and her situation. She made herself one with those who did not already live by faith, but who at the beginning were called to obedience and faith by the word of Jesus. In this she confessed at the same time that her faith can be nothing else but following her earthly Master who is yet to face the cross and resurrection. The Gospels are therefore at the same time the rejection of an eschatological fanaticism which denies the temporal order and proclaims the glory of God's world as already present.

What then of the other question raised by scholarship? With regard to our sources, is an exposition of the history and message of Jesus a sensible undertaking capable of being carried through? Shall we retrogress and once again attempt a detailed description of the course of his life biographically and psychologically? Certainly not. All such attempts, as often as they are undertaken, are doomed to failure. They can only be carried through with a lack of criticism which alleges everything to be historical, or with the display of an imagination no less uncritical, which arbitrarily stops gaps and manufactures connections precisely where the Gospels omit them. They only obscure the fragmentary and incomplete nature of our detailed knowledge and efface the boundary between what is historically certain and uncertain. It is not our most urgent task to establish the possibility or probability of this or that miracle story which criticism calls a legend, or to save this or that word for the historical Jesus which on very good grounds can be shown to have sprung from the faith of the later Church. Such manœuvres, even if called for here and there, can change nothing in the total situation.

Nevertheless, the Gospels justify neither resignation nor scepticism. Rather they bring before our eyes, in very different fashion from what is customary in chronicles and presentations of history, the historical person of Jesus with the utmost vividness. Quite clearly what the Gospels report concerning the message, the deeds and the history of Jesus is still distinguished by an authenticity, a freshness, and a distinctiveness not in any way effaced by the Church's Easter faith. These features point us directly to the earthly figure of Jesus.

It is precisely historical criticism which, rightly understood, has opened up our way anew to this history, by disposing of attempts along biographical, psychological lines. We can now see more clearly. Although the Gospels do not speak of the history of Jesus in the way of reproducing the course of his career in all its happenings and stages, in its inner and outer development, nevertheless they do speak of history as occurrence and event. The Gospels give abundant evidence of such history. This opinion may be boldly stated, despite the fact that on historical grounds so many of the stories and sayings could be contested in detail, despite tendencies evidently active in the tradition, despite the impossibility of finally extracting from more or less authentic particulars a more or less assured whole which we could call a life of Jesus.

As everyone knows, the Gospels tell the story of Jesus in "pericopæ," i.e. in brief anecdotes. These story scenes give his history not only when pieced together, but each one in itself contains the person and history of Jesus in their entirety. None requires explanation in terms of previous happenings. None is directed at later events for the unfolding of what has gone before. We are always being held in the beam of this scene and this scene only. The circle of light is always sharply defined. The description of those who appear in it are limited to the essential. The meeting of Jesus with certain people, which through his word and deed becomes an event of supreme challenge and significance, is clearly and sharply illuminated. This way of telling his story has its exact counterpart in the transmission of his words. Here again each word stands by itself, exhaustive in itself, not dependent on context for its meaning or requiring a commentary on it from some other word. In the same way the so-called discourses of the Gospels—the Sermon on the Mount, the Commissioning of the Disciples, the Parables—are in reality not discourses, but collections of such sayings.

What then is shown us in this style of transmission? Surely these are all characteristics of a popular and unhistorical transmission, evidence that the Gospel tradition, in origin and purpose, is directed to the practical use of the believing Church, to whom mere history as such means very little. Surely the historian is forced thereby to criticise this tradition, which often enough is silent where he seeks an answer, naïvely generalises where he enquires after the individual element in each case, and frequently blurs the distinction between history and interpretation. These are legitimate questions. And yet we must never lose sight of the fact that, precisely in this way of transmitting and recounting, the person and work of Jesus, in their unmistakable uniqueness and distinctiveness, are shown forth with an originality which again and again far exceeds and disarms even all believing understandings and interpretations. Understood in this way, the primitive tradition of Jesus is brim full of history.

CHAPTER 4

The Synoptic Gospels

X. LEON-DUFOUR, S. J.

> This selection reflects recent Catholic thought about critical and historical questions connected with the New Testament. Leon-Dufour is thoroughly familiar with the position of Bultmann and other radical Form Critics, but his own conclusions are more conservative. He recognizes the role of oral tradition but is convinced that the Church prevented serious distortion during the period of transmission. Thus, substantial historicity may be attributed to the Gospel materials. Leon-Dufour is Professor of Biblical Theology at Fouriere, France, and a consultor of the Pontifical Biblical Commission.

§ 1. THE HISTORICAL PROBLEM OF JESUS

I. THE PROBLEM AND THE ANSWERS

THROUGHOUT the preceding chapters, the question was: *Do we reach the Christ of history through the representation which we find in the Gospels?*

The answer varies according to the critics. Bultmann may maintain a thick veil between the primitive community and Jesus Himself, but many others, in spite of the apparent coldness of their criticism, have declared themselves in favor of the possibility of reaching Jesus truly. Some think that at times facts were altered, even described inaccurately, but most hold that they can really hear the word of Christ. Thus in England, V. Taylor, E. Hoskyns, T. W. Manson. Even Goguel wrote recently that "the so-called historicism, against which some conservative theologians like to protest, never existed except in their imagination. The fact of Jesus

Quoted with special permission of the publishers; from A. Feuillet and A. Robert, *Introduction to the New Testament* (New York: Desclee, 1965), pp. 312–324.

54

who is the foundation of Christian faith evidently has besides its historical character a supranatural, suprahistorical significance which may be summed up in the statement that, for faith, Jesus represents an intervention in human history." [1]

For Catholics, the answer is guaranteed by faith; Rome's reaction to Loisy's boldness is significant: the Gospels are historical documents. But this affirmation bears on the fact of the historicity, not on the mode of its transmission.

Too frequently, Catholic apologists are satisfied with a line of argument which indeed is not erroneous, but is not sufficient as an answer to the problem in its present form.

II. A CLASSICAL FORM OF THE ARGUMENT

Frequently, the argument is: The Gospels come from sincere, well-informed authors; therefore, they are historical. Now such an argument implies nothing regarding the manner in which these writings are historical. Furthermore, it places on the authors of the Gospels a burden of modern criticism which seems excessive. The two preceding chapters immediately call it in question. Mark and Luke are not immediate witnesses. Their connection with Peter and Paul is not enough to guarantee their testimony, from a literary point of view, and Matthew comes to us only through a recasting of the work of the Apostle Matthew.

Indeed, we should not ignore the arguments from tradition, but a justification of the historical value of the Gospels should be able to rest ultimately on the internal criticism of the documents. Now can the evangelists Matthew, Mark and Luke be described as witnesses, in the sense required today by a study of historical criticism?

Moreover, the preceding studies positively show them to be primarily "ministers of the Word," carefully transmitting the data they collected after evaluating them. The materials the evangelists admitted imposed themselves in well-defined forms. They were enclosed in a general schema received traditionally (John, a witness, alone disregarded that schema). We can see clearly the points at which they were joined together and thus we can go back to a pre-synoptic stage. At that stage can the "authors" be said to be responsible for materials which had an independent literary existence? Yes, in the sense that they evaluated the solidity of the tradition

[1] "La critique et la foi," *Le Problème biblique dans le protestantisme* (Paris, 1955), p. 32.

which they accepted; no, in the sense that they do not place themselves above the Church which transmits that tradition.

The classical reasoning needs a complement. Indeed, it will always be necessary to establish by external criticism the authenticity of the Gospels, to infer their historicity as a consequence from the authenticity; but it will be necessary to determine besides *how* they are historical.

III. SCHEMA OF A STATEMENT OF THE HISTORICAL VALUE OF THE SYNOPTICS

In order to be treated as fully as it deserves according to contemporary requirements, the question must be solved at different stages so as to include the classical arguments while renewing them. We must go backwards from the second century to the oral tradition. At each stage, external criticism and internal criticism combine to settle progressively in what sense our Gospels are historical.

Three stages may be discerned which correspond to the successive stages at which the Gospel writings can be examined.

1) As they constitute the norm of evangelic faith, the four Gospels were first considered as a unit, as the Gospel in four different forms rather than as four Gospels. According to St. Irenaeus' expression, it was the Fourfold Gospel. To that traditional presentation may be joined, from the modern point of view, an inquiry into the materials contained in the Gospels.

2) A study of the four Gospels considered individually enables one to define the literary genre "Gospel" and to appreciate at that stage in what sense they may be called historical.

3) Lastly, we must go back to the evangelic tradition which preceded the writing down of the four Gospels. A summary study of the milieu in which the tradition lived enable us to state in what sense it deserves our confidence from the historical point of view.

§ 2. FIRST STAGE: THE FOURFOLD GOSPEL

At this stage, it suffices to show that the Gospels are really historical documents.

I. FROM THE TRADITIONAL VIEWPOINT

The Fathers of the ante-Nicene Church regarded the Fourfold Gospel as the source of their faith. They rejected any other Gospel.

They received it as apostolic; they subjected it to a veritable critical treatment. Tertullian appeals against Marcion to the universality and the continuity of the historical tradition which has transmitted those writings.

On the other hand, the Christian faith rests essentially on a historical fact, not primarily on a doctrine. To receive the Gospels as canonical means to recognize their historicity; a general historicity which assuredly does not answer modern exigencies, nevertheless a substantial historicity which later criticism must take into account. According to the saying, *melior est conditio possidentis*, historicity is in possession.

This is confirmed by the New Testament theologians. The study of the point was carried on very carefully in 1931 by Hoskyns. Paul, John, the author of the Epistle to the Hebrews, these theologians base their teaching on a fact: Jesus who died on the Cross, rose from the dead, and is living. This fact has a doctrinal import. It is not simply the symbolic clothing of a more or less mysterious doctrine. These three authors undoubtedly adapt their message to the needs of their correspondents, but all of them lean on the same fact. It would be unthinkable that all this rests on nothing. Better still, the study of their comportment places the critic in the suitable frame of mind to inquire into the historical content of the Gospels: a fact which is inseparable from a doctrinal significance.

Paul's testimony is more particularly cogent. He is a witness independent from the evangelists. It can be said of him that he is sincere and well informed, that he belongs to the very beginnings, that he knows the whole Church. Now, this testimony agrees with that of the evangelists on the main points.

II. FROM THE MODERN POINT OF VIEW

In their way, modern sciences help one to feel confident of the content of the Gospels. They confirm the global historicity affirmed by the tradition by confronting the intrinsic data of the Gospels with the data supplied by other documents or other sciences. At that stage, the question is not yet a literary study, but only an examination of the content. In any investigation concerning a historical work, one determines first the milieu in which the work appeared and thus settles the time of its composition. This first line of inquiry does not exclude the possibility of an archeological reconstruction which the authors might have made on the basis of ancient materials, nor the possible influence of a more or less intentional deformation of the materials. But it increases our confidence in the historical value of the work under consideration.

A milieu before the year 70

The state of things described in the Gospels is that of Palestine before the catastrophe of the year 70. On the other hand, that description cannot be separated from the texture of the Gospel narrative.

From the point of view of language, the accounts written in Greek reveal a contact with the Old Testament and a Palestinian origin earlier than the diffusion and spread in the Hellenistic communities; evidently without prejudging, apart from some nuances to be mentioned later, the argument is valid.

From the geographical point of view, the excavations made for over a century incessantly confirm the Gospel localizations: Capharnaum, Nazareth, Naim, the two Caesareas, the way from Jerusalem to Jericho, the indications supplied recently by Qumran.

From the historical and political point of view, the historian Josephus contributes his confirmation. For instance, the accounts of the opposition between Jesus and Samaritans, Pharisees and Sadducees, etc. The social life of the period, although turned topsy-turvy at the time of the ruin of Jerusalem, appears clearly. Renan's words may be quoted: "I had before my eyes a fifth gospel, torn, but still visible." The religious customs of the time are recognizable: feasts, pilgrimages to the Temple, services in the synagogue, rest on the Sabbath, etc. The currents of thought also are reflected, eschatological, Messianic, even Qumranian.

Facts dating before the year 50

The Acts of the Apostles and St. Paul's Epistles show a fast evolution of the Christian community, both in its organization and in its orientations of thought. One may call evangelic archaism the fact that the writings later than the Pauline Epistles do not take into account the development which took place after the year 50.

The Christian institutions of St. Paul's time already appear distinct from those of the synagogue. A hierarchical organization can be seen clearly. Heresies already appear, universalism is evident, persecutions are taking place. On the contrary, the Gospels present a new religion, but not yet separated from the synagogue, a Master who with His disciples carefully respects the Mosaic laws, a surprising particularism on the part of Jesus (Mt 10, 5; 15, 24), and when allusions are made to persecutions, the terms used are so vague that, supposing that these are prophecies which were written after the event, the effort made to reconstitute the circumstances would be admirable, not to say impossible in view of known pseudepigraphs.

In St. Paul's time, Christian doctrine shows a trend towards a systematization of Christology, soteriology, the doctrine about the Holy Spirit, the Church, knowledge, tradition as a deposit. In the Gospels there is no attempt at synthesis or speculation, for instance about the preexistence or the divinity of Christ. The terminology is primitive: some terms, such as Son of Man, kingdom of heaven, will disappear later on.

The tendencies are quite different. Paul's concern is the fight against the Judaizers and the precursors of Gnosticism. Jesus' opponents are the Pharisees and the Sadducees. We could say that anti-Pharisaism marks a date.

Comparison with the Apocrypha

The Apocrypha are caught in their own trap. They multiply details and fall into anachronism. Thus in the Protevangelium of James, Mary's presentation in the Temple, or the barrenness of Mary's mother, a flagrant imitation of that of Anna, the mother of Samuel.

Their apologetic purpose betrays them; they add miracles without religious significance. Thus in the Arabic Gospel of the Infancy, when Jesus passes, the trees bow to give Him fruit. Jesus causes the children who do not want to play with Him to die, though He raises them afterwards.

The Gospel of Peter is still more significant. At Christ's resurrection, the soldiers see rising from the tomb two enormous forms; they call the centurion on duty, and those objective witnesses, since they are unbelievers, behold a third form coming from the tomb with a cross reaching to heaven. Then they hear a voice: "Did you preach to the dead?" Thus the fact of the resurrection is attested by neutral, impartial witnesses; thereby, however, the freedom of faith is destroyed.

The doctrinarian notes are significant. According to the Gospel of the Ebionites, John the Baptist eats not grasshoppers (ἀκρίς), but as a vegetarian he eats cakes (ἐγκρίς). The Gospel of the Egyptians shows its sectarian hatred of marriage by having Christ Himself express that view of marriage.

III. CONCLUSION: THE PROBLEM WHICH REMAINS

At the end of this first stage, the Synoptic Gospels appear as narratives which have been transmitted in an excellent textual condition. They can be ascribed to first-century writers; they relate the history of a fact which is not contradicted by profane history; they portray a milieu dating from the period in which the fact took place.

Therefore our Gospels are truly historical documents. But in what way are they historical? For indeed there are different kinds of history. The Gospel presentation of the fact is not disinterested, it is doctrinal. From that assured fact there may arise some questions. Was there any influence of certain tendencies, of prejudices of faith which, more or less unconsciously, altered the facts? Was not history reconstructed, "invented" on the basis of religious experience? Why should we not admit, like Bultmann, that most narratives are "ideale Szenen" (ideal scenes) or that myths are the literary clothing of faith? Can we trust the authors and admit that we reach, not their faith alone, but Jesus Himself?

In order to answer these questions, we must pass a judgment of internal criticism which fits perfectly the literary criticism of the documents. This can be expressed in two steps which will be the second and third stages: the historicity of each Gospel, starting from its literary genre; the historicity of the Gospel tradition starting from the preexistent units.

§3. SECOND STAGE: THE FIRST THREE GOSPELS

I. THE LITERARY GENRE "GOSPEL"

The preceding chapters show what the literary genre "Gospel" is. The facts are intrinsically bound up with their interpretation: they are catechetical booklets which record a history. Therefore one should not expect from them the characteristics of modern books of history. Yet at the same time they have a "biographical" purpose which underlies the catechetical purpose. For they are a "gospel," the Good News to be transmitted about the fact which took place before. Essentially, therefore, the Gospels are historical books. But the insufficient amount of information connected with the framework shows that they were not written for a scientific historical purpose. They are not merely historical books.

Modern historical criticism can therefore apply its principles to

the authors of these writings, endeavoring to catch them if they try
to transform facts for the sake of doctrine: has the author exaggerated a fact or point of doctrine, by presenting the fact in a more
marvelous light, by making the doctrine more acceptable or more
coherent, in order to win followers for the religion which they are
teaching?

II. CRITICAL STUDY OF THE BOOKS

A careful study shows that there is no such apologetic purpose,
not even in Matthew. As L. de Grandmaison says, "they are epiph-
anies rather than apologies." The authors do not seek praise, they
vanish behind their work. The apostles are not flattered, and that
at the very time when the Church was extolling them (cf. Gal 2; 1
Cor 9, 1). They are described as lacking understanding, as being
ambitious, quarrelsome, cowards, traitors. Christ appears with
characteristics which are problems to the professional theologian:
He seems to be lower than the Father, He does not know the day
of judgment, He is forsaken by His Father. He flees, hides Himself,
sweats blood. His doctrine is sublime and yet inadmissible, it goes
against received ideas, does not try to make itself acceptable. The
miracles are related soberly, in a manner which at once distinguishes
them from non-evangelic accounts. The Gospels thus seem to be
writings unconcerned with apologetics in the modern sense of the
word, but aimed at transmitting the bare fact to which they testify.

Indeed, they interpret the fact. Yet the simplicity of the account,
of the expression, the difficulties which arise from such artlessness
in the doctrinal presentation, the indissoluble union of the doctrine
and of the fact which makes impossible a purely intellectual ad-
hesion to the Gospel but demands the recognition of the divine
character of Jesus, all this goes to show that the Gospels are not a
doctrinal speculation, but the attestation of a fact.

§ 4. THIRD STAGE: THE GOSPEL TRADITION

I. THE QUESTION OF IDEALIZATION

At the close of the second stage, the Gospels appear as writings
which mean to relate a fact in order to obtain an act of faith. The
fact poses a question: "What is that man?"

This is the intention of the evangelists. But they wrote some thirty or forty years after the event, on the basis of oral and written sources. Does their authority suffice to guarantee these sources as it covered the substances of the Gospel? We cannot appeal to the charism of inspiration, as the inquiry is conducted merely rationally. Nor can we ascribe to them our "critical sense." Unlike modern authors, they were not completely free towards the sources, they were above all "ministers of the Word" who indeed made a choice, but whose prime concern was to transmit with the least amount of modification. The historian has the right and is bound to examine the historical value of the sources in which he can suspect idealization.

Sometimes it is argued that idealization has been avoided in fact: the comparison with the apocrypha is decisive. But some probings do not do away with all doubt. It is further argued that such idealization was impossible "de jure": the very purpose of the Gospels, to base the doctrine on facts, would seem to exclude it. The affirmation may be valid for the work as a whole, but not for the sources, at least at first sight. Only a literary demonstration would be conclusive.

II. THE CHURCH IS THE RESPONSIBLE AUTHOR

The preceding chapter on the sources of the Gospels contains the answer to the question. We may not always have responsible writers of the small presynoptic literary units, but there is the Christian community and this is not an anonymous multitude but a community with structure: the witnesses are there, in charge of the transmission of their recollections. They implant firmly the present life of the young Church in the ground of a past still living through them. Furthermore, the Church consists of a number of communities which can control each other mutually. Between them there are many relations, convergent and divergent (cf. 1 Cor 1-2).

The task of understanding the materials transmitted by the tradition, therefore, was controlled in that multiple yet centered community. Far from having been a source of legends, it rather contributed to preserving the tradition from any substantial departure from the thought of Jesus. In particular the attitude of the community towards the multiplicity of the traditions is illuminating: it regarded minute divergences as negligible. The fundamental concordance subsists; "it proves more when it is limited to a small number of points" (Seignobos).

The presentation of the evangelic doctrinal fact, therefore, is more closely related to painting than to photography, to recollection rather than to a report or a stenographic account, to the parable rather than to allegory. The authors or the traditions give us views of the one fact. It is not possible to overlay two views taken of one object when they are facing each other, and yet it is the same real object.

III. DETAILS AND HISTORY

At the conclusion of the three stages, the Synoptic Gospels present themselves as historical documents. We know how they transmit the facts. However, we have not tried to justify in detail the historicity of each passage. We have shown that we must entertain a favorable assumption regarding their historical value. Each passage has to be studied individually in order to determine its precise genre. This is a matter of exegesis.

That they may be traces of allegorization, of application to the needs of the living Church, is sometimes evident. But what seems to be no less certain is that the deformation of the original traditions was very difficult because of the nature of the community. On the other hand, transformation was sometimes possible, even necessary. This is not surprising, for it is the Church which transmits the understanding of the mere facts. The only way in which the facts and sayings of the past can be understood is to look at them and hear them together with the Church. This is the scientific and traditional method: the Gospels were created and transmitted in a community, and for the believer that community is our holy Mother Church.

One may try to determine more closely the historical character of the particular data of each passage. Evidently the details of the narratives of the Infancy do not have the same historical significance as the details of the account of the Passion. But whatever these details are, they have their own value which hasty criticism could misunderstand. By themselves, torn from the living content which transmits them, they have little significance. Taken with their context they become indispensable in order to grasp the whole of the passage. The Gospel narratives contain details which have the same significance as the details of a parable (not in an allegory): they should not be isolated from the lesson of the whole text; they are indispensable in order to grasp the parable itself. Therefore, it would be an error to neglect the details under the pretext that the literary genre of the passage is not that of a report. They keep, in their place, a full significance.

§ 5.   CONCLUSION: JESUS AND THE "LIVES OF JESUS"

The Jesus of history and the Christ of faith

The one point of convergence in our inquiry is Jesus: Jesus whom the Fathers of the Church thought they could reach through the Gospels, Jesus whom the theologians of the New Testament aimed at knowing, Jesus to whom each of the Gospels testifies, Jesus to whom all the units of the Gospel tradition point. Jesus came as the Son of God to save men by freely accepting death and by rising. This convergence, due to writers and communities living in different places, writing with different concerns and manifesting at times their partial divergences, invites us to see there more than the expression of a religious experience and to recognize the attestation of a fact.[2]

Thus, scientifically and rationally, through the Christ of faith we reach the Jesus of history. There is no chasm between them, but the way which leads to Him. I am not shut in the world of my faith, but rationally I discover in a world of faith the presence of the historical Jesus of Nazareth. The historical inquiry places me in the presence of a mysterious existence of doctrinal significance which urges me to believe in that mysterious man who calls Himself the Savior of men. The answer is a matter of faith.

The fact of Jesus is presented as a life: it is impossible to separate

[2] In Germany, most likely under the impact of the crisis connected with Bultmann's views, many Protestant critics are anxious to determine exactly the extent to which one reaches the historic Christ. F. Mussner, "Der historische Jesus und der Christus der Glaubens," *BZ* (1957), p. 255 mentions the essays of E. Käsemann (1954), N. A. Dahl, O. Michel (1955), E. Heitsch, E. Fuchs, F. Lieb (1956) and shows that most of them declare themselves in favor of a revalorization of history. A similar report was published shortly afterwards by a Protestant, P. Biehl, "Zur Frage nach denn historischen Jesus," *Theologische Rundschau* (1956–1957), pp. 54–75. It shows also that the object proper of the apostolic message is the historical Jesus.

the Gospel's message from that existence, from the life of the Man-God who of His own will underwent death to save men. However, the Gospels do not present themselves as works on the basis of which one could compose the scientific modern life which so many of our contemporaries would like to have.

A solid historical substratum

Indeed, there is an objective historical substratum which imposes itself independently of any belief and of any sympathy for the Christian phenomenon. Goguel made an honest attempt at determining the fact accurately. To a certain extent his undertaking is successful, for it shows more clearly the solidity of the foundation of the historical existence of Jesus. Recently, V. Taylor refused to admit the "intellectual paralysis" which strikes many critics at the mention of a "Life of Jesus."

Jesus, whose origins and comportment were genuinely Jewish, lived in Palestine, healed sick people, gathered some disciples about Him, preached the coming Kingdom; He spoke in such a strikingly personal way that His voice can still be recognized in the Gospels.[3] His teaching is genuinely traditional, according to the Jewish historian Joseph Klausner: "Jesus was a Jew and remained a Jew to His dying breath," but His teaching was "the negation of everything which bound Judaism to life" and it brought Him to an extremism which became non-Judaism. Therefore that teaching of Jesus failed to be understood by His contemporaries, not only by personalities in official positions against whom Jesus rose up, but even by His own disciples.

Finally, He died a violent death under Pontius Pilate, because of His Messianic claims. A last item which the witnesses of that time give us: His disciples affirm that they saw Him alive after His death.

Limits of our historical knowledge

This already is a personal historical knowledge of Jesus, but the historian wants more: to attempt a biographical development of that man. It is not enough to draw a portrait. What is needed is a history. Now it is possible to distinguish several periods. Topograph-

[3] J. Jeremias, "Kennzeichen der ipsissima vox Jesu," *Synoptische Studien für A. Wikenhauser* (Munich, 1953), pp. 86–93.

ically, the impulse begins in Galilee, whence it extends to Judea along the confines of Galilee, to Caesarea Philippi, where Peter's confession took place. Personally, Jesus is situated relatively to John the Baptist, to Herod, to the Pharisees. Doctrinally, the teaching on the necessity of the Passion belongs to a second period. This second period follows the failure in Galilee and the threat of Herod, but especially the incomprehension of the true meaning of Jesus' Messianism.

This is a minimum admitted by every reasonable critic. Is it possible to go further and to work out a detailed chronology of the life of Jesus? Some authors think so. Thus C. Lavergne's *Synopsis of the Four Gospels,* following Fr. Lagrange, dates the Baptism of Christ January 28. Starting from that date, most of the events are themselves dated precisely. The statements of the fourth Gospel are combined with those of the Synoptic Gospels.

Ordinarily, however, the critics hold that such attempts, commendable as they may be, are doomed to failure to the extent that they pretend to fix a precise calendar of the life of Jesus. Dating the Last Supper and the death of Jesus is something indispensable. But one goes beyond the limits of sound criticism when one affirms that the inaugural sermon was delivered on June 19, 28; that the storm was stilled in December 28; that the Transfiguration took place on August 6, 29. This can even result in serious confusions, because it puts assured data such as the date of Jesus' death on the same level as more or less fanciful particulars; questioning these may lead to questioning the former.

Moreover, this attempt at discovering the objective historical foundations means examining the Gospel documents not according to their literary genre, but against their perspective. It pretends to assist at the succession of the events independently of their religious significance. It is right, perhaps even necessary, to force the texts to yield those particulars which were not the chief interest of the evangelists; it would be a serious misunderstanding of their intentions if one were to be satisfied with this: an error of literary criticism.

What is essential is the Gospel of Jesus

The life of Jesus cannot be treated as an ordinary life, intelligible like any other life. Literally, it is presented as a gospel, that is to say as the announcement of Good News which places the hearer before a question. To grasp the person of Jesus, it is not necessary to have faith. It is enough to have some sympathy, the sympathetic attitude of the historian who must communicate as intimately, as scientifically as possible with the faith of the early Christians who transmitted the fact of Jesus. After this is said, it is true that faith only can fully understand Jesus, and faith goes ever more deeply. "The Gospels are the only life of Jesus that can be written. But they must be understood as perfectly as possible" (M. J. Lagrange).[4]

[4] See also "Instructio de historica Evangeliorum veritate," Osservatore Romano, May 14, 1964; Eng. trans. in *CBQ*, 26 (July 1964), pp. 305–312.

CHAPTER 5

Assessment of Form Criticism

ALFRED WIKENHAUSER

Professor Wikenhauser was a member of the Catholic Faculty at the University of Freiburg until his death in 1961. He was one of the editors of the German New Testament commentary series known as the *Regensburger Neues Testament*. His "Assessment of Form Criticism" indicates an approval of its general approach but a more conservative attitude toward the historicity of the individual incidents than is characteristic of Bultmann or even Dibelius.

THIS new method of treatment has quickly established itself in New Testament studies. It marks a notable advance on the one-sided literary criticism which long dominated non-Catholic Gospel studies, and it may be welcomed as a useful means of illuminating the dark period when the Gospel material was transmitted orally.[1]

On the other hand Form Criticism is still in its infancy, and its

---

[1] There have already been attempts to extend it to the other pieces of the NT writings which contain traditional material, i.e. Acts and the paraenetic parts of the Epistles. Cf. Dibelius, *Stilkritisches zur Apg.*: Eucharisterion, Festschrift fuer H. Gunkel 11 (1923) 27–49 and his survey: *Zur FG des NT* (except the Gospels): ThRdsch NF 3 (1931) 207–242, and also the commentary on Acts by Bauernfeind (cf § 29) and E. Lichtenstein, *Die aelteste christliche Glaubensformel:* ZKG 63 (1950) 1–74; M. Dibelius, *Jakobusbrief²*, 1956; D. G. Bradley, *The Topos as a Form in Pauline Paraenesis:* JBL 72 (1953) 238–246. N. A. Dahl, *Fg. Beobachtungen zur Christusverkuendigung in der Gemeindepredigt:* NtlStudien, R. Bultmann, Berlin 1954, 3–9; E. Kaesemann, *Das Formular einer ntl Ordinationsparaenese* (1 Tim. 6, 11–16), ibid. 261–268; E. Lohse, vide ad § 50 (with literature on Paraenesis); W. Nauck, *Freude im Leiden. Zum Problem einer urchristlichen Verfolgungstradition:* Zntw 46 (1955) 68–80.

From *New Testament Introduction* by Alfred Wikenhauser, 1958. By permission of Herder and Herder, the publishers.

founders and chief exponents have come in for justified censure because of the ways in which they have applied it. There is need, therefore, for a correct statement of the principles which should govern this method, and for a demonstration of its inherent limitations.

1. The first and most important premise of Form Criticism is fundamentally correct: the synoptic Gospels are compilations. In them we must distinguish sharply between traditional material and redaction. Only the individual sayings of Jesus and the individual stories are traditional; they must be separated from the framework in which they are embedded, and must be treated by themselves. Only in this way can the original proper significance of a saying or of a narrative be established; exegesis according to the trend of thought, as it was practised in the past, is misleading.

Even if the pericopae are joined by commonly accepted expressions of time, the order in which they stand is not necessarily the chronological order of the incidents recounted in them. The clearest evidence of this is the fact that a number of pericopae have different settings in the individual Gospels; thus, for example, the healing of the leper Mark 1, 40-45 appears elsewhere in Matthew (8, 1-4) and Luke (5, 12-16). The transition from one pericope to another is generally very indefinite (and, when, then, immediately, in those days, at that time), and to interpret these rigorously would be contrary to the Evangelist's intention; they are generally intended to be understood simply as transition formulae. Even in Mark pericopae are grouped according to content without reference to time or place (for example, the five Galilean conflicts, 2, 1 to 3, 6). This applies not only to narratives, but also, indeed even more, to sayings of Our Lord; it may be asserted that all the long discourses of Our Lord in the Synoptics—not excluding the eschatological discourse —are groupings of single sayings according to subject matter. There are, however, some exceptions, of which the most important is the history of the Passion; it may also be assumed that the incidents which Mk. 1, 21-38 reports actually happened on that Sabbath.

Topographical information, when it is given at all, is often as vague as the chronology: 'on the way,' 'in a house,' 'on the sea,' 'on the mountain,' 'in one of the cities.' Although Jesus performed many works in Chorozain (Mt. 11, 21; Lk. 10, 13), the New Testament does not locate a single one there. Only a comparatively small number of the pericopae tell where the incident happened (Nazareth,

Capharnaum, Naim, Bethsaida, the villages around Caesarea, Philippi, Jericho), and it cannot be presumed that these definite indications of place are subsequent additions. So the routes of the journeys of Jesus are not handed down, and it is impossible to reconstruct them.

However, "the framework of the history of Jesus" cannot be dismissed so easily. We must not regard the Evangelists as mere collectors who juxtaposed the words and acts of Jesus quite superficially, and joined them with meaningless connecting words. The outline of the life of Jesus which Mark created and Matthew and Luke adopted, must certainly be considered historical in substance: the imprisonment of the Baptist followed by the Galilean ministry of Jesus which centred around Capharnaum and the north shore of the lake, the lessening of the initial enthusiasm of the people, the withdrawal towards the North (the territory of Tyre, Sidon, and the Decapolis), the gradual revelation to the Apostles that he is Messias and his instructions to them, the journey by Perea to Jerusalem for the Pasch of the Passion.

But while preserving this framework the Evangelists inserted the traditional material with great freedom. We need only think of Matthew's grouping (cf. § 24, 3) and the gathering of most of the non-Marcan material into Luke's so-called "travel document" (cf. § 25, 4); above all the "general accounts" must be regarded as pure redaction (e.g., Mk. 1, 39; 3, 7-12; 6; 7, 54-56; Mt. 4, 23-25; 9, 35 sq.; Lk. 4, 15-44).

For these reasons we are not in a position to write a life of Jesus in the sense of a biography which presents the course of its subject's external and interior development. But this does not mean that the entire tradition about Jesus disintegrates into isolated pieces with no inner connection. On the contrary, in all these individual sayings and stories the speaker and actor is he in whom, according to the belief of the primitive Christians, the time of salvation began. They all deal with the great theme of the New Testament: In Jesus of Nazareth the Messias has appeared on earth. And so the traditional passages which seem separate are joined by a strong bond into an inner unity.

2. The classification of the individual pieces of traditional material into categories or forms is a difficult task, as is shown by the divergent arrangements and nomenclature proposed by the various exponents of Form Criticism.

Classification is easiest and most secure in the case of the discourse material, and Bultmann's arrangement may be accepted as adequate. Here we are dealing with forms which for a long time have been fairly firmly set. The various forms which occur in the traditional material of the Gospels may be paralleled exactly in the Old Testament (especially the Prophets and the Sapiential Books) and in Rabbinical literature, and even up to a point among other nations.[2] In view of these parallels it is certain that these forms did not develop on Hellenistic soil, but that they were shaped by the primitive community in Palestine.

The classification of the narrative material is more difficult. Here it is not a question of sayings which can be expressed with great freedom, but of deeds and incidents in the life of Jesus which, for the narrators, belonged to the immediate past. Historical events cannot be shaped into clear-cut forms so long as the narrator feels tied to recollection or tradition. It would perhaps be better to regard the "apophthegmata" as discourse material, for their climax is a saying of Jesus; of the remaining material—to prescind from the "apophthegmata"—only the miracle stories can be marked off from the point of view of form as a distinct literary category.

Dibelius' choice of the name *Novellen* is unfortunate. It carries with it the unjustified suggestion that they were shaped and published by a particular class of narrators, and that they were designed to meet the needs of pious instruction, not to aid preaching.

The miracle stories have a superficial resemblance (in theme) to Jewish and heathen miracle stories, but this resemblance must not blind us to the profound differences. The Jewish and heathen miracle stories are intended to exalt the person of the miracle worker; the synoptic miracles on the other hand prove that the mission of Jesus is Messianic, and attest the beginning of the era of salvation in which, according to prophecy, illness, distress, and misery are to cease and liberation from sin is to become a reality (Is. 36, 3-6; Mt. 11, 4-6 par; 12, 28 par). A further difference is that bodily manipulations are almost entirely absent from the Gospel stories (only Mk. 7, 31-37; 8, 22-26), and the miracle is worked simply by the word of command of Jesus.

Here we touch a point which is of great importance for the correct application of Form Criticism. Many of its exponents use Form

[2] For the parables see the exhaustive work of M. Hermaniuk: *La parabole évangélique. Enquête exégétique et critique*, Bruges-Paris 1947.

Criticism as a means of historical criticism; against them it must be strongly emphasized that the form of a traditional passage provides no foundation for a judgment concerning its historicity. The study of content must supplement the study of form; Form Criticism must be complemented by the study of facts.

On the other hand Form Criticism has put out of court the false idea of the narrow literary critics about degrees of reliability; they held that the historical reliability of the synoptic material varies according to the written source from which it has been drawn, for example, that the content of the two oldest sources Mark and Q is more dependable than the peculiar parts of Matthew and Luke. Since all the pieces of the synoptic Gospels derive from oral tradition, each must be treated in the light of the category to which it belongs, and the question whether it comes from this or that source is only of minor importance.

3. The ascription to the primitive Christian community of a really creative power is a serious defect in Form Criticism as it is applied by many of its exponents—notably by Bultmann and Bertram, and, less radically, by Dibelius; they maintain that certain parts of the synoptic Gospels were free creations of the community, or that motifs for their forming—especially for miracle stories or *Novellen*, and legends—were borrowed from Judaism and more particularly from Hellenism. According to them our synoptic tradition was formed outside Palestine (perhaps in Syria: Damascus and Antioch) in Greek by hellenized Jewish Christians who understood both Aramaic and Greek, in other words by believers who to a certain extent were under the influence of Hellenistic ideas.

Against this it must be emphasized vigorously that we may not exclude from the formation of tradition the eyewitnesses of the life and work, passion and death of Jesus. Luke says explicitly that the accounts of his predecessors, which he knows and uses, were guaranteed by those "who from the beginning were eyewitnesses and ministers of the word" (that is, of the proclamation of the Gospel), and he intends his own work to be a proof of all that his readers had learned (1, 1-4). Enough firsthand witnesses were still alive in the few decades during which tradition got its final shaping; we have only to think of Peter, James, and John, the "pillars" of the Church of Jerusalem (Gal. 2, 9) at the time of the Council of Jerusalem (cf. also 1 Cor. 15, 6).

It is false to ascribe the making of tradition to anonymous forces, to say that it was the community and the faith of the community which formed and handed on the tradition about Jesus. Creative power belongs not to a mass but only to individuals who tower over the mass.

In addition to the eyewitnesses an important role was played by missionaries (Evangelists, Acts 21, 8; Eph. 4, 11; 2 Tim. 4, 5) and teachers (1 Cor. 12, 28; Eph. 4, 11; Acts 13, 1; Rom. 12, 7; 1 Pet. 4, 11), that is, by those who had the charismatic offices of testifying to the word. Together with the eyewitnesses they provide a strong guarantee of the truth of the tradition concerning the words and deeds of Jesus.

The popular form of the synoptic narratives may be satisfactorily explained by the fact that they derive from men who belonged not to the world of letters but to the ordinary people.

So the testimony of faith which the Gospel tradition expresses has as its theme history itself (Cullmann).

CHAPTER 6

The Historical Value of the Gospel Tradition

VINCENT TAYLOR

> Until his retirement Professor Taylor was Principal and Professor of New Testament Language and Literature at Wesley College, Leeds. He has used the approach of the Form Critics but is generally more conservative than they in his historical conclusions. See his *The Gospel According to St. Mark*, rev. ed., 1966. See also the excerpts from *The Life and Ministry of Jesus* in chapter 22.

FROM the sources of the Gospels and the evangelists' use of different kinds of material we now turn to the vital question of the Gospel tradition. Is the tradition a reliable guide to the investigation of the mind and purpose of Jesus?

In this connection the closing words of R. H. Lightfoot in his *History and Interpretation in the Gospels* (1935) have frequently been quoted:

> It seems, then, that the form of the earthly no less than of the heavenly Christ is for the most part hidden from us. For all the inestimable value of the gospels, they yield us little more than a whisper of his voice; we trace in them but the outskirts of his ways. Only when we see him hereafter in his fulness shall we know him as he was on earth.[1]

Many readers read these words with dismay and some with a mournful acquiescence in their truth.

[1] Lightfoot, p. 225.

From *The Life and Ministry of Jesus* by Vincent Taylor. An expansion of the article "The Life and Ministry of Jesus," *The Interpreter's Bible* Vol. VII. Copyright 1951 by Pierce and Smith (Abingdon Press). Reprinted by permission.

Recently, in his *Gospel Message of St. Mark* (1951) Lightfoot referred to what he called a widespread misunderstanding of this passage. He pointed out that it contains almost a quotation of Job 26:14, and observed that the patriarch would have been even more grievously distressed than he already was, if he had thought that his words would be taken to imply that he had practically no knowledge of his God. This explanation must be accepted, but one may doubt if it meets the real difficulty. We must therefore ask whether the more radical interpretation of the passage represents the facts. Is it only "a whisper of his voice" that we hear in the Gospel tradition?

This inquiry is the more necessary in view of what H. E. W. Turner describes as "the mood of historical pessimism which has come of late years over historical criticism." [2] Echoes of the views of Bultmann and Bertram, to which reference has already been made, and of the skepticism of Loisy [3] and Guignebert, [4] can be heard in Great Britain and America. A gap, it is pointed out, amounting to a generation separates Mark from the ministry of Jesus, and even if it is allowed that Q may be dated about A.D. 50, there is still an interval of about twenty years from the original facts. It is not possible, it is argued, to get behind the primary sources; we can only examine what the evangelists tell us, recognizing that they wrote against the background of the religious ideas of their day.

This skepticism seems to me excessive; it arises from too docile an acceptance of the more radical views of form critics. Several considerations support this claim. (1) The primary sources sometimes overlap, and so provide double or even triple attestation for important sayings and narratives. [5] (2) The study of Mark reveals earlier group forms which, apparently, the evangelist has reproduced with little change, [6] thus enabling us to use some of the advantages of Ur-Markus hypotheses without their embarrassments. (3) The early existence of a primitive and continuous passion narrative is widely acknowledged by form critics and others. (4) The increasing

---

[2] Turner, *Jesus Master and Lord*, p. 93.

[3] Loisy, *La Naissance du Christianisme* (1933, Eng. tr. L. P. Jacks); *Les Origines du Nouveau Testament* (1936, Eng. tr. L. P. Jacks).

[4] Guignebert, *Jesus* (1935, Eng. tr. S. H. Hooke).

[5] Cf. T. W. Manson, *The Sayings of Jesus*, pp. 78, 84, 109–10, 123, 131, 138, 145, 216, 323–27.

[6] I have treated this point and most of the others mentioned in this summary in *The Gospel According to St. Mark*.

degree with which the Gospel sources are held to contain material derived from Aramaic originals carries their tradition to a point much higher up the stream. (5) The Fourth Gospel, along with the interpretative element in it, supplies independent tradition of great value to the historian. (6) The various influences, apologetic, catechetical, liturgical, and doctrinal, which in various ways have modified the original tradition, can be observed and appraised, with results which show that they have by no means always obscured its meaning, but in important respects have elucidated and interpreted its significance.

For these reasons, it may be claimed, within their limitations, the Gospels, while always subject to literary and historical criticism, are a reliable guide to the study of the mind and purpose of Jesus and to the turning points of his ministry in Galilee and Jerusalem. They do not tell us all we should wish to know, and many problems remain unsolved, but we are not left in darkness with no resort but to consider how the primitive Christian communities interpreted his person and mission. In the Gospels, Jesus himself can be seen and the outlines of his ministry can be traced, provided we have courage, imagination, and insight to read the primitive records aright.

Two questions of current interest, in their bearing upon the Gospel tradition, remain to be considered. The first is typology, and the second the suggestion that the Markan outline is liturgical in origin.

The fascinating theme of typology has been treated by Austin Farrer in his book *A Study in St. Mark* (1952), and in a subsequent essay entitled "Loaves and Thousands." [7]

The presence of prefigurings in biblical revelation is undoubted; they can be seen in the teaching of Jesus, the Pauline epistles, the Epistle to the Hebrews, the Gospels, and the Revelation. Jesus saw deep significance in Old Testament messianic ideas, in the teaching of Dan. 7:13 and in the "stone passages" of Ps. 118:22-23 and Dan. 2:34 ff. He claimed that he came, not to destroy but to fulfill the law and the prophets (Matt. 5:17), and he based belief in the resurrection on the fact that God is "the God of Abraham, of Isaac, and of Jacob" (Mark 12:26-27). His choice of the Twelve points back to the twelve tribes of Israel (Luke 22:30), and his action in breaking bread in the wilderness reflects the Old Testament story of the manna and the references to the messianic feast in Isa. 25:6 and other passages.

In Paul's epistles the sense of prefigurings is also manifest, although here the application of the principle is less creative and sometimes artificial. We recall his teaching concerning Hagar and his observation, "Which things are an allegory" (Gal. 4:24); his insistence that the promise was made to Abraham "and his seed" (Gal. 3:16); his reference to the stone which followed the Israelites in their wanderings, with the interpretation "And the rock was Christ" (I Cor. 10:4); his allusions to Jacob, Esau, and Pharaoh in Rom. 9; and, above all, his illustrative use of Old Testament narratives in I Cor. 10:1-11, culminating in the statement, "Now these things happened unto them by way of example; and they were written for our instruction, upon whom the end of the ages has come." In Hebrews an impressive argument is based on the law as "a shadow of the good things to come" (10:1), and deep significance is found in the furnishing of the tabernacle and Old Testament teaching concerning sacrifice. In Matthew the frequent use of the words, "that it might be fulfilled which was spoken by the prophet," is characteristic, and in the Markan tradition it is not difficult to see that the first Christians had Old Testament narratives in mind in relating the stories of the storm on the lake (4:35-41), the feeding of the five thousand (6:30-44), the Transfiguration (9:2-8), and the account of the Passion (15:29). There is a present and a forward look in the narratives of the mission of the Twelve, particularly in Matt. 10, in the account of the Apostolic Council in Acts 15, in many Johannine stories and sayings, and in the visions of the Revelation.

These prefigurings are of much theological importance, provided exegesis avoids the perils of exaggeration and of fancifulness. It is, however, another matter when the Gospel of Mark is described as the symbolic structure of a numerically minded author. Farrer maintains that the evangelist begins with the dominical symbol, "twelve apostles for the twelve tribes," and makes it a framework by adding two equivalent twelves, "twelve loaves for twelve thousands" and "twelve healings of particular persons" corresponding to the calling of the disciples.[8] The correspondence is interesting, but one must

---

[8] We are reminded that four disciples are called in consecutive pairs (Mark 1:16-20) and four persons are healed in consecutive pairs (Mark 1:21-31; 1:40—2:12), that when Levi is called (Mark 2:14) a fifth healing follows (3:1-6), and that after the appointment of the Twelve, seven more healings are

doubt if it is intended and used as a framework by Mark; and still more obscure is the numerical significance of the loaves. More serious is the objection that, contrary to the intentions of typologists, the resolution of the Gospel into cycles and paracycles must compromise its historical value. The claim that Mark was numerically minded must minister to the view that symbolism was a guiding factor in the compilation of the Gospel, and that, in consequence, the order of events and the contents of narratives in it are matters of secondary importance. Typology, I believe, has this tendency, as the *Life of Jesus*[9] written over a century ago by D. F. Strauss abundantly shows.[10]

The second topic of current interest is the attempt of Carrington in *The Primitive Christian Calendar: A Study in the Making of the Marcan Gospel* (1952) to show that Mark was compiled in conformity with a very early Christian lectionary based upon the Hebrew calendar. "The Gospel," he claims, "consists of a series of lections for use in the Christian ecclesia on successive Sundays of the year, and of a longer continuous lection which was used on the annual solemnity of the Pascha (Passover) at which the Passion was commemorated."[11] This theory is based on the alleged "triadic structure" of the Gospel, the connection of its outstanding narratives with Jewish feasts, and the support afforded by the chapter divisions in codex Vaticanus and other manuscripts. A connection is suggested between the seed parables of Mark 4, the feeding of the five thou-

---

recorded. The embarrassment of an additional healing is met by the submission that the Syrophoenician woman's daughter was a Gentile, exorcisms are included among the healings, and summary accounts (Mark 1:32-34; 3:10-12; 6:6) are disregarded, presumably as not being numerically significant. Other members in Mark, the two thousand demons (5:13), the two hundred denarii (6:37), the groups of hundreds and fifties (6:40), the two fishes (6:38), and the three hundred denarii for which the alabaster box of ointment might have been sold (14:5), suggest still fruitful fields for typologists to till.

[9] Eng. tr. Geo. Eliot (1848, 5th ed. 1906).

[10] With reference to the mission of the Seventy (Luke 10:1-20) and the number seventy, Strauss writes: "Had Jesus, then, under the pressing circumstances that mark his public career, nothing more important to do than to cast about for significant numbers, and to surround himself with inner and outer circles of disciples, regulated by these mystic measures? or rather, is not this constant preference for sacred numbers, this assiduous development of an idea to which the number of the apostles furnished the suggestion, wholly in the spirit of primitive Christian legend?" pp. 332–33.

[11] P. xi.

sand, and the confession of Peter followed by the Transfiguration. Each, it is claimed, is connected with withdrawal to a mountain and each has to do with a mystery. "The mystery announced in parables shortly after the First Mountain was enacted in a sacramental act at the Second Mountain, and 'openly' declared shortly before the Third Mountain. It is the death and resurrection of the Son of Man."[12] There are three mountains, three seed parables, and three announcements of the Passion. The events before the Passion cover the Hebrew year: the preaching of John is connected with the end of Tabernacles, the seed parables with the spring sowing, the feeding of the five thousand with the Passover, the feeding of the four thousand with Pentecost, the Transfiguration with midsummer, and the entry into Jerusalem and the cleansing of the temple with Tabernacles.

The interest of this hypothesis is manifest, and it cannot justly be objected that much in it is conjectural. It is probable also that a liturgical interest is to be seen in the Gospels, especially as regards the Last Supper, although I do not think that it goes deep or has corrupted the tradition. Goguel, who has considered the relation between the cultus and the Gospel tradition, rightly points out that to assign a dominant influence to the cultus is to try to explain something which is imperfectly known by something which is absolutely unknown, since we know nothing at all about the form of Christian worship in use at the time when the Gospels were composed.[13] "It was the story which created the cultus," he observes, "and not vice versa."[14] As T. W. Manson has pointed out,[15] the question arises whether the sequence of events in Mark is governed by the exigencies of the liturgical year or vice versa. So far as the cleansing of the temple is concerned Manson himself has independently argued that it falls at the time of Tabernacles,[16] and he says, "If that is so, it would suggest that the early Christian year was anchored at several fixed points, and that these were actual dated events in the ministry."[17]

In several respects, however, misgivings arise. R. P. Casey main-

[12] P. xii.
[13] *Op. cit.*, p. 165.
[14] *Ibid.*, p. 188.
[15] *The Journal of Theological Studies*, N.S., IV, 78.
[16] *Bulletin of the John Rylands Library*, Vol. XXXIII, No. 2, Mar. 1951,
[17] *The Journal of Theological Studies*, N.S., IV, 78,

tains that it is extremely unlikely that Gentile converts were won to a special devotion to the Jewish calendar, and further that there is no reason to believe that the chapter divisions of the manuscripts are earlier than the second part of the third century.[18] Again, the arguments for dating the ministry of John the Baptist, the feeding of the four thousand, and the Transfiguration are slender indeed, if not altogether nonexistent. Finally, it is to be noted that, while Carrington affirms that "historicity was the essential quality of the evangelistic message; but not historicity or historical methods as we conceive them," the value of the Markan outline is likely to be depreciated if the Gospel has been built on the ground plan of a lectionary. How radical may be the results of a liturgical explanation of Gospel origins can be seen in Bertram's *Die Leidensgeschichte Jesu und der Christuskult* (1922), in which the historical element is at a discount and the Gospels are described as cult books. It is not suggested for a moment that Carrington's book is comparable with that of Bertram, but only that Bertram's discussion illustrates the radical possibilities of a full-blown liturgical interpretation. Everyone must agree with Manson's opinion that there is room for a good deal of further investigation, that the task will prove long and difficult and that the Carrington's book, like his earlier volume *The Primitive Christian Catechism* (1940), will be a stimulus to further study.

The fact which emerges from the modern study of the Gospel tradition is its trustworthiness, provided we do not make impossible demands upon it. Bultmann's claim that we must purge it of its mythical trappings and present its teaching in terms of current existentialism [19] rests upon a radical estimate of its contents which is not justified by the most fearless inquiry. The demand that the Gospel must be "demythologized" is sound so far as it asks us to express ancient ideas of demons and spirits and the fantasies of apocalyptic thought in terms intelligible to the modern man, but not if we are to proceed to the task with the assumption that the tradition consists of myths of apocalyptic and Gnostic origin. A problem of special difficulty is the historical interpretation of the nature miracles. This question will arise in the story which follows. Here it is enough to say that in its modern form the issue is not

[18] *Theology,* LV, No. 388, 362–70.
[19] Cf. Bultmann, *Kerygma and Myth* (Eng. tr. by R. H. Fuller, 1953); and Ian Henderson's discussion in *Myth in the New Testament.*

rationalism and orthodoxy, but centers in two different Christologies strongly aligned with those of the ancient schools of Antioch and Alexandria. The question for debate is not whether miracles are possible and may be regarded as forms of divine revelation, but how far the narratives have been affected by tendencies within the tradition, and, above all, by the limitations which inevitably belong to the incarnation of the Son of God.

CHAPTER 7

Some Considerations upon the Historical Aspect of the Fourth Gospel

C. H. DODD

C. H. Dodd, an Emeritus Professor, of Cambridge University since 1949, is the dean of British New Testament scholars. In 1963 he published a further study on John, *Historical Tradition in the Fourth Gospel,* in which he argued for the essential independence of the Johannine tradition from the Synoptic Gospels. The selection quoted below expresses his judgment concerning the historical value of the Fourth Gospel.

IT will have become clear that I regard the Fourth Gospel as being in its essential character a theological work, rather than a history. Nevertheless, the writer has chosen to set forth his theology under the literary form of a 'Gospel,' a form created by Christianity for its own proper purposes. A Gospel in this sense consists of a recital of the historical narrative of the sufferings, death and resurrection of Jesus Christ, prefaced by some account of His ministry in word and deed. To this type the Fourth Gospel entirely conforms, and in this it differs from all other contemporary literature which has the same aim—to set forth the knowledge of God which is eternal life. In one sense it might be said that in the Fourth Gospel the narrative is a dramatic presentation of theological ideas, for the incidents narrated, including, in one aspect, those of the Passion, are treated as 'signs' or symbols of unseen realities; and this symbolical character, as we have seen, goes very deeply into the whole scheme of the work. But this is not an entirely satisfactory description. In tracing the various lines of thought, and comparing them with analogous ideas in con-

Reprinted with the permission of Cambridge University Press from C. H. Dodd, *The Interpretation of the Fourth Gospel* (New York, 1953), pp. 444–453.

temporary theology, we have time and time again been led to recognize the *differentia* of Johannine teaching in the fact that it finds the eternal reality conclusively revealed and embodied in an historical Person, who actually lived, worked, taught, suffered and died, with actual and direct historical consequences. The concise formula for this fact is ὁ λόγος σὰρξ ἐγένετο. We must therefore conclude that the narrative is for the author much more than a dramatic vehicle for ideas. His aim, as I have said, is to set forth the knowledge of God contained in the Christian revelation. But this revelation is distinctively, and nowhere more clearly than in the Fourth Gospel, an historical revelation. It follows that it is important for the evangelist that what he narrates happened.

In the process, however, of bringing out the symbolical value of the facts he has used some freedom. Like many ancient writers, he has put into the mouth of his characters speeches which, since they bear not only the stamp of his own style, but also the stamp of an environment different from that in which the recorded events took place, cannot be regarded as historical.[1] This use of freely composed speeches to elucidate the significance of events does not in itself impugn the historical character of the narrative in the Fourth Gospel, any more than in Thucydides or Tacitus. There is however good reason to suspect that in some cases and in some respects the narratives which provide the setting for such speeches may have been moulded by the ideas which they are made to illustrate. We may perhaps express the evangelist's attitude to history in this way.

[1] The form of discourse selected is mainly that of dialogue. The use of dialogue for the transmission of philosophical teaching goes back to Plato. There is no reason to suppose it had ever entirely lapsed, even though the Stoics preferred the form known as διατριβή. At any rate in the second century it became widely popular. The Hermetic dialogues on the one hand, and those of Lucian on the other, are two obvious examples which attest the renewed popularity of the dialogue form in very different circles. The Fourth Gospel is earlier than these, but it may well have been affected by the same general tendency. In dramatic power, characterization, and general liveliness, the Johannine dialogues are far superior to the Hermetic, while they have a depth and seriousness of purpose which cannot be looked for in the brilliant journalist Lucian. John no doubt was under the influence of the 'dialogues,' if such they may be called, which were used to set forth the teaching of Jesus in the tradition represented by the Synoptic Gospels, and were in turn akin to forms used for the preservation of rabbinic teaching. But in John the Hellenistic influence is stronger. The Johannine dialogue, however, is an original literary creation, for which there is no really close parallel.

He accepts without qualification the general tradition of the ministry, death and resurrection of Jesus, as it was expressed in the apostolic preaching, and entered into the earliest confessions of faith; and he is concerned to affirm with all emphasis the historical actuality of the facts which it transmitted. He has meditated deeply upon the meaning of the Gospel story, taken as a whole. He then turns back upon the details of the story, and seeks in each particular incident the meaning of the whole, expressing that meaning partly by the way in which he reports the facts, partly by the order in which they are placed, and partly through carefully composed discourses and dialogues.

In seeking to interpret the facts he records, the Fourth Evangelist is not necessarily exceeding the limits proper to history. For it is the function of the historian, as distinct from the chronicler, to expose the course of events as an intelligible process, in which the human spirit interacts with its environment; and that means, both to envisage events as arising (on the one side) out of human thoughts and motives, and to make perceptible and intelligible the influence they in turn exert on the thoughts and motives of men, through which fresh events are prepared.[2] From this point of view, the question of the historical value of the Fourth Gospel means asking, To what extent does this work, retelling in a fresh medium of thought the episode out of which Christianity arose, offer a true and valuable account of its significance in history?

In asking that question, we shall still have to pay much attention, as critics have long done, to a comparison of the Fourth Gospel with the Synoptics. But we shall recognize, as some older critics did not, that the Synoptic Gospels also have an inseparable element of interpretation in their record.[3] It is indeed inevitable that an episode which stirred men so deeply (on any showing), and which (in Christian belief) possessed unique spiritual significance, should impose on its reporters the necessity of relating it to their most profound

[2] See what I have said in *History and the Gospel*, pp. 25–9. Cf. Hugh Last in *Journal of Roman Studies*, xxxix (1949), p. 4: 'All the parties so far involved in the present debate would, I think, agree in the view that the primary concern of history is with the various elements—ideas, sentiments, emotions and passions —which together make up the conscious life of men; that events produced by human agency are of very little interest except as clues to the motives and purposes of the agents; that such motives and purposes are the essence of the experiences which the historian has to recreate.'

[3] See R. H. Lightfoot, *History and Interpretation in the Gospels* (1935).

thoughts and feelings, and indeed to their ultimate beliefs about God, man and the universe. For the Synoptic evangelists, that meant relating it to eschatological conceptions derived from Jewish religious tradition. For John, it meant relating it to more rational, and more universal, ideas such as those which we have studied. The question is, whether the fundamental significance of this episode in the history of mankind (in history regarded as an adventure of the spirit in the domain of nature) is expressed more adequately, or less, through the one set of conceptions or through the other; or whether the two modes of expression are complementary to one another, and both essential to a view of the facts which shall be historical in the widest sense. I believe that the course which was taken by *Leben-Jesu-Forschung* ('The Quest of the Historical Jesus,' according to the English title of the most important record of that 'Quest') during the nineteenth century proves that a severe concentration on the Synoptic record, to the exclusion of the Johannine contribution,[4] leads to an impoverished, a one-sided, and finally an incredible view of the facts—I mean, of the *facts*, as part of history.[5] I have elsewhere argued that the early recrudescence in the Church of an over-emphasis on eschatological expectations for the future has in many places tended to overshadow the element of 'realized eschatology' in the ministry, teaching, passion and resurrection of Jesus Christ.[6] John, it appears, drew upon a tradition in which this over-emphasis had at any rate not gone far. His formula ἔρχεται ὥρα καὶ νῦν ἐστιν, with the emphasis on the νῦν ἐστιν, without excluding the element of futurity, is, I believe, not merely an acute theological definition, but is essentially historical, and probably represents the authentic teaching of Jesus as veraciously as any formula could. If that is so, it follows that a picture of the ministry of Jesus largely controlled by that maxim cannot be without historical value.

[4] This proved to carry with it (as might have been expected) the rejection of elements in the Synoptics themselves which seemed to critics reminiscent of the Fourth Gospel: a notable *circulus in probando*.

[5] A great historian of ideas, the late A. J. Carlyle, many years ago admonished me not to neglect the 'implicit history' contained in the Pauline Epistles and the Fourth Gospel; and I have found the observation fruitful.

[6] See *Parables of the Kingdom*, pp. 34–110. The not altogether felicitous term 'realized eschatology' may serve as a label. Emendations of it which have been suggested for the avoidance of misunderstandings are Professor Georges Florovsky's 'inaugurated eschatology' and Professor Joachim Jeremias's 'sich realisierende Eschatologie,' which I like, but cannot translate into English.

It still remains, however, a part of the task of the student of history to seek to discover (in Ranke's oft-quoted phrase) 'wie es eigentlich geschehen ist'—how it actually happened. To what extent and under what conditions may the Fourth Gospel be used as a document for the historian in that sense?

The answer to that question depends upon the sources of information which were at the disposal of the evangelist, if we assume (as I think we may, in view of what has been said) that he intended to record that which happened, however free he may have felt to modify the factual record in order to bring out the meaning.

In the first place, he can be shown to have followed the broad general outline of the ministry, death and resurrection of Jesus Christ which is presupposed in the Synoptic Gospels, reproduced in the apostolic preaching in Acts, and attested up to a point in the Pauline epistles.[7] This outline we have good reason to believe primitive, and by his fidelity to it the evangelist gives proof of his intention to expound the meaning of *facts*, and not to invent a dramatic plot.

In the filling in of this outline in the other gospels, we observe a difference in the treatment of the Passion-narrative as compared with that of the ministry. The Passion-narrative is continuous and detailed, with the succession of incidents well marked, and varying but little in the different accounts. The narrative of the ministry, on the other hand, is largely discontinuous and episodic, and the order is freely varied. These phenomena are consistent with the view that the essential core of a 'Gospel' as such is an account of the Passion, with an introduction which might be expanded at will with a varied selection of material, and which followed no fixed order. The same is true of the Fourth Gospel. The Passion-narrative follows the well-marked pattern. The earlier narrative shows an even greater measure of freedom than the other gospels show.

The actual order of events as they appear even in Mark can no longer be regarded as strictly chronological. It is always in some measure topical, and subject to the more or less arbitrary scheme of arrangement favoured by the particular evangelist.[8] The Fourth Evangelist sits more loosely than the others to any kind of chrono-

---

[7] See my book, *The Apostolic Preaching and its Developments*, 1936, especially pp. 164–75 (in later editions, pp. 65–73).
[8] Yet I believe the tendency to treat the Marcan order as wholly arbitrary has sometimes gone too far. See my article, 'The Framework of the Gospel Narrative,' in *The Expository Times*, vol. xliii (1931/2), pp. 396–400.

logical arrangement. As we have seen, the construction of the Book of Signs is dictated by the order of thought. We should therefore be wasting time in trying to harmonize the order of Mark with the order of John directly, by such puerile expedients, for example, as the assumption that the temple was cleansed twice over, or in attempting to fit the movements between Galilee and Jerusalem into a precise chronological scheme. So far as the Fourth Gospel may be laid under contribution for determining the order of events, it must be through considering single episodes, and connecting paragraphs, severally, on their merits, and attempting to determine from internal indications their probable relations in time.

It is nevertheless true that in one part of the gospel, vi. 1—vii. 1, we seem to have a kind of shadow of the Marcan order, in the sequence of incidents which may be tabulated as follows:

> Feeding of the multitude (vi. 1-13; cf. Mark viii. 1-9).[9]
> Demand for a sign (vi. 30; cf. Mark viii. 11).
> Cryptic saying about bread (vi. 32 sqq.; cf. Mark viii. 14-21).
> Peter's confession and prediction of betrayal (vi. 68-71; cf. Mark viii. 27-31).
> Retirement in Galilee (vii. 1; cf. Mark ix. 30).

In both Mark and John, as it happens, this sequence of incidents is followed by the final abandonment of Galilee.[10] The degree and kind of significance to be attached to this coincidence is bound up with the question whether or not John used the Synoptics as a source. A majority of critics, for many years past, held the opinion, almost as a dogma, that he did so use them—or Mark at least— altering them in accordance with special motives of his own. Since the 'alterations' are so drastic at times, the dogma tended to throw a cloud of discredit upon the Johannine narrative. That opinion however rested upon an assumption, which was not usually avowed, and of which the critic perhaps was hardly aware, that the writings of early Christianity must have formed a documentary series, in literary dependence on one another. It is now widely recognized that the main factor in perpetuating and propagating the Christian

[9] But the Johannine story of the Feeding corresponds (in some respects, including the numbers) with Mark vi. 34-44, and, like it, is followed by the Walking on the Sea (John vi. 16-21, Mark vi. 47-51); which demands consideration at leisure.
[10] See my article, 'The End of the Galilean Ministry,' in *The Expositor*, 8th series, vol. xxii (1921), pp. 273–91.

faith and the Gospel story was oral tradition in its various forms. There is therefore no strong *a priori* presumption that resemblances in early Christian documents are due to literary dependence. The presumption is rather the other way. It is because of specific evidence of various kinds (which need not here be particularized) that we are led to recognize documentary sources behind the Synoptic Gospels (though they may not be so extensive as was formerly believed). Definite evidence pointing to documentary relations between John and the Synoptics is seen to be singularly sparse, when once the presumption in favour of such relations is abandoned. The *prima facie* impression is that John is, in large measure at any rate, working independently of other written gospels.[11]

I am not in this book discussing the question of the authorship of the Fourth Gospel. I should not care to say that the hypothesis is impossible, that the Johannine narrative rests upon personal reminiscences, transformed through the changing experiences of a long life, after the manner imagined by Browning in *A Death in the Desert.* We do not know what effect many years of active intercourse with Hellenistic circles may have had upon a Palestinian Jew —even upon a Galilean fisherman—with an agile and adventurous intelligence. But some of the evidence which has been adduced in favour of authorship by an eyewitness is subject to a heavy discount. For example, the convincing characterization and dramatic actuality of parts of the gospel are urged in its favour. But two of the passages which most powerfully display these features are represented by the evangelist himself as occasions when no eyewitness was present —the conversation with the Samaritan woman,[12] and the examination before Pilate.[13] There are, besides, indications which seem to

[11] See P. Gardner-Smith, *St John and the Synoptics* (1938), a book which at least shows how fragile are the arguments by which the dependence of John on the other gospels has been 'proved,' and makes a strong case for its independence.

[12] Only two persons were aware of this conversation. I find it impossible to imagine a situation in which either of them would have repeated it in this form. If it be replied that either of them may easily have told the evangelist in general terms what the conversation was about, I should be obliged to point out that the dramatic colour—all that was at first invoked to prove eyewitness— would in that case still remain the evangelist's own creation.

[13] I suppose Pilate's secretary was present; but to suggest that he later became a Christian and recited the conversation would be a very long shot; and I do not suppose anyone would wish to argue that the sentry at the door, recruited who knows where, but hardly from the intelligentsia, produced this highly intelligent and most vivid account from memory.

point to the use of previously existing material. It was, I think, Eduard Meyer who first pointed out that the extremely artificial way in which the healing at Bethesda is made to lead up to the discourse in v. 19 sqq. is much more readily explicable if the evangelist was using a narrative that had come down to him (by whatever channel) than if he was composing freely—or, we may add, recollecting what he had himself witnessed—and the same observation may be made elsewhere. Without pronouncing dogmatically upon questions which it would be preposterous to purport to settle in this offhand way, we may say that it is a reasonable hypothesis that the evangelist is giving us a rendering of oral tradition as it had come down to him, sometimes containing material which reached Mark or the others by different channels, sometimes material of similar character which may be supposed to have belonged to the same general store, and sometimes material of a character so different that it is difficult to institute a comparison.

If, taking this hypothesis, we start (as is right) with the Passion-narrative, we find a long and highly wrought passage where the main run of the story is, as we have noted, undoubtedly conformed to the standard traditional pattern. Yet the variation in detail is considerable, and the amount of verbal resemblance to the Synoptics is almost the minimum possible if the same story is to be told at all. Certainly there is not nearly so much as is ordinarily required to prove literary dependence. I have already pointed out that the passages in which definitely Johannine motives are to be recognized are brief and comparatively few, and appear rather to have been inserted into a narrative already shaped than to have determined the course of the narrative. The character of the whole seems to be consistent with an independent rendering of oral tradition, parallel with Mark's, and with the non-Marcan tradition which, as I believe, forms the main basis of the Lucan Passion-narrative. Upon this hypothesis the Johannine Passion-narrative should be examined and estimated; not as a tendentious manipulation of the blameless record of Mark, but as representing a separate line of tradition, to be compared with Mark, with the possibility that it may be inferior to Mark in some respects and superior in others.[14]

[14] Is John's dating the Crucifixion more, or less, probable than Mark's? The question is freely arguable, with no necessary presumption in favour of Mark. Again, for John the political charge against Jesus is the one which clearly decided His fate. Elsewhere he has made Caiaphas explicitly lay stress upon the political danger which His ministry evoked ('the Romans will come and

The examination of other narratives should similarly be conducted in each case on its merits. Some of them evidently refer to incidents also recorded in the Synoptics; for example, the Feeding of the Multitude, the Walking on the Sea, the Cleansing of the Temple, the Anointing at Bethany, and the Triumphal Entry. Others possibly or probably do; for example, the Healing of the Nobleman's Son. Others again reproduce patterns of narrative familiar from the Synoptics, so closely that we may justly regard them as drawn from the same general reservoir; for example, the Healing at Bethesda. Then there are those which, in form and pattern as well as in contents, seem to be peculiar to the Johannine tradition; for example, the Raising of Lazarus and the Meeting of the Sanhedrin. In examining each, it is desirable to have regard, not only to verbal and linguistic similarities and divergences, but also to form or pattern, which may have much to tell about the shaping of the particular narrative in the oral stage.

Similarly, embedded in the discourses and dialogues which are certainly an original creation of the evangelist, we find sayings which appear sometimes to be variant forms of sayings known from the Synoptics, and at other times to have been moulded upon patterns of which the Synoptics also have examples. These are all the more significant when we find a run of such sayings, having some similarity to the sequences of sayings in the Synoptics which some would regard as representing a very early stage in the transmission of the sayings of Jesus (prior to comparatively voluminous collections of sayings such as the hypothetical 'Q'). Such sequences, for example, seem to occur in John iv. 32-8, xii. 24-6; xiii. 13-20.

In examining such passages, whether narrative or didactic, we have always to ask, how far it appears that the specifically Johannine concepts (often indicated by the use of a quasi-technical vocabulary) have worked to produce the form of story or saying. That is why a detailed examination of Johannine thought such as we have here essayed is an indispensable preliminary to any estimate of the historical elements in the gospel. Even when we have a fairly clear

---

take away our place and nation'), as well as recording an abortive attempt to make Him king. On general principles, is it more likely that Mark, writing almost under the walls of the imperial palace at Rome, should have soft-pedalled the suggestion that it was a case of 'another βασιλεύς, one Jesus,' or that John should gratuitously have emphasized this highly dangerous political note in a narrative in which it was not previously prominent?

and comprehensive picture of what the distinctively Johannine types of thought and expression really are, the task of estimating the forms of the various units is a delicate one; but I believe it is not altogether without prospects. Where we have units which have the appearance of having been framed independently of the specially Johannine motives, we may provisionally set them down to the credit of a special branch or channel of oral tradition.

Another question which needs to be asked is how far a given passage, though it does not evidently reflect the theological concepts or vocabulary of the author, may nevertheless have been moulded by special interests in the place where the gospel was written—that is, as I think we are justified in saying, at Ephesus. There is, I believe, at least one element in the narrative which cannot have been due to any such moulding influence; I mean the topographical data. All attempts that have been made to extract a profound symbolical meaning [15] out of the names of Sychar, the city of Ephraim, Bethany beyond Jordan, Aenon by Salim, of Cana and Tiberias, or again, of Kedron, Bethesda (or Bethzatha),[16] and Gabbatha, are hopelessly fanciful; and there is no reason to suppose that a fictitious topography [17] would in any way assist the appeal of the gospel to an Ephesian public. The names, whether we are able to identify them on the map or not, cannot reasonably be supposed to have got into the gospel except out of a tradition which associated certain episodes in the life of Jesus (or of John the Baptist) with those sites.

It may then be of some significance that most of the place-names which occur in John but not in the Synoptics belong to southern Palestine. The only two new names in Galilee are Tiberias and Cana,

[15] Siloam, it is true, is given a symbolical meaning; but that marks it out as an exception. It would be possible to concede that in this case the evangelist introduced a name for symbolical reasons; but I think it more likely that his discovery of the etymology of the name Siloam was a lucky bit of erudition, like some of Philo's etymologies.

[16] A strong case for the originality of the form βηθεσδά, as well as for the identification of the place, has been made out by Joachim Jeremias, *Die Wiederentdeckung von Bethesda*, 1949.

[17] I do not think it can fairly be compared with the fictitious περίοδοι which had some vogue. The suggestion that these names represent a kind of pilgrims' manual is, so far as our evidence goes, anachronistic; and in any case, what would be the point of directing pilgrims to Aenon near to Salim, unless there was a previously established tradition that John baptized there?

while Chorazin, Nain, Decapolis, Gadara (or Gerasa, or Gergesa), Caesarea Philippi, as well as Tyre and Sidon, are absent from the Fourth Gospel. I can see no theological motive for the difference, nor can I think that the Ephesian reader either knew or cared anything about the geographical situation of these places. The natural inference is that the tradition from which the Fourth Evangelist was drawing had some original association with southern Palestine. If so, that might also account for a certain southern, or even metropolitan, outlook which has often been noted.

Along such lines as these I believe that some probable conclusions might be drawn about the pre-canonical tradition lying behind the *prima facie* historical statements of the Fourth Gospel. If it should prove possible to identify such a tradition, then we should have material in hand which we might compare with our other data, drawn from the Synoptic Gospels or from sources outside the gospels altogether. Through such comparative study of different strains of tradition we may hope to advance our knowledge of the facts to which they all refer.

CHAPTER 8

The Gospel According to St. John

CHARLES K. BARRETT

> Professor Barrett of Durham University has produced one of the most instructive modern commentaries on the Fourth Gospel. It ranks with the work of Dodd and Bultmann. In the passage below he asserts that the Gospel is an "impressionistic" combination of "history and interpretation."

THESE conclusions with regard to the purpose of the [fourth] gospel cannot but bear upon the question of its historical reliability. It is evident that it was not John's intention to write a work of scientific history. Such works were extremely scarce in antiquity, and we have seen that John's interests were theological rather than chronological. Moreover, his treatmeant of the only source (Mark) we can isolate with any confidence from his gospel is very free; and there is no reason to think that he followed other sources more closely. He did not hesitate to repress, revise, rewrite, or rearrange. On the other hand there is no sufficient evidence for the view that John freely created narrative material for allegorical purposes. His narratives are for the most part simple, and the details generally remain unallegorized. This means that the chronicler can sometimes (though less frequently than is often thought) pick out from John simple and sound historical material; yet it may be doubted whether John would approve of the proceeding, for he wrote his gospel as a whole, combining discourse material with narrative, in order to bring out with utmost clarity a single presentation, an interpreted history, of Jesus. Neither of these factors, history and interpretation, should be overlooked; nor, for a full understanding of what John intended, should they be separated. From one point of view John is a reaffirmation of history. Both apocalypticism and gnosticism may

From *The Gospel According to St. John,* 1955, pp. 117–119. Reprinted by permission of the publisher, The Society for Promoting Christian Knowledge, London.

be regarded as a flight from history. The apocalyptist escapes from
the past and present into a golden age of the future; the gnostic
escapes from the past and present into a world of mysticism and
fantasy. Over against these John asserted the primacy of history. It
was of supreme importance to him that there was a Jesus of Nazareth who lived and died in Palestine, even though to give an accurate outline of the outstanding events in the career of this person
was no part of his purpose. He sought to draw out, using in part the
form and style of narrative (and that he did use this form is itself
highly significant), the true meaning of the life and death of one
whom he believed to be the Son of God, a being from beyond history. It is for this interpretation of the focal point of all history,
not for accurate historical data, that we must look in John. Yet at
every point history underlies what John wrote. The reader is reminded of ancient Egyptian figure drawing, where the artist has
tried to give a full impression of his subject by incorporating both
full-face and profile in one picture. The result is inevitably like
(from the "photographic" point of view) no man on earth, but it
cannot be said that the general effect is unsuccessful; in some respects it is more successful than a straightforward photograph
would have been. In the same way John presents in his one book
both history and interpretation. The result is not a biography; it is
impressionistic rather than photographically accurate in detail, but
it cannot be denied that the total effect is impressive and illuminating.

By writing in this way John compels us to face one more question:
What was his authority? Those who believe that the evangelist was
the son of Zebedee, the apostle John, will of course have no difficulty
in finding an answer. Those who do not will find themselves confronted also by a wider question of even greater importance: What
is the nature of authority in the Christian Church? For (if the view
suggested in this commentary is right) John assumes a state of
affairs in which all the apostles were dead. The natural authority of
those who from the beginning had been eye-witnesses and ministers
of the Word had been removed; what authority, if any, could take
its place? To this question the gnostics had an answer. Authority
rested with the natural *élite* of the Church, the γνωστικοί *par excellence,* those who were supremely endowed with the charisma
of theosophical speculation. It was an authority at once of the in-
tellect and of religious experience; in effect it meant no authority

at all, and the Church rightly rejected it. But what alternative was available?

The history of Christian thought in the second century may be regarded as to some extent the record of the various attempts that were made to understand, establish, and apply the principle of authority. In the latter part of the century, after Marcion, rapid strides were made towards the fixing of a New Testament canon. Throughout the century, indeed, from New Testament times, we can dimly trace the progressive formulation of a *regula fidei* or *regula veritatis*, which enshrined the essentials of Christian belief. A third line of development in the defining of the authority was the growth, which also goes back to New Testament times, of a permanent ministry, by means of which, as by the Scriptures and the Rule of Faith, apostolic truth was to be preserved and applied. John did nothing to further any of these lines of development. Instead, he asked, and causes his readers to ask, what was the nature of the authority of the apostles themselves; and the answer to this question follows two lines.

First, the authority of the apostles lies in their ability to bear witness to the gospel history. On this, for all his freedom with the details of history, John insists most strongly. See especially 19.35; cf. 21.24. The faith of the Church rests upon the historical testimony borne by eye-witnesses.

Secondly, the authority of the apostles rests upon the commission given to them by Jesus. This appears most clearly in 20.21, but the parallelism between the mission of Jesus from the Father and the mission of the disciples from Jesus is brought out repeatedly and in the strongest terms. It is a parallelism not only of mission but of knowledge, and even of being (10.14f.; 14.20). Together with this mission of the apostles must be taken the mission of the Holy Spirit, "whom the Father will send in my name" (14.26), "whom I will send unto you from the Father" (15.26). It is clear from 20.22 that the mission of the apostles is dependent on the mission of the Spirit. The combined mission of the Spirit and the apostles results in the formation of a further company of believers (17.20; cf. 20.29); and these also enter into the unity and mission of Christ himself (17.21). We reach here the point of transition from the apostles and their authority to the authority under which the Church continued, and which was in fact perpetuated in the life of the Church itself. For the evangelist places not only himself but also his readers beside the apostles both as eye-witnesses and as emissaries. 1.14 is a crucial verse for the understanding of the gospel. It was among "us" that the incarnate Word tabernacled; it is "we" who beheld his glory. This first person plural is to be taken with full seriousness. It does not mean "we men," for it simply was not true that all men (even all who looked upon his person) beheld the glory of Christ; and it cannot mean "we apostles," unless the author was himself an apostle. It remains possible only that it should mean "we, the Church," "we Christians": we beheld the glory of Christ when he abode with us. There is a similar "we" in 21.24, which emphasizes the importance of the testimony of a veracious eye-witness, and adds "we know that his witness is true"—the Church sets its seal upon the veracity of its spokesman. The Church itself is thus the heir of the apostles and of their authority. It is clear that if this statement were left unqualified a door would be left open to a worse anarchy than that of gnosticism; but it is not left unqualified. The Church is the Church—the authoritative, apostolic Church—so far as it rests upon the word of the apostles (17.20), and is obedient to the Spirit, who takes the things of Christ and applies them to generation after generation of Christians.

CHAPTER 9

The New Testament in Current Study

REGINALD H. FULLER

> Professor Fuller, currently of Union Theological Seminary, surveys recent discussion of the sources which stand behind John's Gospel and of that Gospel's Palestinian background. Both of these questions are crucial for an evaluation of the proper use of John as a source for the historical Jesus.

SOURCES

WHEN Streeter wrote the section on the fourth gospel in his *Four Gospels* the quest for written sources was still the order of the day, as it was in synoptic studies. Streeter himself, as we have already noted, maintained the fourth evangelist actually knew and used at least Mark and Luke; and it was widely, if not universally, agreed that he used Mark. In 1938, however, P. Gardner-Smith published a slim, but important and widely influential study,[1] in which he demonstrated (conclusively, to the mind of the present writer) the complete independence of John from all the synoptists, Mark included. It is interesting to find that between his lectures in Cambridge in 1937 and the publication of his book in 1954 . . . C. H. Dodd changed his mind on that question. In 1937 he told us that he accepted John's use of Mark. In 1954 he denies this.[2] Bultmann also, in his commentary (1941) rejects any dependence of John on Mark. Part of the reason for this shift of opinion is undoubtedly the rise of form criticism with its emphasis on oral transmission. Previously even the slightest verbal resemblances were

[1] *St. John and the Synoptic Gospels,* Cambridge.
[2] Dodd, *The Interpretation of the Fourth Gospel,* p. 449.

thought to be sufficient to warrant the conclusion of direct literary dependence. The trend today is to require a high percentage of verbal agreement plus agreement in order before concluding literary dependence. Here again Barrett, although he mentions Gardner-Smith's work,[3] is out of step with the current trend, for he still believes that John knew Mark and Luke.[4]

Quite a new and suggestive approach to the question of sources is found in Bultmann's commentary. He distinguishes between three different classes of material to be found in the fourth gospel. First, there is the "signs source"—which for convenience we will call Σ. This Book of Signs contained a collection of rather crass miracle stories and perhaps other narrative material. Then there is a source which he identifies as "Revelation discourses" (*Offenbarungsreden*). Since these consist of speeches (*logia*) we will call this source Λ. Characteristically, Bultmann thinks that these revelation discourses originated in gnosticism, and were taken over by the fourth evangelist and put to service in the proclamation of the kerygma. By the method of "style-criticism" Bultmann thinks he is able to distinguish between the original material of this source and the evangelist's editing. We are perhaps rather astonished to find that Bultmann considers this gnostic revelation source written originally in Aramaic—unlike the Σ source and the evangelist's own editorial additions. Thirdly, though it is not clear to Bultmann whether this is a separate source from Σ or a continuation of it, John has his own tradition of the passion narrative which again he has heavily edited in the interests of his theology.[5] Occasionally, as for instance in the dating of the passion in relation to the passover, this source contains material of higher value than the Marcan passion narrative.

Bultmann's views on the gnostic character of Λ are the most controversial part of this thesis. What evidence is there for the possibility of Aramaic gnostic revelation discourses? The Odes of Solomon, to which Bultmann appeals, are not discourses, but hymn-like material in verse form. On the other hand only the prologue of St. John is obviously in verse form—and it is only the prologue which offers a sure basis for distinguishing between the original source and the evangelist's additions. It is a tall order to extend the same operation to the discourses throughout the gospel. More-

[3] Barrett, *The Gospel According to St. John*, p. 34, n. 1.
[4] *Ibid.*, pp. 34–36.
[5] Contrast Dodd, *op. cit.*, pp. 423 ff.

over—and this is a characteristic post-Bultmannian objection—is the evangelist merely a commentator? Is he not a creative author in his own right? How can we reduce such a highly individual thinker to the status of a redactor whose prosaic comments interrupt the poetic flow of the original thought? Such are the objections which have been raised against Bultmann's theory by both Käsemann [6] and Haenchen.

That there is considerable pre-Johannine material imbedded in the discourses is becoming increasingly apparent. Two recent studies have been devoted to a study of this pre-Johannine tradition. In 1954 a Danish scholar, Bent Noack,[7] put forward strong grounds for believing that the discourse material as well as the narrative portions of the gospel enshrine traditions which are parallel to, but independent of, the synoptic tradition. Three years later Siegfried Schulz published an important study [8] of the Son of man, Son of God and paraklete logia in the discourses. In the sayings examined he unravels three strata. The earliest he designates "apocalyptic." Here Jesus is identified with the apocalyptic Son of man who is to come again as the future judge and deliverer at the End. If we tie this in with Tödt's later investigations into the Son of man logia in the synoptic tradition (see above, p. 38, n. 27), this stratum may be assigned to the earliest Aramaic speaking church. This conclusion would appear to be warranted from Schulz's observations on the linguistic features of the logia in this earliest stratum. Secondly, there is what he calls the "neo-interpretation" of the Son of man tradition in a "gnostic" sense. The term "gnostic" used in this connection raises many unsolved problems connected with the so-called gnostic redeemer myth (see below, pp. 121ff.). But the character of this re-interpretation at least is clear: Jesus is presented already in his earthly life as the incarnate Son of man, already exercising the functions of the eschatological judge and redeemer. It would be interesting to explore, in the light of Tödt's conclusions (see above, p. 43), how far this re-interpretation also may be assigned to the early Palestinian tradition, which also contains sayings in which

---

[6] In his essay "Neutestamentliche Fragen von heute." *ZTK*, 54, 1957, p. 56.

[7] B. Noack, *Zur Johanneischen Tradition*, Copenhagen, 1954.

[8] *Untersuchungen zur Menschensohn-Christologie im Johannes-Evangelium*, Göttingen, 1957. Schulz has followed up this work with a more comprehensive study of the tradition behind the discourses in *Komposition und Herkunft der Johanneischen Reden*, which is promised for 1962.

Jesus is in his ministry the present Son of man. The difference between Q and this Johannine stratum appears to be that in the Q
sayings the Son of man is used to designate Jesus' present authority
in his ministry, with none of the transcendental functions of the eschatological Son of man, whereas in the Johannine sayings Jesus is
already exercising the transcendental functions of judgment and
salvation. Also the Johannine Son of man is a pre-existent Being
who descends to earth. Here is a subject for further investigation.
As for the third stratum, the evangelist's own specific contribution,
Schulz has very little to say about it. May it be that the evangelist,
in taking over a tradition which represents Jesus as already exercising in his earthly life the functions of the transcendental Son of
man, has himself in turn linked this idea to that of pre-existence
and incarnation? Clearly, there are many questions here for further
investigation.

THE PALESTINIAN BACKGROUND

In other ways the connections between the fourth gospel and
Palestine are becoming increasingly clear. Some of the topography,
which in the past has puzzled critics and thrown doubt on the
author's (or his tradition's) knowledge of Palestine, has been substantiated by archeological discovery. One such puzzle was the lo-
cation of Aenon near Salim (John 3:23). There is a place called
Ainun near Salim by the headwaters of Wadi Far'ah: this sub-
stantiates John's statement that "there were many waters there." [9]
Joachim Jeremias has given an account of excavations in Jerusalem [10] which resulted in the discovery of the pool of Bethesda
(John 5:2ff.). According to Hunter,[11] this has also been confirmed
by the copper scroll from Qumran. The excavations at Shechem
have made it reasonably certain that Sychar in John 4:5 should be
identified with that place. In fact Shechem is the reading of the Old
Syriac version at this point, and it is probably correct. Finally, mention should be made of an article by John A. T. Robinson,[12] who

[9] Hunter, "Recent Trends in Johannine Studies," *The Expository Times,* Vol.
71, pp. 164–167, 219–222.
[10] *Die Wiederentdeckung von Bethesda,* Göttingen, 1949. Cf. also *Unknown
Sayings of Jesus,* tr., R. H. Fuller, London, 1947, p. 44.
[11] Hunter, *loc. cit.*
[12] *NTS,* 6/2 (1960), pp. 117–131.

studies other aspects of the evangelist's presentation, notably his attitude toward the "Jews," resulting in the conclusion that "The *Heimat* of the Johannine tradition, and the milieu in which it took shape, was the heart of southern Palestine." [13]

Yet another point. There is increasing respect in many quarters for some of the distinctive historical traditions enshrined in the fourth gospel. A notable champion of this tradition, who had no conservative ax to grind, was the French scholar, Maurice Goguel.[14] Hunter [15] lists six points in which he thinks the fourth evangelist provides sound historical traditions to supplement or correct the synoptists:

1. Two of Jesus' disciples were formerly disciples of John the Baptist (John 1:35-42).
2. The Judean ministry of Jesus prior to the Galilean ministry (John 3:22 filling the gap implied by Mark 1:14a).
3. The Messianic crisis following the feeding of the multitude (John 6:15, perhaps implied by Mark 6:45: Jesus forces his disciples to leave, while he dismisses the crowd).
4. An extended Judean ministry during the last six months, with an interval of retirement (John 7:14—11:54: the synoptists also contain hints of a more extended ministry at Jerusalem).
5. The dating of the Last Supper on 15 rather than 14 Nisan. This dating is still widely accepted, despite Jeremias' valiant attempts to vindicate the Marcan chronology.[16]
6. Jesus before Annas as the power behind the high priestly throne (18:13).

Some of these traditions have more claim to validity than others, but none is historically impossible.

It is not surprising that quite responsible scholars, and not only those with conservative predilections who would naturally be inclined to "cash in" on the new evidence, are beginning seriously to entertain the possibility that the fourth gospel was written much earlier than has been commonly supposed. If Gardner-Smith is right in denying any dependence on the synoptists a date around 80 or even earlier becomes possible (so Hunter). The Aramaic and Pales-

---

[13] *Ibid.*, p. 124.
[14] M. Goguel, *Jésus*, Paris, 1950 (second ed.).
[15] Hunter, *op. cit.*, p. 219.
[16] This statement of Hunter's view contains an accidental error. He actually wrote "that the Last Supper took place before Nisan 15."

tinian affinities of the author re-open the possibility of a closer connection with John the Apostle than the dominant critical opinion
has allowed (so Mitton). If the idiom of thought is so thoroughly
Palestinian (albeit sectarian), might not the teaching of the fourth
gospel go back ultimately to Jesus himself (so again Mitton)? It
seems to the present writer that these three possibilities are hazardous in the extreme, and great caution is advised. The fatal objection
is that the Q material is our earliest (some of it perhaps with a pre-
resurrection *Sitz im Leben*) evidence for the teaching of Jesus. It
presents him as the proclaimer of the kingdom of God: the fourth
gospel on the other hand completes the process tentatively initiated
by the synoptists by presenting Jesus as the proclaimer of himself: it represents the culmination of the radical reassessment of
Jesus in the light of the Easter event and the church's experience
of the risen Christ. Barrett's views on the origin of the fourth gospel,
modified in the light of the Qumran discoveries, would still seem
best to fit the state of the evidence.

CHAPTER 10

The Value of John in Reconstructing Jesus' Ministry

RAYMOND E. BROWN

> Professor Brown teaches at St. Mary's College in Balti-
> more. A modern, Catholic scholar, thoroughly conversant
> with the modern discussion of the historical Jesus, Professor
> Brown states his own views about the historical element in
> the Gospel of John. He insists that the rather negative atti-
> tude of scholarship toward the historical value of John must
> be reconsidered. His bibliography at the end of the article
> has been included because of its special usefulness.

IT has been a commonplace in the critical investigation of the
historical Jesus that no reliance can be placed on the material
found in John. Even the "new quest" of the historical Jesus among
the post-Bultmannians, especially Bornkamm and Conzelmann,
neglects John. This question deserves reconsideration in view of
the conclusions reached above; namely, that within the material
proper to John there is a strong element of historical plausibility,
and that within the material shared by John and the Synoptics, John
draws on independent and primitive tradition.

But in reopening the question of whether or not the Fourth
Gospel can be a witness to the historical Jesus, we must proceed
with care. . . . We [have] posited [elsewhere] five stages in the
composition of John, with each stage representing a step further
away from the primitive tradition. We cannot ignore the implications of such a development, for it limits the ability of the final form
of the Gospel to give a scientifically accurate portrait of the Jesus

of history. Let us examine the implications in each stage of Johannine development.

(a) The tradition of Jesus' works and words that underlies John (Stage 1) resembles the traditions behind the Synoptic Gospels. In short, these traditions give us variant forms of the narratives about what Jesus did and said. Now, the development of such variants took time. If we ask which of these traditions is the earliest, we are asking a question that admits of no simple answer. Even within the Synoptic family of traditions, one cannot give a blanket rule as to which form of a saying is always to be preferred, the "Q" form or the Marcan form. So too in comparing John and the Synoptics, we find that sometimes the material underlying John's account seems to be more primitive than the material underlying the Synoptic account(s), for example, the story of Jesus' walking on the water in John vi 16-21. At other times, just the opposite is true. Thus, a critical judgment is necessary *for each instance.*

Perhaps we may take this occasion to insist that when in the commentary we do analyze a Johannine narrative or saying and discover that there is primitive tradition underlying it, we are perfectly aware that we are using "primitive" in a relative sense, for the primitive tradition may already represent ten or twenty years of development from the time of Jesus. In general, where possible, we shall try to trace the origins of Johannine material back to Stage 1, and then to show what implications this *may* have for the historical ministry of Jesus. But we make no pretense to try or to be able to decide with any consistency precisely how much scientific history underlies each Johannine scene. Similarly, in pointing out Synoptic parallels for Johannine stories and sayings, we make no presupposition that the Synoptic parallels are necessarily exact historical echoes of what Jesus did and said. Rather, we take for granted some knowledge of the history of the Synoptic tradition. The purpose in presenting such parallels is to show that John's Gospel is not as different as might first seem.

(b) Stages 2 and 3 in our theory of the composition of John saw the dramatic and theological reshaping of the raw material from the Jesus tradition and the weaving of such reshaped stories and sayings into a consecutive Gospel. This same process, *mutatis mutandis,* also took place in the formation of the Synoptic Gospels. At one time John the Evangelist was spoken of as *the Theologian,* almost with the implication that only in the Fourth Gospel did we

have a theological view of the career of Jesus. Today we recognize that each Gospel has a theological view, and that the fourth evangelist is one theologian among the other evangelist-theologians. Nevertheless, it is still true that the fourth evangelist is the theologian par excellence. In particular, the formation of the sayings of Jesus into the Johannine discourses represented a profound theological synthesis. It seems true, for instance, that behind John vi there lies a core of traditional material, containing not only the multiplication of the loaves but also a misunderstanding of what was meant by the scene and the consequent explanation of the bread by Jesus. Yet the formation of this material into the magnificent structure that we now have in John vi represents a unique theological grasp of the ultimate implications of Jesus' deeds and words. The less-developed Synoptic accounts of the scene are not of the same theological quality or mastery. Naturally, in any attempt to use John as a guide to the historical Jesus, such theological development must be taken into account. We are not suggesting that the Johannine theological insight has not been loyal to Jesus of Nazareth; rather it has often brought out implications found in a scene, however far back that scene can be traced. But subsequent development, no matter how homogeneous, is something that is refractive when one's purpose is to establish scientifically the exact circumstances of the ministry of Jesus. And so, although we think that the Fourth Gospel reflects historical memories of Jesus, the greater extent of the theological reshaping of those memories makes Johannine material much harder to use in the quest of the historical Jesus than most Synoptic material.

Even beyond the development that went into the formation of Johannine units is the development that took place when these units were welded into a Gospel. Selection and highlighting were required to make possible the organization now visible in John. Thus, in the first edition of John there came to the fore themes that were probably quite obscure in the hustle and bustle of the actual ministry. It is quite plausible, for instance, that Jesus may have spoken publicly on the occasion of Jewish feasts and may have directed his remarks to a contrast between his own ministry and the theme of the feast. But the systematic replacement of feasts spelled out in John v—x is the product of much reflection by the author, in an attempt to capture the significance of Jesus and his ministry.

If all of this means that John (and this is true of the other Gospels as well) is somewhat distant from a history or biography of Jesus, John xx 30-31 has made it clear that the author's intention was to produce a document not of history but of faith. Yet Sanders, *art. cit.*, is quite right in insisting that John is deeply historical—historical in the sense in which history is concerned not only with what happened but also with the deepest meaning of what happened.

(c) The final redaction of the Gospel, Stage 5 of the composition, places still more obstacles to the use of John in reconstructing the ministry of Jesus. The extra Johannine material that was inserted in the Gospel narrative was not necessarily arranged in any chronological order; and indeed, according to our hypothesis, the addition of material caused the displacement of such scenes as the cleansing of the Temple. Thus, an unqualified acceptance of the present arrangement of the Gospel as truly chronological is not possible.

John mentions at least three Passovers (ii 13, vi 4, xi 55) and therefore implies at least a two-year ministry. Biographers of Jesus have used this indication to form an outline of the ministry, dividing the material found in the Gospels into the activities of the first and second (and third) years. For instance, we may be told that the Sermon on the Mount (Matt v—vii) took place in the first year of the ministry, shortly after Passover (John ii 13). Such a procedure is invalid. Not only does it ignore the fact that the Synoptic material itself is not chronologically ordered (e.g., the Sermon on the Mount, as it now stands, is a composite of words spoken on various occasions), but also it ignores the fact that the Gospels themselves give no real indications for such synchronization of Johannine and Synoptic data. Properly evaluated, the Synoptic tradition and the Johannine tradition are not contradictory; at times they illuminate each other through comparison, as Morris, *art. cit.*, has pointed out. However, the fact that neither tradition shows a scientific interest in chronology betrays itself when we seek to combine them into a consecutive picture. Even the few points of possible chronological contact between the two traditions offer difficulty. For instance, in the early part of the ministry described in John, Jesus makes several journeys into Judea and returns again to Galilee, but it is very hard to match any one of the return journeys with the Synoptic tradition of a return to Galilee after the baptism by John the Baptist. The multiplication of the loaves found in all four Gospels might seem to offer possibility of synchronization, but the issue is confused by the presence of *two* multiplication accounts in Mark-Matthew.

Even were there possibility of synchronization, however, a theory of a two- or three-year ministry as a framework for dividing Jesus' activities ignores the problem created by the purpose for which the Fourth Gospel was written. Since John xx 30 specifically states that the Gospel is not a complete account of Jesus' activities, there is no way of knowing that the three Passovers mentioned were the only Passovers in that ministry. There is no real reason why one cannot postulate a four- or five-year ministry. Furthermore, since the first Passover mentioned in John is intimately connected to the scene of the cleansing of the Temple, a scene which has probably been displaced, some have questioned the value of the reference to this first Passover as a chronological indication.

From all these remarks it should be clear why we must be very cautious about the use of John in scientifically reconstructing in detail the ministry of Jesus of Nazareth, even as we must be careful in so using the other Gospels. We do believe that John is based on a solid tradition of the works and words of Jesus, a tradition which at times is very primitive. We believe that often John gives us correct historical information about Jesus that no other Gospel has preserved, for example, that, like John the Baptist, Jesus had a baptizing ministry for a period before he began his ministry of teaching; that his public ministry lasted more than a year; that he went several times to Jerusalem; that the opposition of the Jewish authorities at Jerusalem was not confined in the last days of his life; and many details about Jesus' passion and death. Yet in evaluating the Johannine picture of Jesus, we cannot neglect the inevitable modifications made in the various stages of Johannine composition.

BIBLIOGRAPHY

The Historical Value of John

Albright, W. F., "Recent Discoveries in Palestine and the Gospel of John," BNTE, pp. 153–71.
Brown, R. E., "The Problem of Historicity in John," CBQ 24 (1962), 1–14. Also in NTE, Ch. ix.
Dodd, C. H., "Le kérygma apostolique dans le quatrième évangile," RHPR 31 (1951), 265–74.
Higgins, A. J. B., *The Historicity of the Fourth Gospel* (London: Lutterworth, 1960).

Leal, J., "El simbolismo histórico del IV Evangelio," EstBib 19 (1960), 329–48. Digested in TD 11 (1963), 91–96.

Pollard, T. E., "St. John's Contribution to the Picture of the Historical Jesus." The Inaugural Lecture at Knox College, Dunedin, New Zealand.

Potter, R. D., "Topography and Archeology in the Fourth Gospel," StEv, I, pp. 329–37.

Sanders, J. N., "The Gospel and the Historian," *The Listener* 56 (1956), 753–57.

Stauffer, E., "Historische Elemente im Vierten Evangelium," *Homiletica en Biblica* 22 (1963), 1–7.

John and the Synoptics

Bailey, J. A., *The Traditions Common to the Gospels of Luke and John* (SNT VII, 1963).

Balmforth, H., "The Structure of the Fourth Gospel," StEv, II, pp. 25–33.

Brown, R. E., "Incidents that are Units in the Synoptic Gospels but Dispersed in St. John," CBQ 23 (1961), 143–60. Also in NTE, Ch. xi.

Gardner-Smith, P., *Saint John and the Synoptic Gospels* (Cambridge: 1938).

Goodwin, C., "How Did John Treat His Sources," JBL 73 (1954), 61–75.

Haenchen, E., "Johanneische Probleme," ZTK 56 (1959), 19–54.

Lee, E. K., "St. Mark and the Fourth Gospel," NTS 3 (1956–57), 50–58.

Mendner, S., "Zum Problem 'Johannes und die Synoptiker,'" NTS 4 (1957–58), 282–307.

Morris, L., "Synoptic Themes Illuminated by the Fourth Gospel," StEv, II, pp. 73–84.

Osty, E., "Les points de contact entre le récit de la passion dans saint Luc et dans saint Jean," *Mélanges J. Lebreton* (RSR 39 [1951]), 146–54.

Wilkens, W., "Evangelist und Tradition im Johannesevangelium," TZ 16 1960), 81–90.

CHAPTER 11

The Framework of the Gospel Narrative

C. H. DODD

Professor Dodd, formerly of Cambridge University, argues that although the oral tradition circulated in the form of isolated units it was accompanied by a tradition providing a general outline of the sequence of events during the ministry. The article appeared first in *The Expository Times* in 1932. It constitutes a major effort to refute the thesis of the more radical Form Critics, namely, that we cannot establish the sequence of events in the ministry. For a critique of Dodd's view see the article by D. E. Nineham "The Order of Events in St. Mark's Gospel—an examination of Dr. Dodd's Hypothesis" in *Studies in the Gospels*, ed. by D. E. Nineham, 1955, pp. 223–239.

THE criticism of the Gospels has achieved at least one secure result. Scarcely anyone now doubts that Mark is our primary Gospel. It offers the earliest extant narrative of the Ministry of Jesus Christ. The general order of that narrative reappears substantially in Matthew and Luke; and even in the Fourth Gospel, which offers at first sight a totally different arrangement of events, traces of the Marcan order can be recognized. Thus the question is important, whether this earliest extant narrative can be trusted to give, if not a complete record, at least a record which so far as it goes follows the chronological order of events, and so enables us to trace the development of the Ministry. That this is the case is the assumption which underlies many of the modern "lives" of Jesus.

From *New Testament Studies* by C. H. Dodd, 1953, pp. 1–11. Reprinted by permission of Manchester University Press, Manchester.

It has, however, been challenged by recent critics. Dr. Rawlinson,[1] for example, in the Introduction to his Commentary on Mark, writes:

> It is the conviction of the present editor, as the Commentary will make plain, that no such developments are to be traced, and that such attempts to treat the Marcan arrangement of the Gospel materials as supplying an outline, in chronological order, of the course of events, are profoundly mistaken;

and again:

> The most fundamental difficulty of all with regard to the 'Marcan hypothesis' is just the intrinsic improbability of anything like a chronological outline of our Lord's Ministry, or an itinerary of His movements, having been preserved, throughout a whole generation of oral tradition, by a Church which was not primarily interested in such matters. It appears to be the clear upshot of the investigations to which reference has been made . . . that it is just the framework and the arrangement of the materials in our Gospels which ought to be set down to the account of the Evangelists, the materials themselves being derived from tradition.

The "investigations" to which Dr. Rawlinson refers are chiefly those of the German school of *Formgeschichte,* and in particular of Professor Karl Ludwig Schmidt, whose book, *Der Rahmen der Geschichte Jesu* ("The Framework of the Story of Jesus"), is the most thorough treatment of this subject that has appeared.

Professor Schmidt's thesis is that the Gospel according to Mark is compiled out of separate *pericopæ,* each transmitted as an independent unit in the folk-tradition of the Church (a typical example is the Leper story in Mark i. 40-45). The arrangement of these *pericopæ* is the work of the Evangelist, who in arranging them has had little regard for chronology or topography, but groups them in the main according to the topics with which they deal, or the features of the Ministry which they illustrate. Only where some *datum* in the story itself anchors it to a particular place—as for example, the appearance of a Syrophœnician woman anchors Mark vii. 24-30 to "the borders of Tyre"—can we accept a topological setting. Similar internal indications of time scarcely exist until we reach

---

[1] Now (1953) Bishop of Derby.

the Passion narrative at the close, so that there is no secure basis for a chronology.

Apart from the arrangement, and the insertion of such insignificant connecting words as εὐθύς and πάλιν, the work of the Evangelist himself is to be recognized in the composition of short generalizing summaries (*Sammelberichte*), which punctuate the narrative, help the transition from one *pericope* to another, and remind the reader that the particular incidents narrated in detail are episodes in a widely extended ministry. These summaries can be recognized by their contrast in manner and content to the traditional narrative units. They lack the concreteness and particularity of the *pericopæ*. They relate nothing which belongs to one point of space and time to the exclusion of all other times and places. Their verbs are more often in the imperfect, the tense of continuous or habitual action, than in the aorist, the tense of action at a definite point. While the traditional units possess a high historical value, the *Sammelberichte* are mere "framework," and are not to be taken seriously as a contribution to our knowledge of the course of the Ministry.

Professor Schmidt seems to have made out his case that the main stuff of the Gospel is reducible to short narrative units, and that the framework is superimposed upon these units. But it seems worth while to inquire whether the order in which the units appear is indeed quite arbitrary, and the framework nothing more than an artificial construction of the Evangelist.

First, Professor Schmidt himself admits certain qualifications to this theory that the Evangelist's materials came to him solely in the form of isolated *pericopæ*. In some portions of the Gospel he recognizes comparatively large blocks which must have reached the Evangelist in substantially their present form. Thus the whole Passion-narrative, xiv—xvi, he thinks took form as a continuous whole long before Mark incorporated it in his work. Similarly, he recognizes as a single whole the story of the Sabbath at Capernaum, i. 23-38, which consists of four *pericopæ*, one of them approximating to the character of a *Sammelbericht*. Not only, he thinks, did it reach the Evangelist in this form, but things actually happened so. Again, he thinks it probable that two further complexes received their present continuous form at an earlier stage of the tradition—one consisting of the Storm, the Gadarene Swine, Jairus's Daughter, and the Hæmorrhoussa; the other of the Feeding of the Multitude, the Voyage and the Landing (vi. 34-53, repeated in viii. 1-10). In these cases, however, he will not admit that the complexes represent an original historical sequence.

Further, in the central portion of the Gospel, where notes of place are most frequent, Professor Schmidt repeatedly refers to "fragments" or "wreckage" (*Bruchstücke, Trümmer*) of an itinerary. I am not quite clear what he means by this. Sometimes he speaks as though the wealth of local indications reflected some real memory of journeyings in particular districts, which *might* have given rise to a formal itinerary; at other times as though some such itinerary had once existed, but had been disintegrated by the Evangelist. I should say myself that if a narrative started with the words ἐκεῖθεν δὲ ἀναστὰς, or the like (vii. 24, xi. 30, x. 1), even the simplest of the simple-minded early Christians would have been disposed to ask πόθεν; in other words, such narratives can hardly have been wholly independent in the tradition. Either they came down linked with other *pericopæ*, or those who heard them told had some kind of outline itinerary in their minds, to which they readily related the separate stories. In any case, some modification of the strict theory of wholly independent units must be admitted. If we should infer that some ancient and traditional itinerary really lies behind the record of journeys in the North, then clearly such an itinerary cannot have been transmitted by itself, or for its own sake, but only as a part of an outline of the Ministry as a whole.

Once again, the theory that the arrangement has been determined by topical considerations calls for critical examination. The clearest case is the series of stories of conflicts with the scribes and Pharisees (ii. 1—iii. 6). But this series Professor Schmidt himself is disposed to regard as having been formed in the tradition before Mark worked upon it. In that case it tells us nothing of Mark's own method of arrangement. In the next great section, iii. 7—vi. 13, the dominant motive, dictating the arrangement of the material, is, according to Professor Schmidt, the πώρωσις, or hardening, of the people, with the allied motive of the "Messianic secret." It is true that this double theme is prominent from time to time in this section; but it appears also in other sections, and even more strongly; and Professor Schmidt himself admits that it is difficult to trace it in all *pericopæ* of this section. This fact he accounts for on the ground that Mark, having decided to place here some one particular *pericope* bearing upon the main theme of the section, took over along with it other material *already* connected with it in the tradition, connected with it, therefore, by links not merely topical. In the two sections which follow, the supposed dominant theme is certainly more consistently prominent: vi. 14—viii. 26 does deal with the theme: Jesus among the Gentiles; and viii. 27—x. 45 is dominated by the thought of the approaching Passion. But even here the topical unity of the sections is not absolute. The refusal of a sign and the saying about leaven (viii. 11-15) have no direct bearing upon the theme "to the Jew first and also to the Greek"; and it is difficult to bring the discussion of Divorce (x. 2-12) under Professor Schmidt's rubric, "Jesus and His Disciples: The Imminent Passion."

But apart from such qualifications, we may legitimately ask, Is this association of narratives dominated by a particular motive necessarily artificial or arbitrary? Let us put it in this way: Was there, or was there not, a point in the life of Jesus at which He summoned His followers to accompany Him to Jerusalem with the prospect of suffering and death? Is it, or is it not, likely that from that point on His thought and His speech dwelt with especial emphasis upon the theme of this approaching Passion? Surely it is on every account likely. Thus, if one particular section of the Gospel is dominated by that theme, it is not because Mark has arbitrarily assembled from all quarters isolated *pericopæ* referring to the approaching Passion, but because these *pericopæ* originally and intrinsically belong to this particular phase of the Ministry. Again, was there, or was there not, a period in the life of Jesus when the outstanding feature of the situation was the obduracy of the people of Galilee? That there was, we have the best authority for stating. A "Q" saying, accepted by Professor Schmidt as unquestionably genuine, represents Jesus as upbraiding the citizens of Capernaum, Bethsaida, and Chorazin because they did not repent. This utterance clearly belongs to some particular occasion, and it looks back on a period of unfruitful work in Galilee which is now regarded as closed. Thus the theme of the πώρωσις of the people lies in the facts themselves, as they were in a particular phase of the Ministry.

To sum up: the theory of arrangement under topical rubrics is on the one hand not sufficient explanation of the order of the Gospel, and on the other hand it is often not needed as an explanation, since the units have an inner connection with one another grounded in the facts themselves.

We may now make a fresh start by considering some of those passsages which Professor Schmidt regards as the most character-

istic elements in the framework supplied by the Evangelist himself
—the *Sammelberichte*, or generalizing summaries which serve as
links between the separate episodes in that portion of the Gospel
where there is least inner connection between them. Professor
Schmidt includes here:

i. 14-15.	Summary of the Galilæan Ministry.
i. 21-22.	Capernaum: Teaching with Authority.
i. 39.	Tour of Galilæan Synagogues.
ii. 13.	By the Sea.
iii. 7b-19.	Concourse of People; Retirement to Hill-country; Appointment of the Twelve.
iv. 33-34.	Parabolic Teaching.
vi. 7. 12-13.	Mission of the Twelve.
vi. 30.	Return of the Twelve.

The most remarkable of these passages is iii. 7b-19. Professor
Schmidt seems to be clearly right in regarding this whole passage as
a generalizing summary. The characteristic features of the narrative
pericopæ are absent. We have two bald and general descriptions of
stages in the Ministry: first, a stage of public teaching by the seashore; and secondly, a stage in which Jesus is in retirement in the
hill-country with a select number of disciples. No single and definite
act is narrated in such a way that we can visualize it as happening
on a particular day in a particular place. The verbs are mostly in
the present or imperfect tense. The nucleus of each of the two
descriptions is a dry catalogue of names—names of the districts
from which people flocked to Jesus, and names of the Twelve
Apostles. Thus we have before us a typical example of the kind of
thing which Professor Schmidt attributes to the Evangelist's own
composition. But what can have been his motive in composing it?
It does not help to give continuity to the narrative, or to link the
preceding *pericope* with that which follows. Nothing in iii. 7b-19
leads up to or prepares for the situation in iii. 20, which, in fact,
does not differ from the situation in ii. 1—iii. 6. A boat is mentioned
but nothing is done with it until ch. iv. Twelve apostles are mentioned, but they play no part until ch. vi. If Mark composed the
passage as part of the framework of his narrative, he has done his
work very clumsily.

But now let us put together these generalizing summaries, as
Professor Schmidt has marked them. We may neglect iv. 33-34, as

belonging rather to an account of Jesus's methods of teaching than to the narrative framework. The remaining summary passages read as follows (with the imperfect tenses emphasized in translation):

> After John's arrest Jesus came into Galilee proclaiming the Kingdom of God in the words, 'The time is fulfilled, and the Kingdom of God has drawn near: repent and believe in the Gospel.' And He enters into Capernaum;[2] and on Sabbath days He would go to synagogue and teach. And all were in a state of astonishment at His teaching; for He was wont to teach them as one with authority, and not like the scribes. And He went proclaiming in the synagogues throughout Galilee, and casting out demons. And He went out to the seaside, and the whole crowd would come to Him, and He would teach them. And from Judæa and Jerusalem, from Idumæa and Peræa, and the districts of Tyre and Sidon, a great throng, hearing what He was doing, came to Him. And He told His disciples to have a boat waiting for Him because of the crowds, so that they should not throng Him; for He healed many, so that all who had plagues kept pressing upon Him to touch Him. And the foul fiends, whenever they saw Him, would fall before Him, and cry out, 'Thou art the Son of God.' And He would enjoin them not to make Him known. And He goes up into the hill-country, and summons those whom He Himself wanted, and they came to Him. And He appointed Twelve that they might be with Him and that He might send them out to preach and to have authority to expel demons. So James son of Zebedee and John his brother; and to them He gave the name Boanerges, i.e. Thundermen; and Andrew and Philip and Bartholomew and Matthew and Thomas and James son of Alpheus and Thaddæus and Simon the Cananæan and Judas Iscariot His betrayer. And He summons the Twelve and began to send them out two by two; and He used to give them authority over foul fiends; and they went out and preached repentance. They kept expelling many demons and anointing many sick folk with oil and healing them. And the apostles gather to Jesus and reported to Him all that they had done and said.

The striking thing here is the way in which the summaries fall naturally into something very like a continuous narrative. We have in fact obtained, merely by putting them together, a perspicuous outline of the Galilæan Ministry, forming a framework into which

---

[2] Mark i. 21, following some MSS. in reading εἰσπορεύεται, with Schmidt.

the separate pictures are set. So continuous a structure scarcely arose out of casual links supplied here and there where the narrative seemed to demand it. But we may raise the further question, whether it is the independent work of the Evangelist at all. The outline gives a conspectus of the Galilæan Ministry in three stages: A. Synagogue preaching and exorcism in Capernaum and elsewhere; B. Teaching, healing, and exorcism by the seashore, in the presence of vast crowds from all Palestine and beyond; C. Retirement in the hill-country with a small circle of disciples, who are sent on preaching and healing tours. This is the frame into which the pictures (the narrative *pericopæ*) are to be fitted. But they fit very ill. Under rubric A we have only two examples of visits to synagogues; the third synagogue episode comes much later on. With rubric B the case is better, for many of the incidents in iv—vi are actually staged on or near the seashore. If this group had followed immediately upon iii. 11 the picture would have fitted the frame at this point; but actually the series of seashore stories is separated from its proper rubric by the third rubric, 'He goes up to the hill-country,' as well as by the twofold episode iii. 20-35, which has no proper setting in the framework. The third rubric is actually an empty one, for there is no particular incident which has its setting in a retirement to the hill-country.

Now if you have in hand a set of pictures, and desire to frame them, you construct a frame to fit the pictures; but if you have in hand a set of pictures *and a frame*, not designed to fit one another, you must fit them as best you can, and the result may be something of a botch. Thus it seems likely that in addition to materials in *pericope* form, Mark had an outline, itself also traditional, to which he attempted to work, with incomplete success.

But Professor Schmidt and Dr. Rawlinson think there is some 'intrinsic improbability' in the idea that oral tradition transmitted an outline of the Ministry of Jesus in chronological order. As against this, we may note that Professor Martin Dibelius, in his *Formgeschicte des Evangeliums*, has pointed to summary outlines of the life of Jesus embedded in the primitive preaching of the Church, appearing in various speeches in the Acts of the Apostles. Fragments of such an outline he recognizes also in I Cor. xv. 3-7 and xi. 23-25. The evidence, he observes, does not suggest that any one outline was universal, but it does suggest that some kind of outline formed a regular part of the *kerygma* everywhere. The fullest examples of such primitive *kerygma* that we possess are those of Acts x. 37-41 and Acts xiii. 23-31. The former passage gives the scheme: preaching of John; baptism of Jesus; beginning of the Ministry in Galilee; healing and exorcism; change of scene to Jerusalem; crucifixion and resurrection. The latter passage contains a much fuller account of the preaching of John at the beginning, and of the Resurrection at the close. Its record of the Ministry is much slighter, but it establishes a journey in company with disciples from Galilee to Jerusalem, ending with the death of Jesus.

In view of this evidence, I cannot see any intrinsic improbability in the supposition that the primitve Church did transmit an outline of the Ministry of Jesus, with some regard at least to its topographical and chronological setting. The outline which we have recognized as existing in fragmentary form in the framework of Mark may well have belonged to a form of the primitive *kerygma*. It implies a somewhat more elaborate form of it than those which are preserved in the Acts of the Apostles; but these, no doubt, are summaries of summaries.

I submit, therefore, that we are led to conceive the materials which Mark took over from tradition as being of three kinds:

(i) Isolated independent *pericopæ*, handed down without any conjunction;

(ii) Larger complexes, which again may be of various kinds: genuinely continuous narratives; *pericopæ* strung upon an itinerary; *pericopæ* connected by unity of theme.

(iii) An outline of the whole ministry, designed, perhaps, as an introduction to the Passion-story, but serving also as a background of reference for separate stories; fragments of this survive in the framework of the Gospel.

In shaping these materials into a Gospel, Mark has attempted to work to the traditional outline, but he is embarrassed by two facts: (*a*) the outline was far too meagre to provide a setting for all the detailed narratives at his disposal, while on the other hand it referred to phases of the Ministry not illustrated by the detailed narratives; (*b*) the materials were already partially grouped in ways which cut across a truly chronological order. Thus he was faced by a difficult problem. I suggest he has solved it, though not wholly satisfactorily, by a compromise between a chronological and a topical order. Where the outline gave a clue to the setting of particular narrative units or groups of units, he has arranged them accordingly.

Where groups of narrative units came down to him already arranged topically, he allowed the arrangement to stand, relating the first member of the group (e.g. ii. 1-12, the first conflict-story) to what appeared to be its most suitable point in the outline scheme. When he was left with wholly disconnected units on his hands, he found place for them as best he could, being sometimes guided by topical considerations, sometimes by a sense of the chronological stage to which the particular episode seemed most naturally to belong. Thus we need not be so scornful of the Marcan order as has recently become the fashion, though we shall not place in it the implicit confidence it once enjoyed. It is in large measure, as Professor Schmidt argues, the result of the Evangelist's own work, rather than directly traditional. But he did that work not arbitrarily or irresponsibly, but under such guidance as he could find in tradition. It is hazardous to argue from the precise sequence of the narrative in detail; yet there is good reason to believe that in broad lines the Marcan order does represent a genuine succession of events, within which movement and development can be traced.

CHAPTER 12

Jesus and His Story

ETHELBERT STAUFFER

Professor Stauffer of Erlangen University is known to
English speaking students through his contributions to New
Testament scholarship, among which are *Christ and the
Caesars*, 1955; and *New Testament Theology*, 1955. In the
opening section of his book Stauffer argues that an investigation of materials contemporaneous with Jesus serves to
establish the accuracy of many sections in the Gospels. For
a specific application of this method see further excerpts in
chapter 23.

THIS book has sprung from the endeavor to find a fresh way to
approach the historical Jesus. It is not a summary of the material
that may be found in many larger Lives of Jesus. Rather, it is intended as pioneer work.

It used to be thought that only the Fourth Gospel had any specific
theological bias, and that the "Synoptic Gospels"—that is, the first
three—were accounts of Jesus which antedated dogmatic theology.
Then, the dogmatic elements in the Synoptic Gospels were uncov-
ered; and today we know that the theological and church-oriented
bias in the traditions is much older than the Gospels themselves.

Twenty-five years ago a prominent Protestant theologian wrote:
"The Passion of Jesus, as it unfolds before our eyes in the Gospels,
must be counted among the most tremendous creations of religious
fiction." [1] Today we must ask ourselves whether this same verdict

[1] Hans Lietzmann: *"Der Prozess Jesu," Sitzungsbericht der Preussischen Akad-
emie der Wissenschaften, Philosophische-historische Klasse*, Vol. XXIII/XXIV
(Berlin, 1931), p. 313.

From *Jesus and His Story*, by Ethelbert Stauffer. Translated by Richard and Clara
Winston. © Copyright 1959 by Alfred A. Knopf, Inc. Reprinted by permission of the
publisher.

does not apply to everything the Gospels have to say about Jesus. What is the meaning of "religious fiction"? What may still be considered historical truth? By what signs can a scholar separate, with any degree of certainty, the historical facts from the dogmatic bias?

The way out of this quandary is to open new sources entirely unaffected by Christian tendencies. The historian's task will then be to carefully evaluate such testimony and check it against the statements of the Christian witnesses.

To this end, we must first muster our "indirect" sources on Jesus —that is to say, the contemporary testimony on the conditions, events, and personalities that played a part in the story of Jesus. In such testimony there is no mention of Jesus himself. For the most part, the authors of these documents knew nothing whatsoever about the existence of Jesus. Consequently, these writings are quite free of religious fiction or dogmatic bias. But they provide abundant information on people and events that are only passingly mentioned in the Gospels, or are even only implicitly in the background. At every step there is the opportunity to check, to supplement, and perhaps to correct the narratives in the Gospels. The chronology of the life of Jesus, as set forth here, is drawn from the synchronization of these accounts with those of the Gospels—and chronology is essential, for upon it is based our picture of the world situation into which Jesus entered.

Virtually nothing is known about the childhood and youth of Jesus. I have made no attempt to fill this regrettable gap with legends. I have thought it useful, however, to say a few words about the historical environment in which Jesus grew up.

I have made a point of evaluating the Jewish legal provisions concerning heretics and the rules of trials. Without these, there is no grasping the legalistic basis of the charges against Jesus, especially as the Gospels deal with this matter but vaguely. And as soon as we attack this problem, we recognize the iron-clad logic that dominated the criminal proceedings against Jesus from the first secret tribunal to the great heresy trial. It becomes clear that everything followed clearly and consistently from the laws, and this may make us reflect a bit on the account given by the Gospels, and its reliability as source material. From this same material it is possible, moreover, to draw up a chronological framework for the course of events in the last years of Jesus' life. I may put it this way: when we train the rays of legal history upon the Gospels, we obtain a historical X-ray

photograph. Upon it stands revealed the clear outline of the life of
Jesus.

In addition to these indirect sources there are the direct statements concerning Jesus in ancient Jewish documents—texts in which
Jesus is mentioned by name (or under a code name). Most of these
texts are the work of the rabbinical authorities; a few spring from
the movement that grew up around John the Baptist. There are not
many; they are all very short, in many cases camouflaged and mud-
dled; and in these texts, also, truth and fiction are closely inter-
twined. These Jewish mentions of Jesus have always been dismissed
with scorn, much to the detriment of research. For in these brief no-
tices lie concealed many an old tradition concerning Jesus, traditions
perhaps reaching back to the days of Caiaphas, and at any rate back
to the first and second centuries. These can be of immense aid to us
in checking, clarifying, and evaluating the Gospel narratives. Naturally these Jewish accounts are at least as tendentious as the stories of
Jesus in the Gospels. They are, we recognize, fresh instances of the
campaign against Jesus which began during his lifetime and won
its victory, of such importance to the history of the world, in his
condemnation and crucifixion.

It is extremely painful to the believing Christian to read these
texts. But we must remember that Jesus stood before the highest
ecclesiastic tribunal of his people as a criminal heretic. Objectivity
demands that the historian hear not only the friends of the defend-
ant, the Christian Apostles and Evangelists, but the friends of the
Great Sanhedrin as well, the rabbis and scribes. However devout a
Christian, one must take these things into account if one wishes to
be a just historian. And it will be well worth one's pain. For in the
course of studying these texts, one will learn to distinguish between
facts and their interpretation—a distinction important in all historical studies, but absolutely crucial in the study of Jesus. The
dichotomy exists in both the Christian and the Jewish traditions
concerning Jesus; only the bias is different. The same facts are employed in the one case to sustain faith in Christ, in the other to attack
that faith.

The sharper the clash, the wider the gulf, the more vital does this
alternation of testimony and counter-testimony become to the historical investigator. For if a confrontation of witnesses yields statements that agree on some points, then these points must represent
facts accepted by both sides. This principle certainly holds true if

the historical traditions of the two groups of witnesses are independent of each other. But it holds true almost as completely in cases where the traditions intersect. For it is highly significant that the witness for the prosecution admits that the witness for the defense is right on certain points; that he agrees with his opponents about certain common facts. But where the two sets of witnesses contradict each other, one side or the other, or both, must be distorting or fabricating the evidence, and it becomes the historian's task to trace the various revisions through the tradition and uncover the nature of the bias.

To this direct and indirect evidence concerning Jesus there has now been added a third category, a group of ancient texts which have long occupied me, and which, with the discovery of the Dead Sea scrolls, have become the center of an international controversy. These are the late-Judaistic Apocalyptic writings. These texts have no particular importance to a study of the *life* of Jesus, but they do have a great bearing on his *message*.

The spate of publications upon the newly discovered manuscripts has given the general public the impression that the scrolls contain everything Jesus ever said. Jesus, we are told, drew at least the key points of his doctrine from the traditional ideas of the Apocalyptists and devotees of the Torah gathered around the Dead Sea. But the historical fact that Jesus took a stand opposed to the Mosaic Torah, to scrupulosity regarding the Torah, and to the authorities of the Torah, would seem to attest to the contrary. Upon closer examination it appears that Jesus himself did not lean upon the Dead Sea school of thought. It was John the Baptist who was most strongly influenced by it, and then the Apostles and Evangelists—in different ways and to various degrees. Thus we obtain a wealth of material which throws great light on the Jesus tradition that prevailed among the Christians of Palestine and antedated the codification of the Gospels.

The preservation, decipherment, and publication of these texts is still proceeding. But it is already possible to make the following statements: many of the sayings of Jesus recorded in the Gospels, which have hitherto been considered authentic because they sounded characteristic of Palestinian Judaism, are more likely to have derived from the doctrinal traditions of the era preceding Jesus (the theology of the group around John the Baptist) or the era succeeding Jesus (the teachings of the Palestinian Christians). These sayings were incorporated into the very oldest traditions concerning Jesus in the course of a major effort to re-Judaicize his message. Jesus himself, however, was far less the child of his times and of his people than has hitherto been thought. He was far more solitary, more bellicose, more revolutionary than has generally been recognized. Judas was, after his fashion, a man who abided by the letter of the law and perhaps also by the instructions of his clerical authorities. But the execution of Jesus was wholly inevitable in any case, and, while it might have taken another form, was basically only a question of time.

So much for the new material on which this book is based. What can be achieved by the use of this material?

First of all, it enables us to form an entirely new, concrete, and dramatic picture of the beginning of the Jesus tradition. We shall come to understand the Christian Gospels and the Jewish texts on Jesus as documents in a passionate controversy centering around the interpretation and the meaning of Jesus of Nazareth. Time and again the question has been raised: what was the actual function of the oldest traditions concerning Jesus? Did they serve for preaching, for liturgy, for the teaching of catechumens, for missionary work of the primitive church? Certainly for all of these. But the oldest and most important function of the traditions was polemical. They originated in the conflict over Jesus. For this conflict reached a pitch of violence even while Jesus still lived. It was revived with fresh passion after the epiphany, and flared up everywhere the message of Christ was proclaimed, in Jerusalem, Samaria, Galilee, Jamnia, Caesarea, Antioch, Rome, and later on, above all, in Ephesus. On either side in the great conflict there were a number of extremely stubborn, belligerent factions. On the one side there were the groups around Peter, James, Matthew, Luke, and John. On the other side stood the scribes, the anti-Roman partisans, the desert sects, the disciples of John the Baptist, and the Samaritans. In the course of these struggles the Christian and Jewish traditions of Jesus were shaped; out of these struggles emerged the Gospels and the rabbinical or Baptistic documents concerning Jesus.

At the beginning of all these struggles stood Jesus himself: "I came to cast fire upon the earth, and would that it were already kindled! I have a baptism to be baptized with; and how I am constrained until it is accomplished." [2]

[2] Luke 12, 49.

It is evident that the figure of Jesus will appear in a new light when seen in terms of this conflict, and when we realize once and for all that both the Christian and Jewish documents on Jesus which we possess are all polemics.

The nineteenth-century ideal was a *biography* of Jesus—that is to say, a representation of the psychological development of Jesus, of his mind and his activities, rendered with narrative vividness, analytic insight, and plausibility. Whether this was a legitimate ideal is a moot question. At any rate, we know today that it was unattainable. What, then, may our ideal be, what ideal am I entitled to set up? I reply: a *history* of Jesus. By this term I mean something extremely modest. I mean a strict clarification of those facts which can be ascertained, possibly of a certain series of events, perhaps too of a number of causal relationships. I shall proceed along pragmatic lines, refraining from any psychologizing. Chronology will be my guide. I shall synchronize but not invent or speculate. This is what I mean by a historical viewpoint.

When I come to a point where presentation of facts and causal relationships stops and interpretation begins, I shall go no further. The Evangelists' interpretation of Jesus, the interpretation offered by the dogmas of the church, and even my personal interpretation of Jesus are barred from this book. However, the oldest and most important of all the interpretations of Jesus must be treated: Jesus' own interpretation of himself. For that necessarily belongs to the story, if only because it reached its historic climax in Jesus' self-witness before the Great Sanhedrin in Jerusalem.

No serious historian can or would wish to penetrate into Jesus' mental processes. Rather, I am concerned here solely with Jesus' witness to himself in the Gospels, in so far as this can be ascertained by the methods of philology. I proceed to examine critically the authentic self-affirmations of Jesus, and to determine their meaning within the history of religious ideas—neither more nor less than this. It will become evident that the historical phenomenon of Jesus was made manifest once again in all its uniqueness and gravity in his declaration before the Great Sanhedrin. This declaration can be set forth clearly, but it is not subject to argument. It can only be accepted or rejected.

CHAPTER 13

The Problem of the Historical Jesus

JOACHIM JEREMIAS

> Professor Jeremias of Goettingen University is one of the foremost interpreters of the Palestinian background of the New Testament. In the excerpt below, particularly points 3 and 4, he indicates and illustrates his concern that background material should be used to validate the Gospel records. He has applied this methodology in his other works. See especially: *The Parables of Jesus*, rev. ed., 1963; *The Eucharistic Words of Jesus*, 1955. It is evident from a full study of his writings that he uses this methodology more cautiously than Stauffer (chapters 12, 23).

HERE I may content myself with suggestions and briefly indicate five aspects of the case.

(1) The critical scholarship of the previous century has thrown up the first bulwark for us in the shape of the remarkable literary criticism which it developed and increasingly refined. We have been taught to distinguish sources or, more correctly (since we are becoming more and more skeptical about the assumption of written sources), strands of tradition: a Marcan tradition, a Logia tradition,[1] the special traditions of Luke, Matthew, and John. Having established this, literary criticism leads us back to the stage of oral tradition antedating our gospels. We have, moreover, been taught to recognize the style of composition of the evangelists, and hence

---

[1] ["Logia," the Greek term for "sayings," is applied to the collection of sayings commonly called "Q" which Matthew and Luke used as a source in addition to their Marcan source. While "Q" is often thought to have been a written book, Professor Jeremias prefers to think of it as an oral stratum of tradition.—EDITOR.]

From *The Problem of the Historical Jesus* by Joachim Jeremias, 1964, pp. 16–21. Reprinted by permission of Fortress Press, Philadelphia.

to distinguish between tradition and redaction. We have been thus enabled to trace the tradition back into its pre-literary stage.

(2) Form criticism has led us a step further back by attempting to determine the laws which governed the shaping of the material; it has thus thrown light from another side upon the creation and growth of the tradition. It is a fact not sufficiently known or heeded that the essential significance of form criticism is that it has enabled us to remove a Hellenistic layer which had overlaid an earlier Palestinian tradition.

(3) We have been carried an important step further on the way back to Jesus himself by studies about the world of his day which have disclosed to us his environment, informing us of the religious climate and of Palestinian customs in his day. I am referring to the study of rabbinical literature and of Late Jewish apocalyptic. As one who was privileged to live in Palestine for some years, I can testify from my own experience how much new light has been thrown in this way upon the gospels. The importance of the study of both ancient and modern Palestine does not lie primarily in the fact that it has revealed to us how Jesus belonged to his own time; its main significance lies rather in the way in which it has helped us to realize afresh the sharpness of Jesus' opposition to the religiosity of his time. And this is the chief significance of the Dead Sea Scrolls for New Testament studies. The Essenism which they disclose to us enables us to realize from their own testimony to what an extent the whole of Late Judaism was imbued with a passion to establish God's holy community. We can now assess more clearly than heretofore the significance of the emphatic denial with which Jesus met all these attempts.

(4) A further result of the study of the environment of Jesus has been to force upon us the necessity of studying his mother tongue. It is barely sixty-five years ago since Dalman proved conclusively, in my estimation, that Jesus spoke Galilean Aramaic.[2] Since then the study of this dialect has been pursued but is still only in an early stage. We still lack critical editions of the texts and a vocabulary of Galilean Aramaic. But the studies made so far have already demon-

---

[2] [Gustav Dalman, *Die Worte Jesu mit Berücksichtigung des nachkanonischen jüdischen Schrifttums und der aramäischen Sprache erörtert* (Leipzig: J. C. Hinrichs'sche Buchhandlung, 1898; ²1930); Eng. trans. by D. M. Kay, *The Words of Jesus considered in the light of post-Biblical Jewish writings and the Aramaic language* (Edinburgh: T. & T. Clark, 1902).—EDITOR.]

strated how rewarding such meticulous philological research can be. It is only necessary to recall in how many cases one and the same saying of Jesus has been transmitted to us in different Greek forms.[3] In most of these cases we are dealing with translation variants, which constitute a reliable aid in reconstructing the Aramaic form of the saying underlying the various versions. For example, the Lord's Prayer, the Greek renderings of which in Matthew and Luke show many divergences, can by this means be retranslated into Jesus' mother tongue with a high degree of probability.[4] Anyone who has ever had anything to do with translations is aware that they can never take the place of the original, and will be able to assess how important it is that we should be able to get back with a high degree of probability to the original Aramaic underlying the Greek tradition. It must of course be remembered that the earliest Christian community spoke Aramaic too; so not every Aramaism is evidence of authenticity. At any rate, however, we are drawing nearer to Jesus himself when we succeed in rediscovering the pre-Hellenistic form of the tradition. In this connection it is of special importance to note that this kind of study reveals peculiarities in the utterances of Jesus which are without contemporary parallels. As a form of address to God the word *abba* is without parallel in the whole of Late Jewish devotional literature.[5] Similarly there is no contemporary analogy to Jesus' use of "Amen" as an introduction to his own utterances.[6] It may be maintained that these two characteristic features of the *ipsissima vox* of Jesus [7] contain in a nutshell his message and his consciousness of his authority.

[3] [On "translation variants," cf. J. Jeremias, *The Sermon on the Mount, op. cit.,* pp. 15–16.—EDITOR.]
[4] [Cf. J. Jeremias, *The Lord's Prayer* ("Facet Books, Biblical Series," 8; Philadelphia: Fortress Press, 1964), p. 15.—EDITOR.]
[5] [*Ibid.,* p. 19.—EDITOR.]
[6] [H. Schlier, *"amen,"* in *Theologisches Wörterbuch zum Neuen Testament,* (ed. G. Kittel), Vol. 1 (Stuttgart: W. Kohlhammer, 1933), pp. 339–42, especially 341–42; Eng. trans. by G. W. Bromiley, *Theological Dictionary of the New Testament,* Vol. 1 (Grand Rapids: Eerdmans, 1964), pp. 335–38. While Schlier speaks of Jesus' use of "Amen" as containing "the whole of Christology in nuce," he does not stress the uniqueness of Jesus' usage or draw out the implications as sharply as Professor Jeremias has.—EDITOR.]
[7] [*Ipsissima vox,* Jesus' own original way of speaking. Cf. J. Jeremias, "Kennzeichen der ipsissima vox Jesu," in *Synoptische Studien: Alfred Wikenhauser zum siebzigsten Geburtstag am 22. Februar 1953 dargebracht von Freunden, Kollegen und Schülern* (Munich: Karl Zink Verlag, 1953), pp. 86–93.—EDITOR.]

(5) Of special significance as a bulwark against a psychological modernizing of Jesus is the rediscovery of the eschatological character of his message. It is not only that we have learned to recognize how extensively Jesus shared the conceptions of contemporary apocalyptic and made use of its language; the decisive importance of this discovery lies elsewhere. We have seen how the whole message of Jesus flowed from an awareness that God was about to break into history, an awareness of the approaching crisis, the coming judgment; and we have seen the significance of the fact that it was against this background that he proclaimed the present in-breaking in his own ministry of the kingdom of God.[8]

It is clear, then, that Jesus was no Jewish rabbi, no teacher of wisdom, no prophet, but that his proclamation of a God who was at the present moment offering a share in salvation to the despised, the oppressed, and the despairing ran counter to all the religiosity of his time, and was in truth the end of Judaism.

At the end of his book *The Quest of the Historical Jesus,* Albert Schweitzer has summed up graphically the outcome of the attempts to write a life of Jesus: "The study of the Life of Jesus has had a curious history. It set out in quest of the historical Jesus, believing that when it had found Him it could bring Him straight into our time as a Teacher and Saviour. It loosed the bands by which He had been riveted for centuries to the stony rocks of ecclesiastical doctrine, and rejoiced to see life and movement coming into the figure once more, and the historical Jesus advancing, as it seemed, to meet it. But He does not stay; He passes by our time and returns to His own." [9] Such was in fact the remarkable outcome of the study of the life of Jesus begun in 1778. It had freed Jesus from fetters; he became a living figure, belonging to the present; he became a man of our own time. Yet he did not stay, but passed by our time and returned to his own. It became clear that he was not a man of our time, but the prophet of Nazareth, who spoke the language of the prophets of the old covenant and proclaimed the God of the old covenant. But we must now extend Schweitzer's metaphor. Jesus did not stay in his own time, but he also passed beyond his own time. He did not remain the rabbi of Nazareth, the prophet of Late Judaism. He receded into the distance, entered into the dim light of Easter morning, and became, as Schweitzer says in the closing sen-

[8] [Cf. J. Jeremias, *The Parables of Jesus, op. cit.*—EDITOR.]
[9] *Op. cit.,* Eng. trans., p. 397.

tence of his book, the One unknown, without a name, who speaks the word, "Follow thou me!" [10]

HISTORICAL STUDY AND JESUS' CLAIM

If we travel the road thus indicated, threading our way amid the five protecting walls which guard us from modernizing Jesus and fashioning him in our own likeness, we are then confronted by a unique claim to authority which breaks through the bounds of the Old Testament and of Judaism. Everywhere we are confronted in the message of Jesus by this ultimate claim, that is to say, we are confronted by the same claim to faith as that with which the kerygma presents us. We must at this point reiterate one of the simplest and most obvious facts, since it is no longer obvious to all. Every sentence of the sources bears witness of this fact to us, every verse of our gospels hammers it into us: something has happened, something unique, something which had never happened before. The study of the history of religions has amassed countless parallels and analogies to the message of Jesus. As far as our knowledge of Pharisaic and rabbinical theology is concerned, for instance, the monumental work of Paul Billerbeck [11] is unsurpassed and will long remain so. Yet the more analogies we amass, the clearer it becomes that there are no analogies to the message of Jesus. There is no parallel to his message that God is concerned with sinners and not with the righteous, and that he grants them, here and now, a share in his kingdom. There is no parallel to Jesus' sitting down in table-fellowship with publicans and sinners. There is no parallel to the authority with which he dares to address God as *abba*. Anyone who admits merely the fact—and I cannot see how it can be gainsaid—that the word *abba* is an authentic utterance of Jesus, is, if he understands the word correctly, without watering down its meaning, thereby confronted with Jesus' claim to authority. Anyone who reads the parable of the Prodigal Son, which belongs to the bedrock

[10] *Ibid.*, p. 401.
[11] [H. Strack and P. Billerbeck, *Kommentar zum Neuen Testament aus Talmud und Midrasch* (6 vols.; Munich: C. H. Beck, 1922–61). The four volumes of commentary from Jewish sources were published between 1922 and 1928 and are exclusively the work of Paul Billerbeck. Volume 4 actually consists of two parts, containing detached notes on various important topics. Vols. 5 and 6 add valuable indices prepared under Professor Jeremias' direction.—EDITOR.]

of the tradition, and observes how in this parable, which describes the unimaginable goodness of divine forgiveness, Jesus justifies his table-fellowship with publicans and sinners, is again confronted with the claim of Jesus to be regarded as God's representative, acting with his authority.[12] One example after another could be cited, but the result would always be the same. If with utmost discipline and conscientiousness we apply the critical resources at our disposal to the study of the historical Jesus, the final result is always the same: we find ourselves confronted with God himself. That is the fact to which the sources bear witness: a man appeared, and those who received his message were certain that they had heard the word of God. It is not as if faith were made superfluous or belittled, when exegesis shows us that behind every word and every deed of Jesus lies his claim to authority. (How could faith ever become superfluous?) Indeed, the truth of the matter is that through the words and acts of Jesus at every turn the challenge to faith is presented. When we read the gospels, even when we read them critically, we cannot evade this challenge. This claim to divine authority is the origin of Christianity, and hence study of the historical Jesus and his message is no peripheral task of New Testament scholarship, a study of one particular historical problem among many others. It is *the* central task of New Testament scholarship.

[12] Cf. E. Fuchs, "Die Frage nach dem historischen Jesus," *op. cit.,* p. 219 (in the reprinted version, p. 154). [Cf. also J. Jeremias, *The Parables of Jesus, op. cit.,* pp. 128–32 in the rev. ed.—EDITOR.]

CHAPTER 14

Kerygma and History

N. A. DAHL

> Professor Dahl, currently of Yale University, discusses
> the problem of establishing criteria by which the histori-
> cally authentic may be distinguished from the inauthentic
> in the Gospels.

ONLY by methodically pure and critical work can the received
traditions be made useful for a historical description of Jesus,
but thereby personal and current views concerning what Jesus may
have said or done may not be made a criterion in the evaluation of
the material in question. The history of research has taught us what
a dangerous source of error this can be. If we want to avoid all subjective arbitrariness historico-critical research on the Gospels becomes an extremely complicated work requiring the highest degree
of precision. The extant Gospels are first of all to be studied and
interpreted as literary wholes. Their relationship to each other must
be accurately examined, but even the relatively certain results of
literary criticism have only limited value for the historical question,
for we must reckon with the fact that the oral tradition still existed
in addition to and following the first written records. The possibility
exists throughout that an older variant of the tradition may have
been preserved in a secondary literary source.[1]

In addition to the literary investigation of the Gospels we must
consider the traditio-historical study of the small or smallest units
of the tradition. In addition to the Gospels, material from later
sources—e.g., quotations from the church fathers—textual variants,

[1] Cf. my essay, "Die Passionsgeschichte bei Matthäus, *New Testament Studies*,
I, No. 3 (1955).

From *Kerygma and History*, pp. 151–159, selected, translated, and edited by Carl E.
Braaten and Roy A. Harrisville. Copyright © 1962 by Abingdon Press.

and fragments of apocryphal gospels has a significance which cannot be ignored. The new material which such sources offer is of course extremely small and of dubious value, but the subsequent history of the Gospel tradition is illuminated, and from it the cautious scholar will be able to draw a few conclusions regarding its earlier history. In further research, critical viewpoints concerning the form, language, and substance are also to be observed. No single road leads to the goal; in spite of the very fruitful beginning of form criticism, the result has been, e.g., that the study of form has not yielded objective criteria for separating older from later traditions to the degree expected. The linguistic criteria, in their turn, lead with great probability to old traditions where the original Semitic tongue shines through but do not allow any positive decision regarding the *ipsissima verba* of Jesus. Preference for one certain method as is shared by the schools should be regarded as a calamity and should, where possible, be replaced by the co-operation of a variety of specialists.

On the basis of numerous individual observations, a more comprehensive picture of the history of the tradition can then be outlined. Certain statistical, not absolute, laws and regularities emerge which leave their imprint on the formation and transformation of the tradition. It is well known that the individual sayings and narratives as such have been relatively faithfully preserved, while the evangelists and the narrators before them were much freer in the collection and arrangement of the material. Within the individual sections of the tradition greater freedom is exercised with respect to rendering introductory and concluding data than with regard to the central point. Among the different variants agreement is greatest in the rendering of the words of Jesus, but the words have not been preserved because of any reverence for the antiquarian, but because they are words of the Lord to his community. Loosed from their original situation, the words have been used and construed in a new way, a factor which has affected not only their arrangement, but also their formation. That can be most easily observed in the case of the parables.[2]

The goal of critical Gospel research is to make clear the history of the tradition about Jesus within the Church. With some certainty, moreover, distinction can be made between the core of the tradition and its later elaboration. It is much more difficult to find objective

[2] Joachim Jeremias, *The Parables of Jesus*, tr. S. H. Hooke (New York: Charles Scribner's Sons, 1955), pp. 20–28.

criteria which can determine whether the core of a tradition is authentic or secondary. It is theoretically possible that migrant sayings have been transferred to Jesus, that words of Jewish wisdom or utterances of primitive Christian prophets have been put in the mouth of the historical Jesus, et cetera, but only very seldom can positive proof be adduced that such is really the case. Here, generally, the total perspective of the scholar is decisive for an evaluation of the case in point, and not vice versa. That can easily be observed in Bultmann's *Die Geschichte der Synoptischen Tradition,* but also applies to scholars who, like myself, are inclined to believe that on the whole the Church did not produce the traditions about Jesus, but rather reproduced them in a new form.

In no case can any distinct and sharp separation be achieved between genuine words of Jesus and constructions of the community. We do not escape the fact that we know Jesus only as the disciples remembered him. Whoever thinks that the disciples completely misunderstood their Master or even consciously falsified his picture may give his phantasy free reign. From a purely historico-scientific point of view, however, it is more logical to assume that the Master is to be recognized from the circle of his disciples and its historical influence. But then it is also possible to work methodically when an attempt is made to advance from the analysis of the Gospel tradition to the description of the historical Jesus.

Even without a clear differentiation between pure history and the Church's theology the Gospel tradition permits us to draw a very clear picture of what was typical and characteristic of Jesus. Cross sections of the tradition bring to the fore what was characteristic, e.g., of his proclamation of the Kingdom of God, of his position toward the law, or of his attitude toward various groups of men. Words and reports of differing form and genre, transmitted within various layers of the tradition, mutually illumine each other and yield a total picture in which there appears something that is characteristic of Jesus. Whether the historicity of individual words or episodes remains uncertain is consequently of lesser importance. The fact that the word or occurrence found a place within the tradition about Jesus indicates that it agreed with the total picture as it existed within the circle of the disciples.[3]

[3] Julius Schniewind's remarks in "Zur Synoptikerexegese," *Theologische Rundschau,* II (1930), 129–89, are still of value, and particularly his discussion of "longitudinal" and "cross-section exegesis." On the questions of method, cf. also C. H. Dodd, *History and the Gospel* (London: James Nisbet & Company, 1938).

The cross-section method must be supplemented by drawing longitudinal lines leading from Judaism beyond Jesus to primitive Christianity. While the time when Zarathustra and Moses lived has long been the subject of debate, we know that Jesus was crucified under Pontius Pilate. The fixed starting point of all our knowledge about him is that he is the crucified One whom the community, originating in his band of disciples, believed to be the risen Messiah. We also know that Jesus worked in Israel and that he himself was born and grew up a Jew, was "born of woman, born under the law." The historical Jesus is to be found at the crossroad where Christianity and Judaism begin separating from each other, although it only became gradually clear that the paths parted in such a way that Christianity appeared as a new religion alongside Judaism.

From the oldest Christian sources we must work our way backwards in the direction of Jesus. It is of great advantage that the most important groups of New Testament writings are independent of each other; Paul, the Synoptists, John, the Epistle to the Hebrews, et cetera, cannot be arranged into one straight line of development. Rather, each in its own way reflects the impression made by Jesus and the events connected with his name. Between the historical Jesus and the New Testament writings there are, of course, the Easter occurrences, but that does not alter the fact that the historian who works backwards from the various formulations of primitive Christianity toward the common starting point by this method also approaches the historical Jesus. The investigation of the tradition lying behind the Gospels is, of course, the most important, but not the only part of this work.

On the other hand, we must view Jesus within the context of Palestinian Judaism. Everything which enlarges our knowledge of this environment of Jesus indirectly extends our knowledge of the historical Jesus himself. Since the results in this area are relatively certain, it is a very real question whether or not the insights gained here in the long run involve the greatest enrichment of our historical knowledge about Jesus. Only by saving the honor of the Pharisees, e.g., has the unheard-of radicality of Jesus' words against the Pharisees really come to light. It is still not possible to estimate what the textual findings from the caves may yield; in any case they impel us to resume the quest of the historical Jesus. As never before we have the possibility of tracing the trends and ideas which, both positively and negatively, form the presuppositions for his ministry.

When, on the one hand, the historian works backwards in this way from oldest Christianity to Jesus and, on the other, attempts to clarify the presuppositions of his appearance on the basis of Jewish sources, quite a clear picture can be gained of the setting into which Jesus appeared and of the changes which his ministry effected. By this method it is also possible to insert the transmitted words and episodes into their original historical situation. Thus we can form an idea of what Jesus wanted to say to the Jews of his own time and can attempt to construct a historical picture of him.

The historian's attempt to reconstruct the historical Jesus by the historico-scientific method may be compared with the work of the archaeologist who attempts to restore an old monument of which only the foundation and a few scattered stones remain. He may try to draw sketches on paper in order to show how the structure probably looked. No one will deny him that, and it can be useful and necessary for his work. He misleads his readers, however, when he publishes his sketch without calling attention to the place where exact knowledge leaves off, where he has good grounds for his reconstruction, and where he has further drawn free hand. When he finds the precise spot where one or a few of the scattered stones originally lay, it means more in the long run than such reconstructive attempts. Similarly, it is permissible to write a description of the historical Jesus, but hypotheses may not be advanced as exact scientific results. If there is an ingenious element in the hypotheses, as e.g., in Albert Schweitzer's case, then they may give important impulse to further research. But over an extended period an expansion of our exact knowledge of primitive Christianity and of Judaism in Jesus' time means more for our historical knowledge of Jesus than many books about his life.

Historical science can only approximately achieve exact results. This does not merely apply to the Jesus-research, but such a general truth is most particularly to be observed in the Jesus-research with its involved problematic. Whoever has to fix an uncertain chronological datum, e.g., the year of the origin of a work, is only seldom in the position of finding new arguments which allow him to make a completely accurate decision. He must begin by establishing the *termini a quo* and *ad quem* and, on the basis of these two limits, try to approach the precise point of time. Even the more involved historical problems will, *mutatis mutandis*, have to be dealt with in a similar way. So far as Jesus is concerned, the scholar must search, on the one hand, for what could be established in any event and cannot justifiably be called into question however great the historical skepticism. Radical criticism, even the most radical, has a necessary, historico-scientific function here provided one adheres to the rule that it is not the nongenuineness, but contrariwise the genuineness of the individual piece which is to be demonstrated and that a genuine transmission concerning Jesus is established only when the "tradition, for various reasons, can be neither derived from Judaism nor attributed to primitive Christianity."[4] This radical criticism and its results may not be dogmatized, but must rather be regarded as one necessary heuristic principle among others. Whatever is discovered in this way is only a critically assured *minimum.*

On the other hand, the total tradition concerning Jesus must be taken into consideration. In its totality it is theology of the Church, but at the same time it is also in its totality a reflex of Jesus' activity —a *maximum* which contains everything of importance for our historical knowledge about Jesus. To delineate this maximum more precisely is a problem for the solution of which Stauffer's "iron rule" applies: *In dubiis pro tradito.*[5] The further task consists in harmonizing the maximum of the tradition with the critically assured minimum to the highest degree possible, in order step by step to approach more closely to the historical Jesus. The chief reason why the older Life-of-Jesus research became sterile and scientifically unfruitful might have been that it set too directly and rashly toward its goal. If today we face a renewal of interest in Jesus-research, we will have to be on our guard against committing the same error again.

Although we are still far removed from the desired degree of exactitude, we may still construct quite a clear picture of the manner of Jesus' appearance as well as of the content of his proclamation and his teaching, and of the impression which he made on the adherents and opponents among his contemporaries. The sources do not permit us to say much regarding his inner life, since they were not interested in it. The question, however, is whether we may detect only characteristic individual features or whether it is possible to give a scientific description of the life of Jesus founded on objective arguments. That a biography of Jesus cannot be written is a truism today. We cannot even write the history of Jesus' develop-

[4] Käsemann, *Essays on N.T. Themes,* 1964, p. 37.
[5] Stauffer, "Der Stand der neutestamentlichen Forschung" in *Theologie und Liturgie,* 1952, p. 93.

ment within the period of his public ministry. The contrast between the Galilean spring and the subsequent period of defection and opposition is not sufficiently attested to in the sources, as Albert Schweitzer correctly emphasized. But Schweitzer's own theory, which did not proceed from the beginning but rather from the climax of Jesus' public life and which found the key for understanding the history of Jesus in the delay of the Parousia at the time the seventy were sent out (Matt. 10:23), rested on an entirely arbitrary combination of the sources.

The difficulty of the task does not mean, however, that it would be senseless to work at it scientifically. There is a point in the life of Jesus which is unconditionally established. That is his death. A historico-scientific description of the life of Jesus would only be possible in the form of a description of his death, its historical presuppositions, and the events preceding and following it. In other areas it has proved a fruitful method to begin with a very definite event in order from out of it to throw light on the preceding and following periods. In our case this could be the only practicable way. Such is due to the nature of the sources. Kähler's statement, "passion stories with a rather lengthy introduction," is important not only for the proper interpretation of the Gospels, but also for their use as historical sources on the life of Jesus. Historical considerations of a more general character point in the same direction. In the historical development which led to the rise of Christianity, the death of Jesus is the axis on which everything turns. "Without his death he would not have become historical at all," said Wellhausen.[6] Historical research must begin with the death of Jesus if it will inquire not only into the preaching but also into the life of Jesus.

Of course, a historical description of the death of Jesus is still a most difficult and complicated task. No doubt the Gospel reports at this point, but only at this point, are somewhat detailed and coherent and up to a certain degree are chronologically arranged. The interest of the evangelists, however, lies in describing Jesus' death as saving event and as the basis of the New Covenant, and not in presenting him as a world historical phenomenon with certain historical causes and effects. Before written Gospels existed, the oldest passion narratives which Christians read were such Old Testament texts as, e.g., Psalm 22, a practice which can often be traced in the Gospel accounts. One must be extremely cautious about employing them in the service of historical reconstruction.

[6] Wellhausen, *Einleitung in die drei ersten Evangelien,* 1905, p. 115.

In other respects, also, our historical knowledge is extremely limited. The debate over the Sanhedrin's authority to levy the death sentence, a debate which still has not been finally settled, provides one example. It is further questionable how much of rabbinic penal law can be traced back to the time of Jesus. Even where that is possible, the gain is dubious, for we must reckon altogether with the possibility that the trial of Jesus was conducted according to the rules of presumably Sadduccean legal practice—if, indeed, there was any intention of conducting before the Sanhedrin a trial against Jesus according to regular juridical forms, which is equally uncertain. The motives which induced the Jewish authorities and Pilate to proceed against Jesus are very difficult for us to detect. With all the existing difficulties, however, the attempt would have to be made once or even several times at beginning with the death of Jesus in order, with all the available means of historical science, to clarify the more proximate details, and from that point on, at attacking the remaining problems of Jesus' life. There will always be much that remains doubtful, but we may be confident that research which works energetically in this direction will attain to significantly surer results than the previous Life-of-Jesus literature.

In any case it is clear that what we know quite certainly of the life of Jesus is that it ended on the cross. That must also be kept in mind in the attempt to understand the preaching and teaching of Jesus. An obvious weakness of many descriptions of Jesus as a very pious and very humane, but somewhat harmless teacher lies in the fact that it is not understood why high priests and Romans had any kind of interest in the execution of this man. The end of Jesus' life helps to sharpen our view of the challenging claim to authority manifest in his appearance and which, e.g., is also evident in the Sermon on the Mount. We must observe the same in the exposition of the parables; in many instances the real meaning becomes clear only when we keep in mind how, in veiled form, they express the decisive meaning which Jesus attributed to his own mission. Accordingly, no one can maintain that historical research has access only to the preaching of Jesus and not to his life. Rather, we must state that an historical understanding of his preaching can be attained only when it is seen in connection with his life, namely with the life which ended on the cross.

CHAPTER 15

Basic Issues, A Survey of Recent Gospel Research

HARVEY K. McARTHUR

The portion of the article quoted here presents a simplified summary of criteria used by historical critics in evaluating the historicity of specific items in the Gospel tradition. It should be noted, however, that these criteria—while intelligible even to the uninitiated—require considerable experience for their optimum use. Even the experts, furthermore, do not agree on their application in specific instances.

A RE there criteria by which authentic material may be distinguished from inauthentic in the Synoptic Gospels?

Since historical research is an art and not a mathematical science, the criteria suggested here cannot be applied in mechanical fashion. They serve as general guides. When they are used in combination by experienced individuals, the results suggest that they provide a significant degree of objectivity. But these results are far from infallible: scholars of equal competence may disagree with one another in their application of the principles; and the work of one generation must be tested by that of another. There is some consensus, nevertheless, concerning the four criteria which are outlined below.

First, there is the criterion of *multiple attestation*. For centuries the church assumed that the four Gospels were independent witnesses to the ministry of Jesus and that multiple attestation occurred when two or more of these Gospels reported the same incident or motif. But the argument from this simple form of multiple attestation disappeared when the interrelatedness of the Synoptic Gospels

Reprinted by permission from *Interpretation;* Vol. XVIII; January, 1964; pp. 39–55.

was recognized. If Matthew and Luke used Mark as a source, then their accounts of events in Mark are clearly not independent witnesses to those events. However, the sources which stand behind Synoptics may be regarded as having a relative independence. (For the present purpose the Fourth Gospel is ignored.) Thus Mark, Q, M (special Matthean material), and L (special Lucan material) may be examined to determine which motifs in the ministry of Jesus have multiple attestation. Generally, the identical incident or saying was not repeated in more than one source, so this methodology is more useful for determining the historicity of particular motifs than for determining the authenticity of specific incidents or sayings. For example, the incident of Jesus' eating with tax collectors and sinners as reported in Mark 2:15-17 is not repeated, so far as we can determine, in Q, L, or M. But the general motif of his concern for the tax collectors and sinners is solidly documented in all strands of the tradition. On the other hand, the Passion predictions, while reappearing in Matthew and Luke, are generally borrowed from Mark. Luke may have had one or two traces of this motif from L, but even these sound like echoes of Mark. Consequently the historicity of the Passion predictions is far less certain than Jesus' concern for tax collectors and sinners.

Admittedly a motif might occur in all four strands of the Synoptic tradition without being authentic; that is, it might have emerged in the earliest Palestinian-Christian community and so have influenced all strands of the tradition, even though unhistorical. Some scholars would place certain types of "Son of man" sayings in this category. On the other hand, it is conceivable that a completely authentic motif might happen to be documented by only one strand of the tradition. But this is merely a way of saying that some material may be authentic even though, from a methodological standpoint, the extant evidence is inconclusive. This is a situation which continually confronts the historian.

It is worthy of note that the Bultmannians do not display any great interest in this multiple-attestation criterion, apparently preferring more esoteric guides. Having indicated some scepticism of British tendencies in Gospel research I should comment that, in my judgment, their regular and faithful use of this criterion is to be commended. While not infallible, it is the most objective of the proposed criteria and one which will undoubtedly have a permanent place in the task of Gospel research.

Second, there is the criterion, or principle, that *the tendencies of the developing tradition should be discounted.* A study of the Gospel tradition from Mark and Q through Matthew and Luke and on to John or the Apocryphal Gospels reveals certain "tendencies" which operate with a fair degree of consistency. Since one may assume that these same tendencies were operative during the earlier, hidden stages of the tradition, the researcher must make allowances for these tendencies when evaluating the earliest available form of the tradition. The tendencies identified here must be stated in highly oversimplified form. Only extended work with the details of the canonical *and* apocryphal Gospels can give any real awareness of the varying degrees to which the following statements are true.

1) Changes in place, time, and sequence of incidents were made without serious historical concern.
2) The beginnings and endings of narratives were subjected to the greatest change; or, conversely, the central section of an incident remained the most stable.
3) Sayings of Jesus changed less than narrative material.
4) Names tended to be added to narratives.
5) Aramaisms tended to disappear.

Perhaps it is necessary to warn the unwary that these tendencies are like actuarial statistics. They indicate what happens on the average; they cannot state categorically what must happen in a specific instance. For example, names may tend to become more numerous as the tradition develops; but this does not mean that every name in the tradition is secondary, or that there may not have been instances in which names were dropped from the tradition. Another necessary caveat is that the tendencies listed here have been identified from a study of the *written* tradition and its development. They may not have been applicable in precisely the same manner during the development of the oral tradition. Nevertheless, they were probably operative in a broad sense during the "tunnel period" of the tradition, and the historian who attempts to recover the earliest version of an incident will need to bear them in mind.

Third, there is the criterion of *attestation by multiple forms.* This criterion was utilized extensively by C. H. Dodd in his book *History and the Gospel,*[1] but it does not appear to have received extended

---

[1] Dodd (New York: Charles Scribner's Sons, 1938), pp. 91 ff.

subsequent discussion. Using the insight of form criticism that the Gospel materials fall into a number of literary forms, Dodd argues that if a motif is present in several different literary forms it is more apt to be authentic than if it appears in only one such form. Actually this criterion points toward a special type of multiple attestation, that is, an attestation not of multiple sources behind our Gospels but of multiple forms within those sources. By way of illustration, Dodd cites six motifs and lists a variety of passages to demonstrate that each of these motifs is attested by its appearance in multiple literary forms.

Many scholars would agree that the motifs he cites are authentic, but that this does not of itself validate his criterion since there is an ambiguity in his evidence. The ambiguity arises from the fact that motifs which he has identified appear not only in a variety of literary forms but also in a variety of sources. Would it be methodologically sound to argue that a motif is authentic if it appears in a variety of literary forms even though all appearances of this motif were confined to a single source? Is the motif of the Passion prediction, which (as has already been said) derives primarily from Mark, made appreciably more secure historically by the fact that it appears in a variety of literary forms in that Gospel? Perhaps a fair answer would be that while the variety of literary forms does not prove that the Passion predictions are authentic, it does prove that they were deeply embedded in the Markan tradition and not simply editorial additions of the final author or editor. Thus the criterion has some value in distinguishing comparatively early from comparatively late traditions, but it is not as decisive as that of multiple attestation by a number of sources.

Fourth, there is the criterion which suggests *the elimination of all material which may be derived either from Judaism or from primitive Christianity.*[2]

This is the most difficult of all the criteria to apply since it may easily be construed so as to leave no space between the Scylla of Judaism and the Charybdis of primitive Christianity. It is a radical

---

[2] See H. Conzelmann, "Jesus Christus," *Die Religion in Geschichte und Gegenwart*, 3rd edition (Tübingen: J. C. B. Mohr [Paul Siebeck], 1959), Vol. III, col. 623; also R. H. Fuller, *The New Testament in Current Study* (New York: Charles Scribner's Sons, 1962), p. 33; also H. Zahrnt, *The Historical Jesus* (New York: Harper & Row, Publishers, 1963), p. 107.

criterion since much of the teaching of Jesus must have been more or less standard Judaism, and the elimination of this from the portrait leaves only a fraction of his original teaching—though perhaps the most distinctive fraction. Finally, it is an ambiguous criterion since scholars differ as to whether a particular item is more "natural" against the background of primitive Christianity or against the background of the ministry of Jesus. Nevertheless, this criterion has received widespread support, and some of its applications are relatively clear-cut.

It is easy to see that the question of the payment of the Temple tax (Matthew 17:24-27) is more natural against the background of primitive Christianity than as an authentic incident during the ministry of Jesus. Of course Jesus and his disciples paid the Temple tax! But as the early Christians steadily differentiated themselves from the main Jewish community, the question may well have become critical. Similarly the saying about cross-bearing is difficult to understand before Good Friday and Easter, but its symbolism is entirely intelligible in the life of the developing church. Again, Mark 9:41 reports that Jesus referred to those who "bear the name of Christ." Even if Jesus was regarded as the Christ by some during his earthly ministry, this particular phraseology seems to suggest a later period when this terminology was in general use. To many scholars these illustrations will seem entirely clear, but there are innumerable passages where a decision would be more difficult to reach.

On the other hand, the idea of eliminating from the words attributed to Jesus those sayings which reflect regular Judaism poses problems of principle as well as of application. Is it too drastic a rule? Should the Markan saying "The sabbath was made for man, not man for the sabbath" (Mark 2:27) be denied to Jesus because similar sayings can be found in Jewish literature? Even if the principle is accepted the problem of application remains. Is Jesus' reply to the question about the Great Commandment (Mark 12:28-34) an expression of Judaism, or is it something distinctive?

Those who accept both halves of this criterion are aware that it is radical, particularly in its elimination of "Judaism" from the materials to be regarded as authentic. They concede that its application eliminates all except a minimal amount of material. However, they accept this limitation for methodological reasons; that is, they are anxious to establish as firm a base of certainty as is possible, even if only for a small amount of material. Some believe that once this minimum has been established with a high degree of probability, it may be possible that materials previously rejected can be reclaimed because of their congruity with elements in the established base.

PART II

The New Historiography

CHAPTER 16

View-Point and Method

RUDOLF BULTMANN

Professor Bultmann, formerly of Marburg University, the most famous and radical of the Form Critics, states in simple language his own attitude toward history and its proper understanding. The position here was developed further, e.g., "The Problem of Hermeneutics" published in *Essays, Philosophical and Theological,* 1955; also *The Presence of Eternity,* 1957.

IN strict accuracy, I should not write *"view-point";* for a fundamental presupposition of this book is that the essence of *history* cannot be grasped by "viewing" it, as we view our natural environment in order to orient ourselves in it. Our relationship to history is wholly different from our relationship to nature. Man, if he rightly understands himself, differentiates himself from nature. When he observes nature, he perceives there something objective which is not himself. When he turns his attention to history, however, he must admit himself to be a part of history; he is considering a living complex of events in which he is essentially involved. He cannot observe this complex objectively as he can observe natural phenomena; for in every word which he says about history he is saying at the same time something about himself. Hence there cannot be impersonal observation of history in the same sense that there can be impersonal observation of nature. Therefore, if this book is to be anything more than information on interesting occurrences in the past, more than a walk through a museum of antiquities, if it is really to lead to our seeing Jesus as a part of the history in which we have our being, or in which by critical conflict we achieve being, then this book must be in the nature of a continuous *dialogue with history*.

Further, it should be understood that the dialogue does not come as a conclusion, as a kind of evaluation of history after one has first learned the objective facts. On the contrary, the actual encounter with history takes place only in the dialogue. We do not stand outside historical forces as neutral observers; we are ourselves moved by them; and only when we are ready to listen to the *demand* which history makes on us do we understand at all what history is about. This dialogue is no clever exercise of subjectivity on the observer's part, but a real *interrogating* of history, in the course of which the historian puts this subjectivity of his in question, and is ready to listen to history as an authority. Further, such an interrogation of history does not end in complete relativism, as if history were a spectacle wholly dependent on the individual standpoint of the observer. Precisely the contrary is true: whatever is relative to the observer—namely all the presuppositions which he brings with him out of his own epoch and training and his individual position within them—must be given up, that history may actually speak. History, however, does not speak when a man stops his ears, that is, when he assumes neutrality, but speaks only when he comes seeking answers to the questions which agitate him. Only by this attitude can we discover whether an objective element is really present in history and whether history has something to say to us.

There is an approach to history which seeks by its *method* to achieve objectivity; that is, it sees history only in a perspective determined by the particular epoch or school to which the student belongs. It succeeds indeed, at its best, in escaping the subjectivity of the individual investigator, but still remains completely bound by the subjectivity of the method and is thus highly relative. Such an approach is extremely successful in dealing with that part of history which can be grasped by objective method, for example in determining the correct chronological sequence of events, and in so far forth is always indispensable. But an approach so limited misses the true significance of history. It must always question history solely on the basis of particular presuppositions, of its own method, and thus quantitatively it collects many new facts *out of* history, but learns nothing genuinely new *about* history and man. It sees in history only as little or as much of man and of humanity as it already explicitly or implicitly knows; the correctness or incorrectness of vision is always dependent on this previous knowledge.

An example may make this clear. A historian sets himself the aim of making a historical phenomenon or personality *"psychologically comprehensible."* Now this expression implies that such a writer has at his disposal complete knowledge of the psychological possibilities of life. He is therefore concerned with reducing every component of the event or of the personality to such possibilities. For that is what making anything "comprehensible" means: the reduction of it to what our previous knowledge includes. All individual facts are understood as specific cases of general laws, and these laws are assumed to be already known. On this assumption the criticism of the tradition is based, so that everything which cannot be understood on that basis is eliminated as unhistorical.

So far as purely psychological facts of the past are the objects of investigation, such a method is (for the psychological expert) quite correct. There remains, however, the question whether such a method reveals the essential of history, really brings us face to face with history. Whoever is of the belief that only through history can he find enlightenment on the contingencies of his own existence, will necessarily reject the psychological approach, however justified that method is in its own sphere. He must reject it if he is in earnest in his attempt to understand history. In such a belief this book is written. Hence no attempt is here made to render Jesus as a historical phenomenon psychologically explicable, and nothing really biographical, apart from a brief introductory section, is included.

Thus I would lead the reader not to any *"view"* of history, but to a highly personal *encounter* with history. But because the book cannot in itself be for the reader *his* encounter with history, but only information about *my* encounter with history, it does of course as a whole appear to him as a *view*, and I must define for him the point of observation. Whether he afterward remains a mere spectator is his affair.

If the following presentation cannot in the ordinary sense claim objectivity, in another sense it is all the more objective; for it refrains from *pronouncing value judgments*. The "objective" historians are often very lavish with such pronouncements, and they thus introduce a subjective element which seems to me unjustified. Purely formal evaluations of the meaning of an event or a person in the immediate historical sequence are of course necessary; but a *judgment of value* depends upon a point of view which the writer imports into the history and by which he measures the historical phenomena. Obviously the criticisms which many historians deliver, favorable or unfavorable, are given from a standpoint beyond history. As against this I have especially aimed to avoid everything beyond history and to find a position for myself *within* history. Therefore evaluations which depend on the distinction between the historical and the super-historical find no place here.

Indeed, if one understands by the historical process only phenomena and incidents determinable in time—"what happened"—then he has occasion to look for something beyond the historical fact which can motivate the interest in history. But then the suspicion becomes most insistent that the essential of history has been missed; for the essential of history is in reality nothing *super-historical*, but is event in time. Accordingly this book lacks all the phraseology which speaks of Jesus as great man, genius, or hero; he appears neither as inspired nor as inspiring,[1] his sayings are not called profound, nor his faith mighty, nor his nature child-like. There is also no consideration of the eternal values of his message, of his discovery of the infinite depths of the human soul, or the like. Attention is entirely limited to what he *purposed,* and hence to what in his purpose as a part of history makes a present demand on us.

For the same reason, *interest in the personality of Jesus* is excluded—and not merely because, in the absence of information, I am making a virtue of necessity. I do indeed think that we can now know almost nothing concerning the life and personality of Jesus, since the early Christian sources show no interest in either, are moreover fragmentary and often legendary; and other sources about Jesus do not exist. Except for the purely critical research, what has been written in the last hundred and fifty years on the life of Jesus, his personality and the development of his inner life, is fantastic and romantic. Whoever reads Albert Schweitzer's brilliantly written *Quest of the Historical Jesus*[2] must vividly realize this. The same impression is made by a survey of the differing contemporary judgments on the question of the Messianic consciousness of Jesus, the varying opinions as to whether Jesus believed himself to be the Messiah or not, and if so, in what sense, and at what point in his life. Considering that it was really no trifle to believe oneself Messiah, that, further, whoever so believed must have regulated his whole life in accordance with this belief, we must admit that if this point is obscure we can, strictly speaking, know nothing of the

[1] Literally, "neither as dæmonic nor as fascinating."
[2] Translated by W. Montgomery. London, 1910.

personality of Jesus. I am personally of the opinion that Jesus did not believe himself to be the Messiah, but I do not imagine that this opinion gives me a clearer picture of his personality. I have in this book not dealt with the question at all—not so much because nothing can be said about it with certainty as because I consider it of secondary importance.

However good the reasons for being interested in the personalities of significant historical figures, Plato or Jesus, Dante or Luther, Napoleon or Goethe, it still remains true that this interest does not touch that which such men had at heart; for *their* interest was not in their personality but in their *work*. And their work was to them not the expression of their personality, nor something through which their personality achieved its "form," but the cause to which they surrendered their lives. Moreover, their work does not mean the sum of the historical effects of their acts; for to this their view could not be directed. Rather, the "work" from *their* standpoint is the end they really sought, and it is in connection with their purpose that they are the proper objects of historical investigation. This is certainly true if the examination of history is no neutral orientation about objectively determined past events, but is motivated by the question how we ourselves, standing in the current of history, can succeed in comprehending our own existence, can gain clear insight into the contingencies and necessities of our own life purpose.

In the case of those who like Jesus have worked through the medium of *word,* what they purposed can be reproduced only as a group of sayings, of ideas—as *teaching*. Whoever tries, according to the modern fashion, to penetrate behind the teaching to the psychology or to the personality of Jesus, inevitably, for the reasons already given, misses what Jesus purposed. For his purpose can be comprehended only as teaching.

But in studying the teaching there is again danger of misunderstanding, of supposing such teaching to be a system of general truths, a system of propositions which have validity apart from the concrete life situation of the speaker. In that case it would follow that the truth of such statements would necessarily be measured by an ideal universal system of truths, of eternally valid propositions. In so far as the thought of Jesus agreed with this ideal system, one could speak of the super-historical element in his message. But here it would again become clear that one has missed the essential of history, has not met with anything really new in history. For this ideal system would not be learned from history, it implies rather a standard beyond history by which the particular historical phenomena are measured. The study of history would then at best consist in bringing this pre-existent ideal system to clearer recognition through the observation of concrete "cases." Historical research would be a work of "recollection" in the Platonic sense, a clarifying of knowledge which man already possesses. Such a view would be essentially rationalistic; history as event in time would be excluded.

Therefore, when I speak of the teaching or thought of Jesus, I base the discussion on no underlying conception of a universally valid system of thought which through this study can be made enlightening to all. Rather the ideas are understood in the light of the concrete situation of a man living in time; as his interpretation of his own existence in the midst of change, uncertainty, decision; as the expression of a possibility of comprehending this life; as the effort to gain clear insight into the contingencies and necessities of his own existence. When we encounter the words of Jesus in history, *we* do not judge *them* by a philosophical system with reference to their rational validity; *they* meet *us* with the question of how we are to interpret our own existence. That we be ourselves deeply disturbed by the problem of our own life is therefore the indispensable condition of our inquiry. Then the examination of history will lead not to the enrichment of timeless wisdom, but to an encounter with history which itself is an event in time. This is dialogue with history.

CHAPTER 17

A New Concept of History and the Self

JAMES M. ROBINSON

> Professor Robinson of Claremont develops his understand-
> ing of the new historiography and of the possibilities it offers
> for a true encounter with the historical Jesus. He is perhaps
> the most vigorous American exponent of the new quest of the
> historical Jesus.

IF the possibility of resuming the quest lies neither in the *kerygma*,
nor in new sources, nor in a new view of the Gospels, such a
possibility *has* been latent in the radically different understanding
of history and of human existence which distinguishes the present
from the quest which ended in failure. 'Historicism' is gone as the
ideological core of historiography, and with it is gone the centrality
of the chronicle. 'Psychologism' is gone as the ideological core of
biography, and with it is gone the centrality of the *curriculum vitae.*
Consequently the kind of history and biography attempted unsuc-
cessfully for Jesus by the nineteenth century is now seen to be based
upon a false understanding of the nature of history and the self. As
a result it has become *a completely open question,* as to whether a
kind of history or biography of Jesus, consistent with the contemporary view of history and human existence, is possible.

This open question has been obscured during the past generation
by the necessary polemics against the impossible and misguided
kind of quest. But these polemics have been successful enough for
the urgent task of our day no longer to be their mechanical perpetuation, but rather the investigation of the possibility of writing
the kind of history or biography of Jesus consistent with our modern
understanding of history and human existence.

Nineteenth-century historiography and biography were modelled

James M. Robinson, A New Quest of the Historical Jesus, SCM Press, London, 1959,
pp. 66–72. Distributed in the U.S.A. by Alec R. Allenson. Reprinted by permission.

153

after the natural sciences, e.g., in their effort to establish causal relationships and to classify the particular in terms of the general. Today it is widely recognized that this method placed a premium upon the admixture of nature in history and man, while largely bypassing the distinctively historical and human, where transcendence, if at all, is to be found. It was primarily Wilhelm Dilthey who introduced the modern period by posing for historiography the 'question about the scientific knowledge of individual persons, the great forms of singular human existence.'[1] Today history is increasingly understood as essentially the unique and creative, whose reality would not *be* apart from the event in which it becomes, and whose truth could not be *known* by Platonic recollection or inference from a rational principle, but only through historical encounter. History is the act of intention, the commitment, the meaning for the participants, behind the external occurrence. In such intention and commitment the self of the participant actualizes itself, and in this act of self-actualization the self is revealed. Hence it is the task of modern historiography to grasp such acts of intention, such commitments, such meaning, such self-actualization; and it is the task of modern biography to lay hold of the selfhood which is therein revealed.

This implication of the modern view of history for biography is only strengthened when one turns to the modern concept of selfhood, and its more direct implications for biography. The self is not simply one's personality, resultant upon (and to be explained by) the various influences and ingredients present in one's heritage and development. Rather selfhood is constituted by commitment to a context, from which commitment one's existence arises. One's empirical *habitus* is the inescapable medium through which the self expresses itself, but is not identical with the self, even when one seems to make it so. For even if one avoids commitment and merely drifts with life's tide, or even if the commitment is merely to hold to one's own past or absolutize one's personality, the resultant selfhood is decisively qualified by the mood of inauthenticity in the one case, or by one or the other form of doctrinaire self-assertion in the other.

[1] 'Die Entstehung der Hermeneutik' (1900), *Ges. Schr.* V, 317 Dilthey is becoming increasingly known in the English-speaking world through such works as H. A. Hodges, *Wilhelm Dilthey; An Introduction,* 1944; R. G. Collingwood, *The Idea of History,* 1946, 171–6; Rudolf Bultmann, *History and Eschatology* (Gifford Lectures, 1957), 123 ff.

Consequently it would be a basic misunderstanding of selfhood, to describe the causal relationships and cultural ingredients composing the personality, and assume one had understood the self. Selfhood results from implicit or explicit commitment to a kind of existence, and is to be understood only in terms of that commitment, i.e., by laying hold of the understanding of existence in terms of which the self is constituted.

To be sure, neither the modern view of history nor the modern view of existence involves necessarily a dimension of transcendence. To this extent the classical philologian Ernest Heitsch[2] is correct in sensing that the historian's awareness *'tua res agitur'* is 'nuanced in a particular way' by the New Testament scholar: 'It is a matter of *thy blessedness,* however one may understand this.' The secular historian does not have this particular and narrow concentration of interest, but thinks *'tua res agitur'* in the comprehensive sense that 'nothing human is foreign to thee.' Yet it is precisely because of this complete openness to all that is human, that the historian must open himself to encounter with humans who understand their existence as lived out of transcendence.

The first effect of the modern view of history and human existence upon New Testament study was, as we have seen, to focus attention upon the *kerygma* as the New Testament statement of Jesus' history and selfhood. This involved also a positive appraisal of the kerygmatic nature of the Gospels, so that one came to recognize the legitimacy in their procedure of transforming the *ipissima verba* and brute facts into kerygmatic meaning. Thus the modern approach to history and the self made it easy to emphasize the rarity of unaltered sayings and scenes.

There is however another aspect which is equally true, and yet has not been equally emphasized. If the Church's *kerygma* reduced the quantity of unaltered material, it deserves credit for the quality of the unaltered material. The kind of material which the 'kerygmatizing' process would leave *unaltered* is the kind of material which fits best the needs of research based upon the modern view of history and the self. For the kerygmatic interest of the primitive Church would leave unaltered precisely those sayings and scenes in which Jesus made his intention and understanding of existence most apparent to them. Of course the very fact that the earliest Church could on occasion go on saying it in Jesus' way makes it

[2] *ZTK* LIII, 1956, 193.

difficult to be certain that any given saying originated with Jesus rather than in this earliest phase of the Church. And areas where Jesus differed from his first disciples would tend to have disappeared from the tradition. Yet in spite of such difficulties, the 'kerygmatic' quality of the material the primitive Church preserved unaltered means that this material is especially suitable for modern research concerned with encountering the meaning of history and the existential selfhood of persons.

Now that the modern view of history and the self has become formally more analogous to the approach of the *kerygma*, we need no longer consider it disastrous that the chronology and causalities of the public ministry are gone. For we have, for example, in the parables, in the beatitudes and woes, and in the sayings on the kingdom, exorcism, John the Baptist and the law, sufficient insight into Jesus' intention to encounter his historical action, and enough insight into the understanding of existence presupposed in his intention to encounter his selfhood. 'If it is by the finger of God that I cast out demons, then the kingdom of God has come upon you' (Luke 11.20). 'From the days of John the Baptist until now the kingdom of heaven has suffered violence, and men of violence take it by force' (Matt. 11.12). Such authentic sayings, whose exact wording cannot well be reconstructed, whose translation is uncertain, whose out-of-date thought patterns are obvious, are none the less more important historical sources for encountering Jesus' history and person than would be the chronological and psychological material the original quest sought in vain. Consequently Jesus' history and selfhood *are* accessible to modern historiography and biography. And *that* is the crucial significance of Käsemann's remark: 'There are after all pieces in the synoptic tradition which the historian must simply acknowledge as authentic, if he wishes to remain a historian.' *This* kind of quest of the historical Jesus *is* possible.

The positive relevance of the modern view of history and the self to the problem of Jesus has not gone completely undetected. As a matter of fact, Bultmann's *Jesus and the Word* of 1926 was prefaced with a classic statement of the modern view of history, and on this basis he states that his book reflects his own encounter with the historical Jesus, and may mediate an encounter with the historical Jesus on the part of the reader. And Käsemann's brief analysis of the authentic sayings of Jesus [3] concludes that, in spite

[3] *ZTK LI*, 1954, 144–51.

of the absence of messianic titles, Jesus' understanding of his existence can be deduced from his intentions revealed in his sayings.
We have already noted how Fuchs derives his understanding of
Jesus' work and person from his conduct and its interpretation in
the parables.[4] Similarly Bornkamm [5] recognizes that the possibility
of his *Jesus von Nazareth* resides in a new view of history. 'If the
Gospels do not speak of the history of Jesus in the sense of a repro-
ducible *curriculum vitae* with its experiences and stages, its outward and inward development, yet they none the less speak of
history as occurrence and event. Of such history the Gospels provide information which is more than abundant.' And his presentation of 'The messianic question'[6] is permeated by the new view
of existence, when he explains that Jesus presented no independent
doctrine of his person precisely because 'the "messianic" aspect of
his being is enclosed *in* his word and act, and in the immediateness
of his historical appearance.' It is consequently not surprising that
Peter Biehl [7] has introduced into the discussion of a new quest a
thematic discussion of the interpretation of history in terms of the
historicity of the self, as found in Martin Heidegger and R. G.
Collingwood.

It is apparent that a new quest of the historical Jesus cannot
be built upon the effort to deny the impossibilities inherent in the
original quest; rather a new quest must be built upon the fact that
the sources *do* make possible a new kind of quest working in terms
of the modern view of history and the self. Whether one wishes to
designate this possible task of historical research a history or life
of Jesus, or whether one prefers to reserve these terms for the kind
of history or life envisaged by the nineteenth century, is not of
crucial importance. The German ability to distinguish between
Historie and *Geschichte* has made it possible, from Bultmann's *Jesus*

[4] He also derives Jesus' selfhood from his call for decision (ZKT LIII, 1956,
221 f., 227): 'This requirement is simply the echo of that decision which Jesus
himself had made. We must understand Jesus' conduct as equally determined
by a decision, and consequently we can infer from what he required what he
himself did.' 'Believing on Jesus means now in content repeating Jesus' decision . . . Jesus' person now became the content of faith,' Cf. also his essay
'Jesus Christus in Person. Zum Problem der Geschichtlichkeit der Offenbarung,'
Festschrift Rudolf Bultmann, 1949, 48–73.
[5] *Jesus von Nazareth*, 21–23, esp. 22.
[6] *Ibid.*, Ch. VIII, esp. 163.
[7] *TR*, n.F. XXIV, 1956–7, 69 ff.

and the Word on, to look upon oneself as presenting the history (*Geschichte*) of Jesus. Such has not been the case with the terms 'life,' 'biography,' and '*bios*,' which continue to be avoided,[8] for the reason Käsemann gives:[9] 'In a life of Jesus one simply cannot give up outer and inner development.' Since usage determines meaning, it may be that such a nineteenth-century definition of biography is still accurate.[10] But this should not obscure the crucial fact that Jesus' understanding of his existence, his selfhood, and thus in the higher sense his life, is a possible subject of historical research.

[8] Cf. Käsemann, ZTK LI, 1954, 132; Bornkamm, *Jesus von Nazareth*, 11; and even Stauffer, *Jesus: Gestalt und Geschichte*, 12. It is interesting that Maurice Goguel entitled the second edition of his *Life of Jesus* merely *Jésus* (1950).

[9] *ZTK* LI, 1954, 151.

[10] Cf. Martin Kähler's definition (*Der sogenannte historische Jesus und der geschichtliche, biblische Christus* (1892, reprinted 1953), 23: 'More recent biography seeks its strength in psychological analysis, in demonstrating the quantity of causes and the causal chain out of which the appearance and performance of the person being portrayed has arisen.' The continuation of this definition in the modern period is evident, e.g. in the statement of D. W. Riddle ('Jesus in Modern Research,' *The Journal of Religion* XVII, 1937, 177) that we know 'general features' of Jesus, but not such as to write a 'biography,' or in the ambiguous statement of C. J. Cadoux ('Is it Possible to Write a Life of Christ?,' *ExpT* LIII, 1941–2, 177): 'We do not possess for the life of Jesus anything approaching that knowledge of chronology which is usually deemed necessary for a "biography." . . . I do not concur in the modern view that it is impossible to write a life of Christ.'

PART III

The Results of Research, "Lives" of Jesus

CHAPTER 18

The Primitive Christian Kerygma and the Historical Jesus

RUDOLF BULTMANN

In this article which was given first as a lecture in Heidelberg in 1959, Bultmann pays his respects to those of his students who have been agitating for a "New Quest." He remains skeptical. In this connection he summarizes what he believes may be affirmed with reasonable certainty about the historical Jesus. Actually this summary relates to the events of the ministry. For the teaching of Jesus, Bultmann's basic statement is still *Jesus and the Word*, 1934.

HENCE, with a bit of caution we can say the following concerning Jesus' activity: Characteristic for him are exorcisms, the breach of the Sabbath commandment, the abandonment of ritual purifications, polemic against Jewish legalism, fellowship with outcasts such as publicans and harlots, sympathy for women and children; it can also be seen that Jesus was not an ascetic like John the Baptist, but gladly ate and drank a glass of wine. Perhaps we may add that he called disciples and assembled about himself a small company of followers—men and women.[1]

In this connection, where we are dealing with the life and portrait of Jesus, we can only say of his preaching that he doubtless appeared in the consciousness of being commissioned by God to preach the eschatological message of the breaking-in of the king-

[1] Cf. Hans Conzelmann, "Jesus Christus" in *Religion in Geschichte und Gegenwart*, 1959.

From *The Historical Jesus and the Kerygmatic Christ*, selected, translated and edited by Carl E. Braaten and Roy A. Harrisville (Heidelberg: Carl Winter Universitatsverlag, 1960), pp. 22–24. Copyright © 1964 by Abingdon Press, New York. Reprinted by permission.

dom of God and the demanding but also inviting will of God. We may thus ascribe to him a prophetic consciousness, indeed, a "consciousness of authority." We will speak of this in another connection; that is, with regard to the second attempt to assimilate the activity of Jesus to the kerygma.

One more thing must be said here. The greatest embarrassment to the attempt to reconstruct a portrait of Jesus is the fact that we cannot know how Jesus understood his end, his death.[2] It is symptomatic that it is practically universally assumed that Jesus went consciously to his suffering and death and that he understood this as the organic or necessary conclusion to his activity.[3] But how do we know this, when prophecies of the passion must be understood by critical research as *vaticinia ex eventu*?[4] That Jesus, after learning of the Baptist's death, had to reckon with his own equally violent death[5] is an improbable psychological construction, because Jesus clearly conceived his life in an entirely different fashion than did the Baptist from whom he distinguished himself (Matt. 11:16-19).

Why was Jesus drawn to Jerusalem at the end of his career? If the assumption is correct that "first and foremost his journey to Jerusalem was undertaken in order to confront the people there, in the holy city, with the message of the kingdom of God, and to summon them at the eleventh hour to make their decision;" if it is correct that "only on the journey with his followers to Jerusalem

[2] *Ibid.*, p. 646: The passion narrative "takes its shape entirely from the perspective of the Easter faith. It is this faith which provides the key to the interpretation of Jesus' death." Robinson wants to avoid the problem by speaking of "Jesus' death as his own existential act of accepting his death." Cf. Robinson, *A New Quest of the Historical Jesus*, 1959, p. 89.

[3] This is Robinson's point of view. He states that "only Jesus' death as his own existential act of accepting his death and living out of transcendence is really a historical event in distinction from a natural occurrence." Cf. Robinson, *loc. cit.*

[4] Cf. Conzelmann, *op. cit.*, p. 630: "Their [sc. the prophecies of the passion] genuineness cannot be defended by stating that Jesus had to reckon on a future encounter with death and life. These prophecies do not offer a keen analysis of the situation, but rather express a divine necessity for suffering. That is, they already contain an interpretation of the passion from the Easter point of view."

[5] Thus Ernst Fuchs, "Die Frage nach dem historischen Jesus," *Zeitschrift für Theologie und Kirche*, 53. Jahrgang (1956), p. 222.

and the temple did Jesus seek the final decision," [6] then he scarcely reckoned on execution at the hands of the Romans, but only on the imminent appearing of the kingdom of God. But these are only assumptions. What is certain is merely that he was crucified by the Romans, and thus suffered the death of a political criminal. This death can scarcely be understood as an inherent and necessary consequence of his activity; rather it took place because his activity was misconstrued as a political activity. In that case it would have been—historically speaking—a meaningless fate. We cannot tell whether or how Jesus found meaning in it. We may not veil from ourselves the possibility that he suffered a collapse.

[6] Bornkamm, *Jesus of Nazareth*, 1960, p. 155. For Bornkamm, of course, this is not a conjecture but a certainty. Conzelmann also states: "In any event it is certain that Jesus journeyed to Jerusalem . . . in order to confront his people at the center, at the site of the temple and the highest authorities, with the final decision." *Op. cit.*, p. 647.

CHAPTER 19

Jesus of Nazareth

GUENTHER BORNKAMM

One of the leaders in the "New Quest," Professor Bornkamm of Heidelberg University was the first of the group to
present a full scale study of the historical Jesus. The chapter
quoted is his summary of Jesus' career. Additional details
are affirmed as historical in Chapter VI "Discipleship," and
Chapter VII "Jesus' Journey to Jerusalem." Still other chapters deal with the teaching of Jesus. See also chapter 3.

THE nature of the sources does not permit us to paint a biographical picture of the life of Jesus against the background
of the history of his people and his age. Nevertheless, what these
sources do yield as regards the historical facts concerning the personality and career of Jesus is not negligible, and demands careful
attention. We shall, therefore, try first of all to compile the main
historically indisputable traits, and to present the rough outline of
Jesus' person and history. In doing this, we must, of course, desist
from rash combinations of the biographical data and must use the
greatest critical caution in order to be able really to focus those
facts which are prior to any pious interpretation and which manifest
themselves as undistorted and primary.

The childhood and adolescence of Jesus are obscure for us from
the historical point of view. The birth narratives in Matthew and
Luke, which differ from one another not inconsiderably, are too
much overgrown by legends and by Jewish as well as Christian
messianic conceptions to be used for historical assertions. The importance and meaning of these texts lie in a different area. The

home of Jesus is the semi-pagan, despised Galilee. His native town is Nazareth. His family certainly belonged to the Jewish part of the population which, since the times of the Maccabees, had reattached themselves to the temple cult in Jerusalem and the legal practices of Judaism. Only a criticism blinded by racial ideologies could deny the Jewish origin of Jesus. Jesus' father was a carpenter, and possibly he himself was too. We know the names of his parents, Joseph and Mary, and those of his brothers, James, Joses, Judas and Simon (Mk. vi. 3). His brothers—as well as his mother—were originally unbelievers (Mk. iii. 21, 31; Jn. vii. 5), but later belonged to the Church and to its missionaries (Acts i. 14; I Cor. ix. 5). The tradition occasionally also mentions Jesus' sisters (Mk. vi. 3; Mt. xiii. 56). Jesus' mother tongue is the Aramaic of Galilee, the same dialect by which the servants of the high priest recognise Peter when he denies his Master in Jerusalem (Mt. xxvi. 73). Hebrew was at that time no longer a spoken language, but rather only the language of religion and of scholars (somewhat comparable to the ecclesiastical Slavonic of the Orthodox Church). As a Jewish rabbi he must have been able to understand the ancient language of the Bible. On the other hand, we do not know to what extent he and his disciples knew Greek, widely used in administration and commerce. At any rate we find in Jesus no trace of the influence of Greek philosophy or of the Greek manner of living, just as nothing is known of activity on his part in the Hellenistic towns of the country. Rather we hear of his activity in the smaller hamlets and villages—Bethsaida, Chorazin, Capernaum—in the hill country and round the Sea of Galilee.

According to an isolated note in Luke, Jesus' public ministry begins, following the work of John the Baptist, at about his thirtieth year (Lk. iii. 23). His own baptism by John is one of the most certainly verified occurrences of his life. Tradition, however, has altogether transformed the story into a testimony to the Christ, so that we cannot gather from it what baptism meant for Jesus himself, for his decisions and for his inner development. But that this event was of far-reaching importance nobody will deny. It is all the more important that Jesus, without ever questioning the mission and the authority of the Baptist, nevertheless does not continue the work of the Baptist and his followers in the Jordan valley, but starts his own work in Galilee—like John, as a prophet of the coming kingdom of God. The instrument of his activity, however, is no longer baptism, but his spoken word and helping hand. We can no longer say with certainty how long Jesus' activity lasted. The first three Gospels create the impression that it lasted but a year. But they do not give a reliable chronology. We learn a great deal about his preaching, the conflict with his opponents, his healing and the additional help he granted the suffering, and the powerful influence which went forth from him. The people flock to him. Disciples follow him, but his enemies also arise and increase. All this will have to occupy us later. Here we are only concerned with the rough outlines of his life and his work. The last decisive turning point in his life is the resolution to go to Jerusalem with his disciples in order to confront the people there with his message in face of the coming kingdom of God. At the end of this road is his death on the cross. These meagre, indisputable facts comprise a very great deal. There is little enough in this enumeration, and yet it contains most important information about the life story of Jesus and its stages.

Much remains hidden in the obscurity of history. Tradition does not yield a logical and detailed account of the course of Jesus' life. Nevertheless, the Gospels furnish much more material as regards the outlines of his historical person seen in the setting of his own world. We shall, therefore, recall the picture of that world in which he appeared.

As we saw, time and history, the past and the future, determine in a unique way the thought, experience and hopes of the Jewish people. This people finds its God and itself in the past, in which its life and character were given to it; and in the future, in which its life and its character are to be restored to it. It knows no other security, even in a present which reveals nothing of this certainty and seems to mock this people's claim. It knows its sole task as that of guarding faithfully this past and this future. Thus the world in which Jesus appears is a world between past and future; it is so strongly identified with the one and with the other that, according to the Jewish faith, the immediate present is practically nonexistent. The whole of life is caught in a network of sacred traditions. Everyone has his place within a structure determined and ordered by the law and promise of God. Whoever lives up to this divine system can claim eternal salvation; whoever does not is rejected. All time is time between, and as such it is a time of stewardship, founded in God's decisions of the past and looking forward to God's decisions in the future, which mean salvation or destruction for each one. We can now understand the strange picture presented by the historical milieu in which Jesus lived. It is comparable to a soil hardened and barren through its age-long history and tradition, yet a volcanic, eruptive ground, out of whose cracks and crevices breaks forth again and again the fire of a burning expectation. However, both, torpidity and convulsion, petrifaction and blazing eruption have, at bottom, the same origin: they are the outcome and expression of a faith in a God who is beyond the world and history.

This world comes alive and is immediately present in the story of Jesus, as told by the writers of the Gospels. All the characters who encounter Jesus bear the stamp of this world: the priest and the scribe, the Pharisee and the publican, the rich and the poor, the healthy and the sick, the righteous and the sinner. They appear in the story in a matter-of-fact and simple fashion, chosen at random and of great variety, and appearing in no particular order. Yet all the characters, however great their diversity, present a very human appearance. In their encounter with Jesus—whatever they experience in this encounter and whatever their attitude towards it—they come to this amazing event, their meeting with Jesus, as fully real people.

Jesus belongs to this world. Yet in the midst of it he is of unmistakable otherness. This is the secret of his influence and his rejection. Faith has given manifold expression to this secret. But even he who, prior to any interpretation, keeps his eyes fixed upon the historical appearance of Jesus, upon the manner of his words and works, even he meets with this his insoluble mystery. We become aware of the fact when we try to fit this figure into any of the descriptions and categories then prevalent in Judaism. He is a prophet of the coming kingdom of God. Indeed the title of prophet is occasionally used by the tradition (Mk. viii. 28; Mt. xxi. 11, 46, etc.). Yet he is in no way completely contained in this category, and differs from the customary ways of a prophet. A prophet has to produce his credentials, somewhat as did the prophets of the old covenant in telling the story of their calling and in accompanying their message with the sacred prophetic saying: " . . . says the Lord . . . " (Amos vi. 8, 14; Hos. ii. 16; xi. 11; Is. i. 24; and elsewhere). Jesus, on the other hand, never speaks of his calling, and nowhere does he use the ancient, prophetic formula. Even less do we find any trace of that self-justification typical of the apocalyptic visionaries of later Judaism, who claim the authority of ecstatic states of mind and visions, secret revelations of the next world, and miraculous insight into God's degrees. Jesus refuses to justify himself and his message in this way. But those who listen to him have to accept the saying: "And blessed is he who takes no offence at me" (Mt. xi. 6).

The prophet of the coming kingdom of God is at the same time a rabbi who proclaims the divine law, who teaches in synagogues, who gathers disciples, and who debates with other scribes in the manner of their profession and under the same authority of scripture. The forms and laws of scribal tradition are to be found abundantly in his sayings. Prophet and rabbi—how does this go together? How does the message of the kingdom of God agree with the proclamation of the divine will? And what is the meaning of becoming a follower, and of the discipleship for which he calls, in view of this unity of prophet and rabbi? All these questions will concern us later.

This rabbi differs considerably from the other members of his class. Even external facts reveal this difference. Jesus does not only teach in the synagogues, but also in the open field, on the shores of the lake, during his wanderings. And his followers are a strange crowd. Even those people are amongst them whom an official rabbi would do his best to avoid: women and children, tax collectors and sinners. Above all, his manner of teaching differs profoundly from that of the other rabbis. A rabbi is an interpreter of Scripture. This lends authority to his office, an authority which has to prove itself from the given letter of Scripture and the not less authoritative exegesis of the "Fathers." Their authority is thus always a derived authority. Jesus' teaching, on the other hand, never consists merely in the interpretation of an authoritatively given sacred text, not even when words from Scripture are quoted. The reality of God and the authority of his will are always directly present, and are fulfilled in him. There is nothing in contemporary Judaism which corresponds to the immediacy with which he teaches. This is true to such a degree that he even dares to confront the literal text of the law with the immediately present will of God. (See Ch. V, 1.)

We shall meet this feature again in his similes and parables, no less than in the words of wisdom which speak with manifest relevance and utmost simplicity: for example, that "a city set on an hill cannot be hid" (Mt. v. 14); that "men do not light a lamp and put it under a bushel" (Mt. v. 15); that "no one can add one cubit to his span of life" (Mt. vi. 27); that one should "let the day's own trouble be sufficient for the day" (Mt. vi. 34); etc. In all these utterances Jesus draws into the service of his message the world of nature and the life of man, and those everyday experiences which everyone knows and shares, without using the established structure of sacred traditions and texts. The listener is never obliged to look for premises which would give meaning to Jesus' teaching, or to recall the theory about doctrines and traditions which he would be supposed to know beforehand. For Jesus never talks 'over' God, the world and man, the past and the future, from any particular "point of view."

This directness, if anything, is part of the picture of the historical Jesus. He bears the stamp of this directness right from the very beginning. The immediate present is the hallmark of all the words of Jesus, of his appearance and his actions, in a world which, as we said, had lost the present, because it lived between the past and the future, between traditions and promises or threats, in security or anxiety, conscious of its own rights or under sentence for its own lawlessness.

What the Gospels report on numerous individual occasions about Jesus' attitude to and influence on the different people he encounters is important in this context. We are not concerned here with the question whether all these scenes can claim historical reliability, how far we have to consider in them the influence of legends, and to what extent typical stylistic devices are used which are to be found elsewhere in the presentation of teaching and disputes, of healings and the performance of various miracles. We have left no doubt that these factors do play a considerable part. Nevertheless, tradition has caught an essential feature of the historical Jesus, a feature which accords exactly with what we have said about his way of teaching.

Every one of the scenes described in the Gospels reveals Jesus' astounding sovereignty in dealing with situations according to the kind of people he encounters. This is apparent in the numerous teaching and conflict passages, in which he sees through his opponents, disarms their objections, answers their questions, or forces them to answer them for themselves. He can make his opponent open his mouth or he can put him to silence (Mt. xxii. 34). The same can be seen when he encounters those who seek help: miraculous powers proceed from him, the sick flock around him, their relatives and friends seek his help. Often he fulfils their request, but he can also refuse, or keep the petitioners waiting and put them to the test. Not infrequently he withdraws himself (Mk. i. 35 ff.), but, on the other hand, he is often ready and on the spot sooner than the sufferers dare hope (Mt. viii. 5 ff.; Lk. xix. 1 ff.), and he freely breaks through the strict boundaries which traditions and prejudices had set up. Similar characteristics can be seen in his dealings with his disciples. He calls them with the command of the master (Mk. i. 16 ff.), but he also warns and discourages them from their discipleship (Lk. ix. 57 ff.; xiv. 28 ff.). Again and again his behaviour and method are in sharp contrast to what people expect of him and what, from their own point of view, they hope for. He withdraws from the people, as John reports, when he is to be made king (Jn. vi. 15). In his encounters with others we see time and again that he knows men and uncovers their thoughts, a feature which the Gospels have frequently elaborated to the point of the miraculous.[1] The two sons of Zebedee meet with this quality when Jesus turns down their ambitious desires (Mk. x. 35 ff.). Peter experiences it when, in answer to his confession of the Messiah, he is given Jesus' words about the suffering of the Son of man, and when, wanting to make Jesus forsake his path, he receives the sharp retort: "Get behind me, Satan! For you are not on the side of God, but of men" (Mk. viii. 27-33). The same is expressed by the scenes which describe Peter's denial (Mk. xiv. 29 ff.), and the betrayal of Judas (Mk. xiv. 17 ff.). It would be possible to go on quoting other tales at random, even if they belong to the traditional store of legends. The important point is that in all of them the same feature recurs, by which the historical Jesus can be recognised. We need recall only two more stories from the synoptic Gospels. The first is the scene where Jesus in the guest of Simon the Pharisee, and a woman, known throughout the town as a sinner, enters, wets Jesus' feet with her tears, dries them with her hair and anoints them with ointment. When the Pharisee is secretly indignant at the awkward scene, he said to himself: "If this man were a prophet, he would have known who and what sort of woman this is who is touching him." Jesus gives him this answer: "Simon, I have something to say to you," and tells him the parable of the unequal debtors, to one of whom the creditor forgave a large sum and to the other a small one. "Which of them will love him more?" (Lk. vii. 36-50). A most il-

---

[1] Especially in Jn., cf. 1:40 ff., 47 f.; 2:24 f.; 4:17 ff.

luminating illustration of Jesus' insight into the character of his interlocutors is the story of the rich man who asks him about eternal life. Jesus points him to the ten commandments (which shows that the right way has long since been made evident and does not need any specific new revelation), and the rich man professes that he has kept them all since his youth. The story ends, "And Jesus, looking upon him, loved him, and said to him: You lack one thing. Go sell what you have and give to the poor, and you will have treasure in heaven; and come, follow me." This is a demand on which the rich man founders (Mk. x. 17-22). The passages in the Gospels which deal with Jesus' perception and penetrating insight ought to be assembled without fear that this would be a merely sentimental undertaking. In reality we are here concerned with a most characteristic trait in the historical Jesus, one which quite accurately is confirmed by the nature of his preaching.

The Gospels call this patent immediacy of Jesus' sovereign power his "authority." They apply this word to his teaching: "They were astonished at his teaching, for he taught them as one who had authority, and not as the scribes" (Mk. i. 22; Mk. vii. 29). They also use it for the power of his healing word (Mt. viii. 5 ff.). The word "authority" certainly contains already the mystery of Jesus' personality and influence, as understood by faith. It therefore transcends the merely "historical" sphere. Yet it denotes a reality which appertains to the historical Jesus and is prior to any interpretation. In his encounters with the most different people, Jesus' "authority" is always immediately and authentically present. But the people to whom he talks and with whom he deals are also there, undisguised and real. They all contribute something towards the encounter with him. The righteous contribute their righteousness, the scribes the weight of their doctrine and arguments, the tax collectors and sinners their guilt, the needy their sickness, the demoniacs the fetters of their obsession and the poor the burden of their poverty. All this is not eradicated or irrelevant, but it does not count in this encounter. This encounter compels everyone to step out of his customary background. This bringing to light of men as they really are takes place in all stories about Jesus. It happens each time, however, simply and as a matter of course, without in any way being forced, without that awkward compulsion toward self-disclosure which is well known from a certain type of later Christian sermon.

Jesus' aid bears, therefore, the stamp of a genuine involvement and a passionate tackling of the situation, when he is wrathful over the power of disease (Mk. i. 41) and commands the demons (Mk. i. 25); but also in the blessing when he calls the children to himself and lays his hands upon them or upon the sick (Mk. x. 13 ff.; vii. 31 ff., etc.).

Many of the texts mentioned will concern us later. We are here only concerned with that prevailing feature of Jesus' authority, equally recognisable in his words and in his deeds. It also character- ises Jesus' way, the consistency with which he sticks at it and keeps on it to the very end; both when he takes up a certain position, contends and helps, and when he withdraws and withholds him- self, not only from his opponents, but also from his followers.

The Gospels give us the right to discuss all this in a very human manner, without immediately using interpretations with which faith has invested the mystery of his person as far back as the early Christian tradition. We have, therefore, not begun straight away with the question of Jesus' "messianic consciousness," and we will not enter upon it until the end of the book (cf. Ch. VIII). For, how- ever it may be answered, so much is certain: it is not a separate or prevailing theme in his preaching to which everything else is sub- ordinated. He certainly does not make it the condition for the un- derstanding of his message and actions. The very nature of his teaching and his actions, so vulnerable, so open to controversy and yet so direct and matter of fact, doom to failure any attempt to raise his Messiahship into a system of dogma through which his preach- ing, his actions and his history would receive their meaning.

We shall have to guard against any rash attempt to fit these features which we have tried to describe in rough and most incom- plete outline into the usual categories of the religious genius, the person of great originality, and particularly into the picture of the pastor *par excellence*. What is essential is the indissoluble connec- tion between what has been said here and Jesus' message about the reality of God, his kingdom and his will. This alone lends to Jesus' history and person the character of unmediated presence, gives the force of an actual event to his preaching, and makes his words and deeds so incomparably compelling. To make the reality of God present: this is the essential mystery of Jesus. This making-present of the reality of God signifies the end of the world in which it takes place. This is why the scribes and Pharisees rebel, because they see Jesus' teaching as a revolutionary attack upon law and tradition. This is why the demons cry out, because they sense an inroad upon their sphere of power "before the time" (Mt. viii. 29). This is why his own people think him mad (Mk. iii. 21). But this is also why the people marvel and the saved praise God.

The story told by the Gospels signifies the end of the world, although not, it is true, in the sense of an obvious drama and a visible catastrophe. On the contrary, it is not the world which ends here obviously and visibly; rather it is Jesus of Nazareth on the cross. And yet, in this story, the world reaches its end. The story breaks off, and the people who belong to it have to bear witness to what has happened, everyone in his own way. Pharisees, scribes and priests, as the guardians of law and tradition. The rejected, who, according to the prevailing standards of the same world, have no right and no place before God because of their guilt and fate, and who are now suddenly accepted as Jesus' boon companions. Those whom Jesus' word has freed from demonic powers. The sick who become healthy. But also the disciples, who leave everything and obey Jesus' call to "follow me." In each case a world has come to its end, be it for salvation or judgment. Its past is called in question. Its future is no longer secure—that future towards which it has been moving, according to all those traditions and laws which had been valid until then. In this sense its "time" has ended. In the encounter with Jesus, time is left to no one: the past whence he comes is no longer confirmed, and the future he dreams of no longer assured. But this is precisely why every individual is granted his own new present. For life, world and the existence of every individual, now stand in the sudden flash of light of the coming God, in the light of his reality and presence. This is the theme which Jesus proclaims.

CHAPTER 20

The New Testament in Current Study

REGINALD H. FULLER

> Professor Fuller, presently of Union Theological Semi-
> nary, comments on current views concerning what may be
> known about the historical Jesus. It is clear that he does not
> assume a full scale life can be written but rather only a
> sketch which indicates basic motifs of the ministry. Profes-
> sor Fuller's article indicates not only his own views but also
> others which are presently under discussion.

WHAT CAN BE KNOWN OF JESUS

IN his article on "Jesus Christus," [1] Hans Conzelmann, has summarized the material which passes these criteria. Jesus proclaimed the Reign of God. This Reign, while future, was effectively
engaging men already in the present in the word of Jesus himself.
It demands decision, response, acceptance of the challenge. It is
making itself felt in advance in the words and works of Jesus, so
that men's lives here and now are "decisively qualified" in the
present by the future Reign of God. At this point Ernst Fuchs [2]
contributes the important addition that Jesus' gracious activity in
eating with publicans and sinners (what Fuchs calls Jesus' conduct,
Verhalten) is a special concentration of the redeeming activity of the
Reign of God already making itself felt in advance. We might add
too that Jesus' healings and exorcisms point in the same direction.
Jesus' *eschatology* implies a present confrontation with the future
Reign of God.

[1] In *Religion in Geschichte und Gegenwart,* Vol. III, p. 621 ff., 1959.
[2] See his article, "Die Frage nach dem historischen Jesus," *ZThK,* 53, 1956,
pp. 210–229.

The ethic of Jesus points in the same direction. Jesus demands absolute, radical obedience to the will of God, sweeping away all qualifications and evasions ("You have heard that it was said . . . but I say"). In Jesus' ethic there is an immediate confrontation with the demanding God.

The teaching of Jesus about God (Conzelmann calls it his "cosmology") and his providential care (e.g., Matt. 6:19-34) has similar implications. Here Jesus confronts men with God's direct lordship over human life, which rules out anxiety. We might also include under the rubric of Jesus' teaching on God what he says about faith. Gerhard Ebeling has paid particular attention to this subject.[3] Faith is not a subjective attitude of the soul, but being on the receiving end of the divine action. Faith implies an act of God at the other end. Ebeling calls attention to Hans Schlier's remarkable article on "Amen" in the *Theologisches Wörterbuch* (Vol. I). Whereas the Jew *concluded* his prayer to God with Amen, thus expressing his faith that God would act, Jesus *prefaces* his words with an "Amen," thus denoting that prior to his utterance there is his total engagement to the act of God, of which his words thus become the channel. As Schlier pertinently remarks, "Amen I say unto you" includes the whole of Christology in a nutshell.

Günther Bornkamm[4] can also speak of a general impression made by Jesus in the gospels which is quite independent of the authenticity of this or that particular saying. We are, he says, impressed by Jesus' humble submission to God on the one hand, and his tremendous sense of authority expressed both in word and in deed on the other. Jesus is always master of every situation. His gracious service of man is combined with a penetrating insight into human motives and a radical judgment of their behavior ("He knew what was in man," says the fourth gospel in an editorial comment which is nevertheless completely justified by Jesus' history). Yet this same judgment of men is combined with the acceptance of sinners and their forgiveness. There is nothing in this portrait, says Bornkamm, which could have been read out of or created either by the Messianic expectations of pre-Christian Judaism or by the post-

[3] "Jesus und der Glaube," *ZThK*, 55, 1958, pp. 64–100; "Die Frage nach dem historischen Jesus und das Problem der Christologie," *ZThK*, 1959, Beiheft I, pp. 14–30. He has also written a full-length work on the subject, *Das Wesen des Christlichen Glaubens*, Tübingen, 1959.
[4] *Jesus of Nazareth*, Ch. III.

Easter Christology of the church. In fact, it is just these elements which tend to be toned down in the later strata of the gospels. Yet at the same time the impression survives all the way through, even down to the fourth gospel. Here is an encounter with Jesus independent of the kerygma (though of course it has been filtered through the kerygma). It is often said, both by radicals and conservatives, that you cannot get back behind the apostolic witness. In a sense this is true: all we know of Jesus is through the apostolic witness. Yet the techniques of historical, literary and form criticism do enable us to dig through the apostolic witness and come to a pre-Easter stratum which their witness has taken up and used. Thus, as James M. Robinson claims,[5] we have for the first time since the apostolic age a second line of encounter with Jesus additional to the kerygma. It is true of course that the gospels are kerygmatic in intention, not historical or biographical, and that in using them in this way we are using them in a way for which they were not originally intended. But in the service of the kerygma the Evangelists actually use authentic traditions and logia of Jesus, and if they contain such authentic memories, it is certainly legitimate for us to find them and use them in this way.

JESUS' SELF-UNDERSTANDING

But what of the Messianic problem? Did Jesus claim to be Messiah? Did he possess a "Messianic consciousness"? Form criticism had eliminated the Messianic categories from the sayings of the historical Jesus on the ground that these categories reflect the faith of the post-Easter church. This elimination is still maintained by the post-Bultmannian scholars, and in fact, as we shall see, it is carried to even greater lengths by some of them. Of course, let us remind ourselves, this is not because these scholars do not personally believe in Jesus' Messiahship, or rather in what that mythological confession of faith stands for—they are not unbelievers, or even liberal Protestants who subtly modernize what is meant by Messiahship and eliminate the redemptive act of God. They are not trying to recover a simple Jesus who was just a teacher or a Jewish reformer. Their concern is simply to apply objectively a sound and relevant historical methodology. What then are the results? Bult-

[5] *A New Quest of the Historical Jesus,* p. 90.

mann, it will be remembered, allowed [6] some of the Son of man sayings to stand as authentic logia of Jesus, namely those which speak of the future work of the apocalyptic Son of man. But he held that Jesus did not identify himself with that Son of man, but looked for his coming as a figure quite distinct from himself, as Mark 8:38 and Luke 12:8f. (a saying testified both by Mark and Q) clearly show. There is an interesting divergence of opinion among the post-Bultmannian scholars on this matter. Some of them (we might call them the right-wing school [7]) follow Bultmann in accepting as authentic those sayings about the coming Son of man which distinguish between Jesus and the Son of man. Since the post-Easter church came to identify Jesus with the coming Son of man, it is unthinkable for these scholars that the church should have created logia which make the distinction between them. This distinction is removed in the Son of man logia created by the post-Easter church. The sayings in question, however, speak of the coming Son of man, not as judge and redeemer, but as advocate (paraklete), and are wholly in line with Jesus' proclamation of the Reign of God as something which, though future, is presently operative in his word and work. A man's acceptance of Jesus and his message determines his acceptance or rejection at the coming of the kingdom of God. This distinction between Jesus and the coming Son of man corresponds to the distinction between the kingdom as it is breaking through in Jesus, and its final consummation. Now just as in the sayings about the kingdom Jesus' intention is not to impart teaching about the future kingdom, but to convey the decisiveness of the present moment of confrontation ("Blessed are you poor, for yours is (now) the (future) kingdom of God"), so Jesus, in speaking of the future Son of man, is not imparting teaching about that figure, but reinforcing the decisiveness of his own word and work for salvation. Hans Tödt puts it in this way: while there is not a Christological identity between Jesus and the Son of man, there is a soteriological continuity between the work of the one and the work of the other. As a result of the Easter revelation the church came to see that Jesus was now identified with the coming Son of man, for God had vindicated Jesus and his eschatological message. Consequently, the church was able

---

[6] *Theology of the New Testament* I, p. 30.

[7] These include Günther Bornkamm, *Jesus of Nazareth*, p. 206, and H. E. Tödt's extensive monograph, *Der Menschensohn in der Synoptischen Überlieferung*, Gütersloh, 1959.

to carry the term "Son of man" as it were over to the other side of the equation, to Jesus in his earthly work. This happened very early, already in the oral tradition before it diverged into Q and Mark. Thus we get the sayings which speak of Jesus in his earthly work speaking of himself as Son of man. This, however, is not a mere self-designation: it expresses precisely that authority of Jesus which is apparent in the authentic sayings such as Mark 8:38, and which there is to be vindicated by the Son of man.

The "left wing" Bultmannians [8] take what at first sight appears to be a more radical line. They agree in eliminating from the authentic logia of Jesus not only those sayings which speak of the Son of man in his earthly work and in the passion, but even those which speak of him as coming at the End. Even these are, for them, creations of the post-Easter church, words of primitive Christian prophets. Conzelmann and Vielhauer are so impressed by the immediacy and finality of God's presence in Jesus that there can be no room for a second soteriological figure between Jesus and the coming Kingdom, as Bultmann and his right wing pupils had postulated. This is analogous to the more conservative positions of E. Schweizer and John A. T. Robinson,[9] who accept the sayings which identify Jesus in his earthly work with the Son of man, and tend rather to eliminate the sayings which speak of the coming Son of man as post-Easter creations. Conzelmann then seeks to answer the problem why it is that the title Son of man is found only on the lips of Jesus, not as a confession of faith on the lips of others —an argument often used in favor of the authenticity of the Son of man logia. The reason for this, he says, is that in the early church Jesus was not *confessed* as Son of man, but *expected* to come as such. Thus the term Son of man is used only in creations of early Christian prophets, in which the exalted Jesus speaks as the coming Son of man, revealing himself as such to his expectant church. Vielhauer's attempt to eliminate even the future sayings is much

[8] E. Käsemann, "Sätze heiligen Rechtes im neuen Testament," *NTS*, 1, 4, 1954–55, pp. 248–260; Hans Conzelmann, *ZThK*, 54, 1957, p. 281, and art., "Jesus Christus," *RGG* (see p. 26); and Philipp Vielhauer, "Gottesreich und Menschensohn in der Verkündigung Jesu," in *Festschrift für Günther Dehn*, ed., W. Schneemelcher, 1957, pp. 51–79.

[9] E. Schweizer, *ZNW*, 50, 1959, pp. 185–209; John A. T. Robinson, *Jesus and His Coming*, London, 1957.

more thorough-going. Following a line of argument which had already been put forward by an American scholar, H. B. Sharman,[10] Vielhauer points out that the Son of man sayings never speak of the kingdom of God, and conversely the kingdom of God sayings never speak of the Son of man. The two sets of logia therefore belong to different strata of the tradition. The question is, which of them goes back to Jesus? It is, argues Vielhauer, universally accepted that the kingdom of God was the central concept in the proclamation of Jesus. Therefore the kingdom of God logia must in general be accepted as authentic, and the Son of man sayings of all three types as creations of the post-Easter church. This is further substantiated by the fact that in the pre-Christian Jewish tradition also the combination of Son of man with kingdom of God is never found. It is true that the combination seems to appear in Dan. 7, but there, according to Vielhauer, the Son of man is not an individual redemptive figure, but a symbol for the saints of the Most High. In Enoch the term, kingdom of God, never occurs, and in IV Ezra 13 the actual term, kingdom of God, is studiously avoided. In the Rabbinic tradition the term, kingdom of God, is never combined with the expectation of the Messiah,[11] nor conversely when they speak of the Messiah do the Rabbis mention the kingdom of God. Whereas the right wing Bultmannians postulate the resurrection encounters as the cause of the transference of the term Son of man from the coming One to Jesus in his earthly work, the left wing postulate it as the cause of the creation of all the Son of man logia. This forces Vielhauer to overlook the distinction between Jesus and the Son of man in such sayings as Mark 8:38. However, he concludes on a positive note. The resurrection revealed to the disciples that Jesus now lives in the glory of God. It therefore becomes necessary for them to insert Jesus' person into their proclamation of the kingdom of God, since with his death and resurrection the kingdom of God had now broken in. The early church therefore picked up the term, Son of man, in order to express the identity of the earthly Jesus with the exalted one. They had prece-

[10] *Son of Man and Kingdom of God,* New York and London, 1944. Sharman's theological presuppositions, however, were those of an old-fashioned liberal.
[11] As Tödt points out, *op. cit.,* p. 300, Vielhauer has slipped up here: if the Rabbis spoke of the *Son of man* rather than of the Anointed One, this observation would be pertinent. Since they do not, it has no bearing on Jesus' usage.

dent for this in Enoch 71, where the man Enoch is exalted as Son of man. Vielhauer's essay concludes with words which are worth quoting:

> From this, the oldest faith in the Son of man, the sayings about the coming Son of man are derived. They objectivize a particular moment in the proclamation of Jesus by isolating it, and thus they introduce that concentration of the interest of faith in the person of Jesus which has left its deposit in the various christologies of the New Testament. Just as these christologies with all their variety and contradictions point to the essentially provisional character of all christology, so does the starting-point of christology, the faith in the Son of man, point to their necessity. Yet the problem of christology cannot be solved by recourse to the so-called historical Jesus, any more than it can by taking refuge in the so-called historical, biblical Christ.[12]

AN IMPLICIT CHRISTOLOGY

Since this subject is so important, a few personal reactions would seem to be in place here. It is hard to believe that the church, if it had come as a result of the impact of the Easter revelation to identify Jesus with the coming Son of man as the expression of its faith, should either have coined such logia as Mark 8:38, Luke 12:8f. par., which expressly distinguish between Jesus and the coming Son of man (a point which, we have seen, Vielhauer conveniently ignores), or that it should have created Son of man sayings on such a wholesale scale had not Jesus himself used the term in authentic logia. In fact the rejection of Mark 8:38, Luke 12:8 par., as post-Easter creations offends against the primary criterion of tradition history, which is that sayings which conflict with the post-Easter faith of the church are *prima facie* authentic. They must therefore be retained as Jesuanic, and precisely in the sense that they distinguish between Jesus and the Son of man. But does this conflict with the insight derived from Jesus' eschatology, ethics and teaching about God, that they all imply a Christology? Does this insert another figure between Jesus and the coming kingdom? Far from it. Rightly understood, these sayings do not introduce the figure of the Son of man for his own sake, but precisely *for the sake of Jesus' own implicit*

---

[12] Vielhauer, *op. cit.*, p. 71.

christological self-understanding. The Son of man merely acts as a kind of rubber stamp for the authority of Jesus' own word and person as the final eschatological self-communication of God. In calling men to fellowship with himself Jesus is giving them already here and now, by anticipation, the final salvation of the Kingdom of God. Once, however, the explicit identification of Jesus with the Son of man had been reached after Easter, the effect on Jesus' logia is a two-fold one. Sayings in which he had spoken simply as "I" now become sayings in which he speaks of himself as the Son of man. This has for instance clearly happened at Matt. 16:13 compared with Mark 8:27. It may equally have happened with at least some of the "present" Son of man sayings, e.g., Matt. 8:20 par. On the other hand, there was the opposite tendency to replace an original Son of man with "I," where Jesus had spoken of the Son of man, on the other side of the equation, the transcendental side, as a figure distinct himself. This has clearly happened at Matt. 10:32f. compared with Luke 12:8f.

THE DEATH OF JESUS

Günther Bornkamm's *Jesus of Nazareth* does not stop, as Bultmann's *Jesus and the Word* did, with the proclamation and teaching of Jesus, but goes significantly further. He includes a chapter on "Jesus and His Disciples," and another on his journey to Jerusalem, his passion and death, as essential and ascertainable parts of his history.[13] Though with Bultmann he regards Marcan predictions of the passion as *vaticinia ex eventu*, and creations of the post-Easter kerygmatic theology, and although like John Knox [14] he will not allow that Jesus went up to Jerusalem deliberately to die (which would be tantamount to suicide), yet he thinks that the final journey to Jerusalem was deliberate. Its purpose was to confront Judaism at its very center with the challenge of his eschatological message. But with the fate of John the Baptist before him he could very well have known [15] that death was a possible, and indeed probable, outcome of this challenge. Bultmann in his only published (to

---

[13] Cf. my criticism of Bultmann in *The Mission and Achievement of Jesus*, pp. 50f.
[14] *The Death of Christ*, New York, 1958, esp. Ch. III, "The Psychological Question."
[15] Cf. E. Fuchs, *ZThK*, 53, 1956, p. 225; Knox, *op. cit.*, p. 120.

1960) reaction to the post-Bultmannian discussion [16] objects to this
as psychological speculation: "It may be legitimate to say that Jesus'
relationship to God presumed the passion right from the outset. But
this ought not to be based on biographical and psychological considerations. All we ought to say is that Jesus' understanding of the
will of God included the possibility that suffering might be necessary." However, Bornkamm's view is not entirely speculative, for
it is based on Luke 13.31-33, which he regards as substantially authentic. Moreover, we do have one saying, which Bornkamm, like
many other recent, highly critical writers [17] accept as authentic,
and in which Jesus speaks of the meaning of his death (at a time
when it was a certainty), explicitly relating that death to the com-
ming of the kingdom of God. This is the eschatological prediction
in the Supper narrative (Mark 14:25 par., Luke 22:16, 18). Unlike
the other eucharistic sayings, this logion is above suspicion. It can
hardly be a creation of the church's liturgical tradition, for as a
matter of fact it was very early dropped from the liturgical formula. In I Cor. 11:23-26 it survives in tenuous form in the words,
"until he comes," and in the early liturgies it has completely disappeared. The eschatological prediction is of paramount importance
and is the clue to Jesus' interpretation of his death. In it Jesus declares that between him as he sat at supper and the coming of the
Reign of God there stood the decisive event of his death. Only on
the other side of it would he be re-united with his disciples in the
Messianic banquet. To that death he must go alone, without them.
But they will be restored to fellowship with him on the other side
of that death when the Reign of God comes. Of that reunion the
Last Supper is the pledge and promise.

THE CHURCH

On the question whether Jesus intended to found a church, the
Bultmann school see the church as the outcome of the Easter event.
Jesus envisaged only two things—the present in which he was in-

[16] "Allgemeine Wahrheit und christliche Verkündigung," in *Glauben und
Verstehen* III, 1960, pp. 176f. Bultmann has since published a more extended
reaction entitled *Das Verhältnis der urchristlichen Christusbotschaft zum historischen Jesus*, Heidelberg, 1960.
[17] E.g., E. Schweizer, art., "Abendmahl" in *RGG*, third ed.; cf. Knox, *op. cit.*,
p. 120.

volved, and its vindication in the coming of God's Reign. There was for him no room for an intervening period between the present and the future. Also, the passage, Matt. 16:18, while certainly Palestinian [18] is a creation of the post-Easter church. But this is not the whole story. With N. A. Dahl [19] one must say that insofar as the kingdom of God, the end time, implies a people of God to enjoy it, the notion of a reconstituted, eschatological community was implied as a part of Jesus' hope. The post-Bultmannians are divided on the authenticity of the Twelve within the lifetime of Jesus, but those who accept it would regard their number as a prophetic sign of the reconstitution of the people of God. But at the same time this qualification must be added: Jesus did not look for a continuing people of God in history, as the church turned out to be. He did not think in terms of an ecclesiastical organization, still less did he legislate for it. In that sense, the church is the end-result of his work, rather than his deliberate intention.

[18] So even Bultmann, *Geschichte der synoptischen Tradition*, 1957, pp. 147–150, and *Theology of the New Testament* I, p. 37.
[19] *Das Volk Gottes*, Oslo, 1941.

CHAPTER 21

We Jews and Jesus

SAMUEL SANDMEL

> Dr. Sandmel, Provost and Professor of Bible and Hel-
> lenistic Literature, Jewish Institute of Religion, provides in
> this selection some indication not only of his own under-
> standing of the historical Jesus but also of the thinking of
> other Jewish scholars present and past.

THE growth of communication between Jews and Christians was
inevitable in the freedom of Western countries. There is a
sense in which Montefiore and Klausner, however sturdily Jewish
they are and however limited their scholarship may appear to be,
represent an honest quest to discover the historic role of Jesus the
Jew. Where Jews live in some amity with next door neighbors who
are Christians, it is inevitable that Jews ask themselves who and
what was Jesus, and Christians ask them what their point of view
toward Jesus is. However much some Jews have been disturbed by
the mere asking of this question, the fact remains that it is a recurrent Jewish and Christian question.

The level on which the question has been asked, or the manner
of its asking, has not uniformly pleased Jews. I suppose that in the
1920's no American rabbi was more beloved of the Jewish "masses"
than Stephen S. Wise of New York. In January 1925, Wise spoke at
his services on Klausner's book and, going beyond Klausner, reclaimed Jesus for Judaism. Within two weeks Wise had undergone
a considerable amount of personal abuse, and he felt impelled to
resign his presidency of both the American Zionist Organization and
the American Jewish Congress.

I have read Wise's address, and I can comment that it had at
least this infelicity, it was not a well-informed sermon. Yet the con-

clusion seems inescapable that the uproar was caused not so much by what Wise had said, but who it was who was saying it, and at what juncture. American and German rabbis had earlier delivered many a sermon on Jesus with a comparable viewpoint, but they had escaped the public notice that Wise's sermon attracted.

A French priest, Joseph Bonsirven, collected the sermons on Jesus, mostly of American rabbis, mostly Reform, and in 1937 published a little book, *Les Juifs et Jésus; attitudes nouvelles*; this book, "The Jews and Jesus; New Attitudes" has not been translated into English. Bonsirven cited the most eminent rabbis of the time, even quoting their words. He expressed himself as pleased that the historic Jewish aversion to Jesus has been replaced by a friendly attitude. He went on to say, however, that what the Jewish writers he cited were doing was reclaiming Jesus for themselves, and he lamented that they were not bringing themselves to Christ.

Bonsirven was exactly right on both counts. There is a quite long tradition among Jews in the West of reclaiming Jesus for Judaism and I suspect that in some Jewish circles not only is there no questioning of the propriety of reclamation, but it is even an axiom in the form that Jesus was a Jew, and therefore "ours." Before Hitler, one could document a Jewish interest in Jesus which, during and after Hitler, understandably receded.

In the same period, Christian biblical scholarship tended to divert its interest from Jesus the man to an interest in Jesus the Christ. Since I deal here with movements and trends and not with individuals, my point is that whereas one might have thought in the 1900's and 1910's that Jewish and Christian scholars were on the threshold of some incipient common understanding of Jesus, today that common understanding has again become remote. The older Gospel scholarship was easy for Jews to read and understand; today's scholarship has so shifted to the theological as to be very hard to understand and even to read.

It is my opinion that Jews and Christians are farther apart today on the question of Jesus than they have been in the past hundred years, this despite other ways in which Judaism and Christianity have drawn closer to each other than ever before.

Then what has the accumulated scholarship of the past century and a half contributed to our knowledge of Jesus? The answer has to be that the Jewish backgrounds have become better understood, the Graeco-Roman environment, especially the religious quests among pagans, better known, and the relations of the Gospels to each other and to other Christian writings better assessed; also, archaeology has broadened and deepened our knowledge of both late Judaism and early Christianity.

A little attention to the Dead Sea scrolls may be a good prelude to move us on to our conclusions. Like many an archaeological discovery, the Dead Sea scrolls were newsworthy enough to be reported in the general press, but they had the additional attraction that they were, if their date between the years 100 B.C. and A.D. 100 could be accepted, the first and only major discovery of documents from the age of Jesus. Since the public impression had already been that archaeology in some way confirmed Scripture, it was hoped, expected, and prematurely announced that the scrolls were verifying Christian claims. Sometimes this alleged verification took the form of finding in some of the scrolls, through misreading them, or through supplying readings where the texts had gaps, so-called precursors of Christianity. The result has been that materials in the scrolls have been deemed to anticipate similar material in the Gospels and Epistles of Paul. One line of such reasoning has run in the peculiarly perverse way that there was nothing essentially new in Christianity because its main theological contentions were already found in the Dead Sea scrolls. An opposite view has seemed to concede that the scrolls show a connection with the direct source from which the raw materials of Christianity were drawn, but that Christianity developed these raw materials in its own unique ways. These related but conflicting conclusions have rested on the premise that there was some special connection between the community which had created the scrolls and Christianity, a revival, often unconscious, of the view of Heinrich Graetz noted above. The scroll community was identified with the Essenes, and a good many nineteenth-century theories about the Essenic origin of Christianity were revived. Again, John the Baptist was made a member in good standing of the Essene community, and either through John, or even through his own direct membership, Jesus himself was brought into relationship with the Essenes.

Indeed, one scholar, William F. Albright, has used the evidence from the scrolls to repudiate the common opinion of Gospel scholars that the Gospel According to John was the latest Gospel; he believes it to be the earliest, and that what has antecedently seemed to scholars to be Grecian was in reality a product of that type of Palestinian Judaism which the scroll community represents. He goes still further and expresses the judgment that the scrolls have demonstrated that the discourses in John, universally attributed to an age much later than that of Jesus, were quite apt to be Jesus' own words, and that a Jesus who spoke in one way in the Synoptic Gospels did not rule out his speaking in a different way in John, and hence the discourses in John are *ipsissima verba*. In a word, there have been those scholars who hailed the scrolls as confirming the reliability of the Gospel records, this after a century and a half of Gospel scholarship had gone in exactly the opposite direction.

With the progressive study of the scrolls a good many of the initial enthusiastic judgments turned out to be unpersuasive. Even for those willing to date the scrolls between 100 B.C. and A.D. 100, there are two important factors which have attracted more continuing attention. The first of these is that the scrolls contain very little material of that kind which enables them to be dated around specific known events, and lack even more noticeably the names of people. Jesus, Peter, and Paul go unnamed in the scrolls. Hence, the attribution of a relationship between earliest Christianity and the scrolls is a matter of disputed inference, and not a case in which mere citation could clinch the issue. The second factor, consequently, is that the scrolls serve at best as adding illumination to the Jewish background of Christianity. The question, next, is whether the scrolls throw light on the specific background of Christianity, or whether they merely add to the material already available relating to the general background. (Some scholars seem unaware that, even prior to the discovery of the scrolls, illuminating background materials were already at hand.) There appears to me to be as yet no consensus among scholars on this latter issue, for there are those who insist that the scrolls point to the specific background, and others (which is the view that I favor) that their contribution is only general and not specific. I would personally emphasize that the scrolls have contributed in quantity little to what we already had, and that in quality this little is worthy but of much less significance than it was sometimes initially deemed. The scrolls are "important," in my opinion, only in themselves, and not in the light that they shed on Christianity. For the scrolls turn out not to have added one jot to the previous knowledge about Jesus.

We are still dependent for knowledge about Jesus only on New

Testament materials, the chief of which are the Gospels. The century and a half of Gospel study can be summarized in this way: Strauss began by denying virtually everything in the Gospels, but without studying the relationship of the Gospels to each other. Renan differed from Strauss in that he was arbitrary in rejecting some materials as legendary and accepting other materials as historical. The testing of the theory of the priority of Mark, by inquiring into the relationships of the Gospels to each other in the interest of discovering an objective way by which to approach the question of reliable history, was an initial step corrective of Strauss's wholesale denial and of Renan's arbitrariness. The "discovery" of Q seemed to provide, in itself and in Mark, two sources which by virtue of their earliness suggested a greater reliability in them than in Matthew and in Luke. But, in turn, the work of Wrede undermined the theory that the early source was more historical, for Wrede's conclusions made Mark as unhistorical as Matthew and Luke. Since neither the "two source" nor the "four source" hypothesis solved the problem of historical reliability, form criticism was resorted to in an effort to recover the materials which went into the early sources and to sift this material in order to isolate the historical form from the unhistorical. While form criticism set forth a way by which historical materials could be recovered, the conclusions of form criticism chanced to be abundantly negative and its method unpersuasive, even to those who were willing to receive the negative results, on the basis of their opinion that form criticism was marred by extreme subjectivity.

By and large the opinion of scholars has been that the Gospels reflect more adequately the piety of the Church than they reflect Jesus himself. Out of this general opinion there has arisen in very recent years what is called the "new quest" for the historical Jesus. These questers believe that it will be possible through continued study to find in the teaching and preaching of the early Church some set of reliable reflections of Jesus, on the premise that his impact on early preachers and teachers was vivid enough to create unmistakable specifics. As yet this type of investigation has been proposed as a method but not carried to the point of conclusions.

There is, then, no unmistakable agreement on the Jesus of history to be found in the labors and written works of New Testament scholars. What Schweitzer said almost sixty years ago is just as true now, that the Jesus of history is beyond recovery, and that the Jesus of Gospel scholars of the nineteenth century, and of the twentieth, never existed, for that Jesus emerges more from the intuition and from the anachronisms of the scholars than from the pages of the Gospels.

THE MEANING

It would be easy for someone like me to set forth some ingenious statement about Jesus. I have ample Jewish predecessors to rely on if I were to wish to choose one of the several options. I could with Graetz term Jesus an Essene, with Geiger term him a Pharisee, with Montefiore term him a prophet, and with countless others term him a rabbi (even though rabbi, *as a title*, appears to be later than the age of Jesus). I am withheld from such a statement by the very nature of the problems which have created the variety of opinion among the Christians. It is the problem that the Gospels, the primary sources, are writings from an age at least four decades or more removed from the time of Jesus, and that the Gospels so intertwine authentic material about Jesus with the pious meditation of the Church that I know of no way to separate the strands and to end up with some secure and quantitatively adequate body of material. I simply do not know enough about him to have an opinion, and I surely do not have enough to set him, as it were, in some one single category.

But beyond this, it is my conviction that the Gospels are not telling about the man that scholarship seeks, but about the human career of a divine being. To search the Gospels for the man seems to me to involve a distortion of what is in the Gospels. New Testament scholarship has not succeeded in isolating the man Jesus, Jesus the Jew.

Yet, suppose someone were to say, "You keep stressing the scholars. Aren't you making too much of scholarship? Forget for a moment the problems of historical reliability. Here are the Gospels; they tell you about Jesus. Isn't it possible for you to have some view of him which is the essence of the Gospels but kept free from the piddling questions of whether this or that detail is historical?"

Possibly something of this kind is possible, though just how satisfying it would be is a different matter. I have at various times tried to formulate some such thing, but I have not succeeded in satisfying myself. I once spoke, on the spur of the moment, of likening the portrait of Jesus to an oil painting rather than a photograph; if one stands too near to an oil painting, he sees the brush marks rather than the portrait.

It seems to me not to violate the documents or that scholarship which I have imbibed to think of Jesus as someone who had gifts of leadership and who was something of a teacher. I believe too that I discern in him a Jewish loyalty at variance with the views both of Christian and Jewish partisans who, through opposing motives that cancel each other out, detach him from Judaism. I believe that Jesus firmly believed that the end of the world was coming soon. I believe that he believed himself to be the Messiah, and that those scholars who deny this are incorrect.

I own to seeing no originality in the teachings of Jesus, for I hold that those passages which deal with his supernatural role reflect not his authentic words but the piety of the developing Church. As to those teachings which are conceivably his, they seem to me to be of a piece with Jewish teaching, and that they range from the commonplaces of that Jewish teaching through a sporadic flash of insight that other Jewish teachers also achieved. Yet I feel that all too often the question of originality is a misguided one, for it can often resolve itself into the unimportant question of mere priority. To my mind the crux of the issue about the Golden Rule is not the question of whether Hillel said it before Jesus, or Jesus before Hillel (Hillel chances to be a little earlier than Jesus), nor whether Hillel's formula in the negative is superior or inferior to Jesus' formula in the affirmative (the "Western Text" of Acts gives the Golden Rule in the negative formula!), nor whether both are, or are not, derived from Leviticus 19. To my mind the issue is that of value, not of priority; I find that there is more in the teachings of Jesus that I admire than that I do not; indeed, purely by chance I would deny that the hateful and hating chapter Matthew 23 goes back authentically to Jesus. There is, then, a general sense in which I see abiding values in many of the teachings of Jesus, and I also see that Christians have found affirmative values in passages which do not stir me; for example, I believe that Christians have been motivated to noble act and deed by the injunction not to resist evil, but I cannot in good conscience agree with this sentiment.

I cannot ascribe to the teachings of Jesus a striking uniqueness in particulars which in honesty I do not discern. The uniqueness of

Jesus would lie not in single particulars, but in the combination of facets, in the totality of what we may perhaps glimpse of him, and not in any one isolated way. Thus he was in part a teacher, a Jewish loyalist, a leader of men, with a personality unquestionably striking enough to be a leader, and his career must have been exceedingly singular for his followers to say that he had been resurrected.

He was a martyr to his Jewish patriotism. So many Jews became martyrs at the hands of later Christians that his martyrdom seems to us perhaps too unexceptionable for special notice. We Jews have so suffered, because Christians in ages past made us suffer, that it is difficult for us to acknowledge that Jesus suffered unusually. I believe that he did. There is to my mind both in the Epistles of Paul and in the Gospels the recurrent note that the career of Jesus was one of triumph; I can certainly acknowledge that martyrdom partakes of the overtone of triumph. Yet the dominant note to me of his career is overwhelmingly one of pathos, of sympathy, that a man, with the normal frailties of men, aspired and labored and worked, and yet experienced defeat.

I must hasten to add that I do not see this as exclusive in the instance of Jesus, or even, for I must be honest, the pre-eminent motif in his experience. But I do see it. Perhaps I would see it in even greater clarity if I could leap across the centuries of the Jewish-Christian tragedy, for just as often as I begin to find myself in warm sympathy with Jesus, I find this sympathy obstructed by a feeling that he remains always in some measure alien to me. When I ask myself why this is so, I do not ascribe it to any conscious bias— this may be the case, but I do not think so—but rather because I am inherently unable to see in Jesus that extra attribute which Christians and quasi-Christians see in him. Perhaps the impediment is not so much what my mind and heart may tell me about Jesus, but simply my resistance to what admirable and noble Christians tell me about him. I can agree that he was a great and good man, but not that he exceeded other great and good men in the excellency of human virtues.

I discern no possible religious assessment of Jesus, either by me or by other Jews. I cannot share in the sentiments of Montefiore which seem to me to fly in the face of prudent scholarship, nor in Klausner's distant dream of a reclaimed Jesus.

I must say most plainly that Jesus has no bearing on me in a religious way. I am aware that some Christians declare that they see in Christianity, with its figure of Jesus, a completeness which eludes them in Judaism. I am not sensible of any such incompleteness, for I neither feel nor understand that my Judaism is in any way incomplete. A religion is, after all, a complex of more than just theological viewpoints, for a religion has its own tone and texture which arise from its history, its group experience, its mores and norms, and even its folkways. I confess that there arises in me from time to time, in moods of self-criticism, some occasional feeling about certain inadequacies in Judaism. For example, I could wish that our exalted Jewish intellectual tradition were less remote than it has been from the Western stream of intellectual history; I could wish that our music had developed beyond the modal, and into Jewish counterparts of Bach, Mozart, and Beethoven; I could wish that we had a richer tradition of art. In such areas, then, I confess to recognizing deficiencies, and, in such a sense, incompleteness. But I do not discern any religious incompleteness which the figure of a Jesus would fill in, just as I see no incompleteness which a Mohammed or a Confucius would fill in.

Culturally, however, the situation is quite different. I own to an affinity for Mozart's liturgical music and to Beethoven's; and if to me by chance Bach does not appeal in the same way, then it is my idiosyncrasy and my loss. The figure of Jesus is part of Western culture, and I hold myself in all truth to be a legatee of and a participant in Western culture. In this sense, the figure of Jesus comes into my ken inevitably, just as he comes into the ken of all Western Jews. I cannot value him above the martyr Socrates, but I cannot conceive of myself as unaware of him, or isolated from him. Since I chance to enjoy folk music, whether from the robust voices of Israeli sabras or from the nasal tones of the Tennessee mountaineers, I also enjoy Christian music, especially the medieval English carols. I am eternally grateful to live in a land and in an age in which I am not constrained, through having felt the hostility of Christians, to cut myself off from that place in Western culture which Jesus occupies. Near Jerusalem there is a Byzantine church to which Israelis go in great numbers to hear organ recitals of Bach; they do not cut themselves off from the great music of Western civilization.

I see no valid reason for Jews to insulate themselves from the Jesus of Western culture, any more than they should, or would, from Plato. If it is retorted that in this attitude there is a risk, that it is hard to mark off the Jesus of culture from the Jesus of religion, then my reply is that Jews are going to run this risk, and only renewed Christian persecution, God forbid, will deter them from it. Here and there some Jew will cross over to Christianity. I know that this happens and will continue to happen. I venture to suppose that these crossings arise much more from Western freedom, and freedom to court and woo, than from theological concessions. To my mind there is a greater likelihood of the perpetuation of Jewish loyalties through the understanding by Jews of where they stand religiously in respect to Jesus than in their retaining this as a somewhat forbidden area, even though it enters into our ken and into our lives.

In context, I am saying that since Jesus occupies a position in Western culture, and since Jews in the West are part of Western culture, Jews will inevitably encounter his figure. Jews need not shy away from such cultural encounter. They will not, and they should not, compromise their convictions about the Christ Jesus of the Christian religion. They should know and understand the Jewish religion, certainly as a higher priority to their understanding Christianity. But Jews can be trusted to discern the difference between the Jesus of religion and the Jesus of Western culture.

CHAPTER 22

The Mission of the Twelve

VINCENT TAYLOR

Professor Taylor, formerly of Wesley College, Leeds, has written a study of Jesus which occupies a middle position between the radical skeptics among the Form Critics and the more conservative scholars such as Ethelbert Stauffer. It is impossible to give more than an excerpt here, but Taylor's chapter illustrates his use of the sources. More skeptical scholars suspect that the concept of the "Twelve" is a creation of the later community projected back into the ministry.

A T some time subsequent to the rejection at Nazareth, Jesus sent forth the Twelve, two by two, to announce the imminent coming of the kingdom of God. Like Jesus himself, they were to go to "the lost sheep of the house of Israel" (Matt. 10:6) with the message, "The kingdom of God is come nigh unto you" (Matt. 10:7; Luke 9:2; 10:9), to summon men to repent, to cast out devils, and to heal the sick. The importance of this event in the primitive tradition is shown by the fact that versions of the charge given to the disciples are found in every one of our four main Gospel sources, in Mark, in Q, in M, and in L.[1] Moreover, the instructions themselves reveal its climacteric character. The equipment of the Twelve was to be reduced to the barest essentials. They were to take with them no bread, no begging bag, and not a copper in their girdles. According to Mark, they were allowed a staff and sandals, but in Q even the

[1] See Mark 6:8-11; for Q see Luke 10:2-3, 8-12, 13-16 (with parallels in Matt.); for M, Matt. 10:5-8, 9-16, 23-25, 40—11:1; for L, Luke 10:1, 4-7, 17-20. So T. W. Manson, *The Sayings of Jesus*, pp. 73–76, 179–84, 256–59.

staff and shoes are prohibited and only a single undertunic is allowed (Matt. 10:10). Contrary to the immemorial custom of the east, like Gehazi (II Kings 4:29) of old they were to salute no man in the way. They were to accept the first hospitality that was offered; to pay no attention to the kind of food provided; to bespeak peace on the house that received them; to shake off the dust under their feet against the place that would not hear them. The time was one of harvest, but the laborers were few, and they were to pray the Lord of the harvest that he would send forth laborers into his harvest (Matt. 9:37-38). They were the representatives of Jesus, *sheluhim*, "men sent," so that to receive them was to receive him, and to receive Jesus was to receive him that sent him (Matt. 10:40).

Everything in the records goes to show that the Twelve were sent out under an overwhelming sense of urgency. A crisis was imminent; it was the eve of expected events. Nothing could be more mistaken than to think of their mission as a simple evangelistic tour, in which, so to speak, they were "tried out" as healers and preachers. The instructions show that they were to be "like an invading army, and live on the country." [2] They were heralds of the swift advent of the kingdom of God.

The general rejection of the "thoroughgoing eschatology" of Schweitzer has tended to obscure the emphasis he rightly laid upon the crucial importance of the mission and its decisive importance for Jesus himself.[3] Schweitzer was fully justified in insisting that "the whole history of 'Christianity' down to the present day . . . is based on the delay of the Parousia."[4] He was mistaken in supposing that Jesus looked for the end of history in the coming of a supernatural Son of man from heaven, but not in the view that for him the inbreaking of the Kingdom was near. What Jesus expected, and what he sent forth the Twelve to announce, was the speedy coming of the rule of God and the setting up of the messianic community of the Son of man. It was in this expectation, I think, that he assured

[2] Manson, *The Sayings of Jesus,* p. 181.
[3] "The thoroughgoing eschatological school makes better work of it [the withdrawal of Jesus from public work and his resolve to die]. They recognise in the non-occurrence of the Parousia promised in Matt. 10:23 the 'historic fact,' in the estimation of Jesus, which in some way determined the alteration of his plans, and his attitude towards the multitude," *The Quest of the Historical Jesus,* p. 358.
[4] *Ibid.*

the Twelve that they would not have gone through the cities of Israel before the Son of man would be come (Matt. 10:23).

In recent exposition the genuineness of Matt. 10:23 has been widely disputed on the ground that it appears in a section of Matthew which is a compilation and in which the interest is centered on the early Christian mission to the Gentiles. It is said to be the Judaistic-Christian explanation of the prohibition in Matt. 10:5, "Go not into the way of the Gentiles, and enter not into any city of the Samaritans" (E.R.V.).[5] As Streeter puts it, "It is not that Gentiles cannot or ought not to be saved, but the time will not be long enough to preach to all, and Israel has the first right to hear."[6] "It reflects," says Manson, "the experience and the expectations of the primitive Palestinian Church."[7] This explanation may well be a correct account of the meaning of Matt. 10:23 in its present context and as Matthew uses it, but only, I suggest, if it already existed in the tradition as a genuine saying of Jesus. In Matt. 10:5-23 it is exploited, but not invented, for who would have invented a prophecy of Jesus which was not fulfilled? It is probable therefore that criticism will need to look again at a saying which may have an important bearing on the mission of the Twelve.

Another saying which throws light upon the mind of Jesus at this period[8] is given by Luke in his account of the return of the Seventy (10:17-20). When the disciples returned, exulting that even the demons were subject to them in his name, Jesus replied, "I was beholding Satan fall as lightning from heaven" (10:18). The downfall of Satan in the last days was a current Jewish-Christian eschatological expectation, as we see from Rev. 12:9, where in the oracle it is said that Satan "was cast down to the earth, and his angels with him." In Luke 10:18 Jesus plainly has this idea in mind and speaks of it in terms of "realized eschatology." But what is the tone of the saying, and how does it bear upon the mission? In his *Die Gliechnisse Jesu,*[9] Jeremias mentions the Dutch scholar, M. van Rhijn, who explains the saying as ironical. Jesus sees that his disciples are in

---

[5] Cf. B. T. D. Smith, *The Gospel According to St. Matthew,* p. 123.
[6] *The Four Gospels,* p. 255.
[7] *The Sayings of Jesus,* p. 182.
[8] The saying is relevant whether we regard the mission of the Seventy as a doublet of the mission of the Twelve or whether we interpret them as successive events.
[9] P. 101n.

danger of overestimating their success in the matter of exorcisms, and wishes to say that not so quickly will Satan be overcome. Jeremias himself thinks that the saying does not suggest irony. Does it, however, suggest disappointment? Is the meaning that Jesus had looked to see [10] Satan fall from heaven, in whatever sense we may interpret the figure, but, alas! in vain? Certainly there is reproof in his address to the disciples, "Rejoice not that the spirits are subject to you; but rejoice that your names are written in heaven" (Luke 10:20), but it is difficult to be sure about the tone of a recorded saying. In any case Luke 10:18-20 is significant. The passage contains two eschatological concepts, the allusion to the fall of Satan and a reference to the Book of Life; it suggests that the mission was no ordinary missionary tour, but an event of crisis connected with the kingdom of God and with the community of the Son of man.

It may be objected that we are reading more into the incident than the Gospels relate. This objection is valid; but there is every justification for going beyond the bare records. All the sources give extracts from the charge to the Twelve, but the narrative passages —Mark 6:7, 12-13; Matt. 10:1, 5; Luke 9:1-2, 6; 10:1, 17—are of the scantiest and most general character. It is manifest that at the time the Gospels were written, the significance of the mission had long been forgotten. It is from this cause, it may be added, that the place of the Twelve themselves in the earliest tradition is so obscure. The justification for reading more into the incident is the disparity between the narrative passages and the extraordinary character of the injunctions laid upon the disciples. It was not for simple evangelistic activity that they were charged to ignore the traditional salutations of the East, to travel surprisingly light, to receive without comment the barest sustenance, to hurry on from place to place, to reject even the dust of unreceptive towns, always announcing the imminence of the kingdom of God. They are not preachers, but delegates; not teachers, but heralds; and their hearers are tested by their response, by whether they receive their message and repent. The mission presents the challenge of an impending event. For this reason it is entirely unique in the annals of evangelic activity. The task of the preaching friars and of the leaders of the Evangelical Revival offers only a faint analogy. For a closer parallel we have to think rather of the despatch of a fiery cross among the

[10] In this case the imperfect ἐθεώρουν is conative. Unfortunately, whether an imperfect is conative or not depends on the context. Cf. Acts 7:26 and 26:11.

Highland clans, except that the message is not a call to arms but a summons to hear. It is this fact, hidden but visible behind the tradition like the lower writing in a palimpsest, which justifies the belief that the mission and its sequel are fundamental to the understanding of the story of Jesus.

No small part of the significance of the mission is that it failed. In the words of Schweitzer, but with a different interpretation of the title "Son of man": "The disciples returned to him; and the appearing of the Son of Man had not taken place." [11] But the failure was immensely fruitful. In this respect the record is an epitome of the earthly life of Jesus, which is the story of victory through defeat, of rejection followed by exaltation. Jesus was not mistaken, and never was mistaken, in believing that the kingdom of God was at hand, for it is always at hand, even today. Had the expectation of the coming of the Kingdom been an error, it would have been renounced; but Jesus did not renounce, and never withdrew, his conviction that the rule of God was near, as the subsequent sacramental meal in the wilderness and his solemn reply to the challenge of Caiaphas so clearly show. The disappointment was one of clock time. Expectation had been foreshortened. The consummation looked for had not happened. Nevertheless, it lives on in the story of Jesus, and from now on it appears in grander but crimson colors. Through the failure of the mission, the fate of John the Baptist, and his own profound meditation upon the servant teaching of Isa. 53, Jesus was led to seek a deeper interpretation of the doctrine of the Son of man. It is to the birth and elucidation of the conviction that "the Son of man must suffer" that we must trace his withdrawal from public teaching, and apparently for a time from his daily association with the Twelve, during the period when he retired to the borders of Tyre (Mark 7:24), thence to emerge in renewed contact with his disciples in the villages of Caesarea Philippi, when he asked of them, "Who do men say that I am?" and more pointedly, "Who do *you* say that I am?" (Mark 8:27-29 R.S.V.), and finally to go to Jerusalem to suffering, death, resurrection, and victory.

[11] *Op. cit.*, p. 357.

CHAPTER 23

Jesus and His Story

ETHELBERT STAUFFER

Professor Stauffer of Erlangen has surprised most New Testament scholars by the confidence with which he has argued from non-Biblical materials to the literal historicity of incidents in the Gospels. The following excerpts provide two illustrations of this methodology. The chapter, "The Son of Mary," utilizes primarily Jewish materials in this way; "The Star," involves the use of materials from the general Mediterranean culture. Using this method Stauffer regards it as possible to reconstruct a remarkably detailed life of Jesus.

THE SON OF MARY

IN both the major Gospels (Matthew and Luke) Jesus is accounted the son of the Virgin Mary.[1] Is the miraculous birth of Jesus a historical fact? Or is it only a fable that first won acceptance in the late apostolic age, inspired by Isaiah 7, 14, and by the numerous legends of parthenogenesis which were rife in antiquity? "Parallels" in the history of religion are of no import in themselves against the authenticity of a historical account. But that only Matthew and Luke speak of the virgin birth gives rise to question. Nothing is said about it in the *Logia*, or in Mark and John.

However, this silence is only apparent. When the Fourth Evangelist relates the story of the wedding at Cana, with Mary already counting upon Jesus' power to work miracles,[2] he appears to take

[1] Matthew 1, 20 ff.; Luke 1, 35.
[2] John 2, 3.

it for granted that the mother knows from the beginning of the secret of her son. Still older and more impressive as evidence are two items from the *Logia* and the Gospel of Mark which concern the beginnings of the attacks upon Mary.

In the *Logia* we learn that Jesus was berated for being a "glutton and drunkard." [3] There must have been some grounds for this charge. For it fits in with all that we know about the attitude of Jesus and about the Pharisaical groups' reaction to it. Now, among Palestinian Jews this particular insult would be flung at a person born of an illegitimate connection who betrayed, by his mode of life and his religious conduct, the stain of his birth. This was the sense in which the Pharisees and their followers employed the phrase against Jesus. Their meaning was: he is a bastard. [4]

The First Evangelist gives us no background, and therefore has no occasion to deal with chronology in connection with the birth of Jesus. But in Mark 6, 3, we hear what Jesus' fellow countrymen in Nazareth thought about these matters: "Is not this the carpenter, the son of Mary and brother of James, and Joseph, and Judas, and Simon, and are not his sisters here with us? And they took offense at him."

This account, which appears only in Mark, does full justice to the situation. [5] The Jews had strict rules governing name-giving. A Jew was named after his father (Jochanan ben Sakkai, for example) even if his father had died before his birth. He was named after his mother only when the father was unknown. [6] The same custom prevailed among the Arabs, as well as in Egypt, [7] and, *mutatis mutandis,* still does in Western countries.

---

[3] Matthew 11, 19; Luke 7, 34.

[4] See Deut. 20, 18 ff.; Targ. Jer. Vol. 1, *ad loc.* For the after-effects of the controversy about Jesus, see Kalla 18 b; 41 d; Sanh. 107 b; Sota 47 a.

[5] See Matt. 3, 13; John 2, 12. It is also possible that the Christology of the early Church, based on priestly theology, presupposes Jesus being born by parthenogenesis of Mary of the House of Aaron.

[6] A person is characterized as an illegitimate child when he is named with the name of his mother. For he "has no father." (Lev. 24:11; Mek. Ex. 12:6; Lev. r. 24:10; Num. r. 6:2; 25:1; Mishle r. 7:23, end.)

[7] A list of ditch-diggers on a Vatican papyrus enumerates several hundred persons. In about 65 cases there appears, instead of the usual patronymic, the note *"apatōr."* See Friedrich Preisigke, *Sammelbuch* (Berlin and Leipzig, 1913), No. 5124.

Therefore, the Jews mentioned in Mark 6, 4, were saying: Jesus is the son of Mary and only the son of Mary, not of Joseph. This, of course, was meant to defame him. The people of Nazareth had hitherto held their peace, out of consideration for the feelings of Jesus. But now when the man turned out to be an apostate who was making all kinds of blasphemous claims, they spoke out.[8] The intention was to drive the apostate from his native town by shaming him. For the present the dishonoring name sufficed: Jeshua ben Miriam.

After the death of Jesus the matter was spoken of more plainly. In a genealogical table dating from before A.D. 70 Jesus is listed as "the bastard of a wedded wife."[9] Evidently the Evangelist Matthew was familiar with such lists and was warring against them.[10] Later rabbis bluntly called Jesus the son of an adulteress.[11] They also claimed to know precisely the "unknown father's" name: Panthera. In old rabbinical texts we find frequent mention of Jesus ben Panthera, and the eclectic Platonist Celsus around 160 retails all sorts of gossipy anecdotes about Mary and the legionary Panthera.[12]

Among the Samaritans and Mandaeans also Jesus was referred

[8] As long as a *mamser* leads a life pleasing to God, nothing insulting shall be said about his birth. (Tos. Eduy. 3:4 [459]; Kid. 70 b; 71 a Baraitha; Tos. Kid. 5:2 [341]; Lev. r. 24:10; Rashi on Ex. 12:38, and Lev. 24:10. Also Aboth V 20 ff. in Codex M. [in Karl Marti-Georg Beer: Aboth (Giessen; 1927), p. 157]: Everyone who casts aspersions [upon another because of the circumstances of his birth] is himself tainted.")

If the *mamser* becomes an apostate, his illegitimate birth shall be spoken of publicly and unsparingly. (Lev. 24:10 f.;Tos. Eduy. 3:4 [459]; Lev. r. 24:10; Meg. 25 b; Soph. 9:11).

[9] Yebamoth 4,13.

[10] Hence the striking mention of Tamar, Rahab, Ruth, and Bathsheba in Matt. 1, 3 ff.—four women in the genealogical table of the Israelite kings who became mothers under more or less dubious circumstances. An Arabic parallel to this is the courtesan Zarca in the family tree of the Omayad Caliph Merwan I, which provided his enemies with many occasions for attack. See W. R. Smith, *Kinship and Marriage in Early Arabia* (London, 1907), p. 171.

[11] Shabb. 104 b; Sahn. 67 a; Pesikta rabb. 100 b. Such phrases were typical of polemical writings. Thus, for example, Rabbi Nehemia (c. A.D. 150) calls the hated Emperor Titus, in S. Deut. 328, p. 139 b, the "son of Vespasian's wife"— "*ben ishtho shel Ispasianos.*"

[12] Tos. Hul. 2, 24 and *passim;* Origen, *Cels.* 1, 32 and frequently. But the Greek Celsus is the first to offer an explanation of Luke 1, 26 ff., from the point of view of the "history of religion"; see Origen, *Cels.* 1, 37.

to as the son of Mary, Jesus ben Miriam, with polemic intent.[13] We must ask ourselves whether these charges did not originate in the Palestinian community of the Baptist. For Luke, in 1, 41 ff., already seems aware of slander of Mary within that group, and takes issue with these slanders, just as Matthew 1, 3 ff., assumes and combats a similar movement in rabbinical circles.

The Islamic tradition of Jesus presents the exact opposite of these taunts against Mary. In the Koran we find Jesus referred to regularly as Isa ibn Maryam—Jesus, the son of Mary.[14] And Abdullah al-Baidawi, the classical commentator on the Koran, remarks with full understanding of the Semitic practice in nomenclature: the name of the mother is borne when the father is unknown. But this name and explanation are here intended in a thoroughly positive sense. In Islam Jesus is regarded as the son of the Virgin Mary who was begotten by the creative Word of God.[15]

To sum up: Jesus was the son of Mary, not of Joseph. That is the historical fact, recognized alike by Christians and Jews, friends and adversaries. This fact is significant and ambiguous, like all facts in the history of Jesus. The Christians believed him to be begotten by an act of the Divine Creator. The Jews of antiquity spoke of Mary as an adulteress. Out of this struggle between interpretation and counter-interpretation—which, according to Mark 6, 3, and Matthew 11, 19, had already begun during the lifetime of Jesus— the account of the ancestry of Jesus in the major Gospels emerged. They lay stress on Joseph's having himself bowed to the miracle of God. He neither denounced nor abandoned Mary, but rather took her into his house as his lawful wife and legitimized the son of Mary by personally naming him. By this act Jesus was admitted in a formal, legal sense to the house of David.

[13] See Nathan Adler and M. Seligsohn, *Une Nouvelle Chronique samaritaine* (Paris, 1903), p. 41 ff.; *Ginza,* Right-hand part, 382 (Lidzbarski, p. 410, 32). But the Mandaeans gave a perverted account of the virgin birth from the demonological, not pornographic, aspect; see, e.g., *Ginza,* Right-hand part, 56 (Lidzbarski, p. 50, 15 ff.). The counterpart to this, in a positive sense, is the mythological story of the birth of John the Baptist in the *John Book,* p. 116 ff. (Mark Lidzbarski, *Das Johannesbuch der Mandäer* [Giessen, 1915], p. 115 f.) For the connections among the disciples of the Baptist, the Samaritans, and the Mandaeans in traditional history, see Stauffer, *Z.N.W.,* Vol. 46 (1955), p. 13 f.
[14] Sura 3, 40, etc.
[15] Sura 19, 16 ff.

Among the Jews of Palestine a betrothed bride was under the same strict obligation to fidelity as a wedded wife. If she proved unfaithful, the prospective husband could repudiate her or go to law. Stoning was the penalty for breach of faith on the part of a bride.[16] Completion of the wedding ceremonies was marked by fetching the bride home to the bridegroom's house.[17] If the husband gave a newborn child his name, he recognized the child as his own in blood, or at least in law, and accepted it into his family with all the legal consequences involved.[18]

[16] Matt. 1, 19; cf. Deut. 22, 23 f.; Deut. § 239 f.; 242; Sanh. 7, 9; Git. 6, 2; John 8, 5.
[17] Matt. 1, 20. 24; Luke 2, 5; cf. 3 Macc. 4, 6 ff.; Gen. r. 26; Tos. Keth. 1, 4.
[18] Matt. 1, 25; Luke 2, 22 ff.; cf. Isa. 43, 1; Ps. 2, 7. An Arabian example is given in W. R. Smith, op. cit., p. 169 f.: the Omayad Abu Sofyan had a son by a courtesan. His name was Ziyad, "Son of his father"—i.e., an unknown father. Abu Sofyan later adopted the child, thus legally admitting him to the dynasty of the caliphs of Damascus. An example of the opposite in familial law is the disowning of a child; see Gen. 21, 9 ff.; Luke 15, 19; Ex. r. 46, 4 ("They are not my sons; I know them not; their mother committed adultery and bore them"). See P. M. Meyer, *Juristische Papyri* (Berlin, 1920), p. 25 ff., for the disinheriting of a daughter by the formula of disowning.

THE STAR

"Where is he who has been born king of the Jews? For we have seen his star in the East, and have come to worship him." Thus the Magi from the East speak in Matthew 2, 2. Perhaps Paul in Galatians 4, 3 f., was also thinking of this appearance of the star. Thus, at any rate, he was understood by Ignatius of Antioch when he combined the motifs of Matthew 2 and Galatians 4 in one apocalyptic advent hymn to the Star of Bethlehem.[1]

As long ago as the seventeenth century, Kepler ascribed the star of Bethlehem to the unique orbit of the planet Jupiter in the year 7 B.C.[2] In the spring of that year there was a conjunction of Jupiter and Venus. In the summer and autumn of that year Jupiter encountered the planet Saturn in the Sign of the Fishes—this being the extremely rare Great Conjunction that takes place in this form

[1] Ignatius, Letter to the Ephesians, 19:2 f.
[2] Johannes Kepler, *De Stella Nova*, 1606, pp. 129 f., 134 f.

only once every 794 years. According to the account in Matthew, the Magi noted only the beginning of the conjunction, only the appearance of Jupiter "out of the east." Upon this they based their astronomical and astrological forecast and thereupon set out for Palestine; when they reached Palestine they witnessed the crucial phenomenon in the heavens.[3] The rarity of that conjunction of Jupiter could not have escaped the astronomers of antiquity. But was astronomical science in the days of Jesus sufficiently developed to forecast the orbits and conjunctions of the planets?

Two recent finds provide the answer to this question: the "Berlin Planetary Table" and the "Celestial Almanac" of the ancient observatory of Sippar,[4] the Greenwich of Babylonia. The Berlin Planetary Table is a list of forthcoming movements of the planets drawn up in the year 17 B.C., and extended to A.D. 10; it was copied on an Egyptian papyrus dating from A.D. 42. It proves that even then astronomers were able to calculate the positions of the planets decades in advance. The Celestial Almanac of Sippar is one of the most recent cuneiform tablets which have come down to us. It contains predictions of the positions of the planets for the year 7 B.C., probably drawn up at the beginning of that year. On this clay tablet all the principal motions and conjunctions of the year 7 were calculated in advance, precise to the month and day. The main subject of the tablet, however, was the impending conjunction of Jupiter and Saturn in the Fishes, annotations for which appear about five times, with exact dates. In sum, astronomers of the day knew accurately what events were to be expected in the firmament, and were looking forward with special eagerness to the rare conjunction of Jupiter in 7 B.C.

What opinions did contemporary astrologers hold concerning this phenomenon? Today we can answer this question also. Jupiter was regarded as the star of the ruler of the universe, and the constellation of the Fishes as the sign of the last days. In the East, Saturn was considered to be the planet of Palestine. If Jupiter encountered Saturn in the sign of the Fishes, it could only mean that the ruler

---

[3] Matthew 2, 9 f.
[4] W. Spiegelberg, *Demotische Papyrus aus den Kgl. Museen zu Berlin* (1902), p. 29 ff.; P. Schnabel, "Der juengste datierbare Keilschrifttext," *Zeitschrift fuer Assyrologie*, Vol. 36 (1925), p. 66 ff. Cf. also F. X. Kugler, *Sternkunde und Sterndienst in Babel* (Muenster, 1907 ff.), Vol. 1 ff.

of the last days would appear in Palestine.[5] Such were the passages that prompted the Magi of Matthew 2, 2, to go to Jerusalem.

Evidently, then, there is substance to the account in Matthew; it agrees excellently with the original documents of the period. The clay tablet of Sippar may be regarded as the astronomical pocket-almanac with which the wise men set out from the East, and it is understandable that their astrological deductions would cause a great stir in Herod's Jerusalem.[6]

Undoubtedly the unique orbit of Jupiter of the year 7 B.C. was also noticed and commented on in the western parts of the Roman Empire. We know that Augustus was deeply interested in astronomical phenomena, and it is evident from the Berlin Planetary Table that in Rome and Alexandria the movements in the heavens were followed with the closest attention. In the Roman Empire, Augustus was regarded as Jupiter in human form, and thus ruler of the *ultima ætas,* the last age. Venus was considered the star of the Julian family, and Saturn the symbol of the Golden Age. In these circumstances the extraordinary path of Jupiter in 7 B.C. could only be taken as referring to the career of the Emperor Augustus: surely this year would bring the glorious climax of his splendid career.

As a matter of fact, we possess a number of documents of the period which directly or indirectly confirm this deduction.[7] We may count among these the Augustan inscription at Philae, which I have discussed in detail elsewhere.[8] In the spring of 7 B.C. there took place the conjunction of Jupiter with Venus, which in Egypt was regarded as the star of Isis. On March 8 of that year an eminent Alexandrian erected a memorial tablet in the temple of Isis on the island of Philae in the Nile. The inscription upon the tablet of Philae

---

[5] Rabbinical writings on the constellation of the Last Days (*the Fishes*) in Strack and Billerbeck, *Kommentar zum Neuen Testament,* Vol. 4, pp. 1046, 1049. Mandaean material on Jupiter, Saturn, the Fishes, and the time of the Messiah in *Ginza,* Right-hand part, 18 (Lidzbarski, p. 408 ff.) and *The Book of the Zodiac* (ed. E. S. Drower, London, 1949), pp. 60 ff., 70, 119 and *passim.* Cf. also Test. Lev. 18:3; Dmd. 7:18 ff. A special study of this subject is in preparation.

[6] Matt. 2:3. Perhaps we may also synchronize this with the oracle of the approaching downfall of Herod in Jos. ANT. XVII 2:4.

[7] We mention only the Gemma Augustea, the triumphal reliefs on the bowl of Boscoreale, and the coins of the year 7 B.C.

[8] Stauffer, *Jerusalem und Rom,* Ch. 2.

hailed the Emperor as Zeus Eleutherios (that is, freedom-giving Jupiter).

Thus, the star of Bethlehem, too, is a historical fact. It, too, however, was a sign of God as ambiguous as all the other events in the story of Jesus. Whose coming was presaged by the heavenly phenomena of the year 7 B.C.—Augustus' or Jesus'?

PART IV

Historical Uncertainty and Christian Faith

CHAPTER 24

Jesus and the Word

RUDOLF BULTMANN

While Professor Bultmann, now retired from the University of Marburg, is profoundly concerned with the *kerygma*, i.e., message, which emerged as the Christian community's understanding of the significance of Jesus, he is not concerned—theologically—with the rediscovery of the details of that ministry. It is sufficient for modern man that he confront the "self-understanding" which is implicit in the *kerygma*. See the article "The Primitive Christian Kerygma and the Historical Jesus," in *The Historical Jesus and the Kerygmatic Christ*, ed. Carl E. Braaten and Roy A. Harrisville, 1964. See also the article, "The Problem of Hermeneutics" in *Essays, Philosophical and Theological*, 1955. For critiques of Bultmann's view, see especially chapters 29, 30.

THERE is little more to say in introduction. The subject of this book is, as I have said, not the life or the personality of Jesus, but only his teaching, his message. Little as we know of his life and personality, we know enough of his *message* to make for ourselves a consistent picture. Here, too, great caution is demanded by the nature of our sources. What the sources offer us is first of all the message of the early Christian community, which for the most part the church freely attributed to Jesus. This naturally gives no proof that all the words which are put into his mouth were actually spoken by him. As can be easily proved, many sayings originated in the church itself; others were modified by the church.

Critical investigation shows that the whole tradition about Jesus which appears in the three synoptic gospels is composed of a series of layers which can on the whole be clearly distinguished, although the separation at some points is difficult and doubtful. (The Gospel of John cannot be taken into account at all as a source for the teaching of Jesus, and it is not referred to in this book). The separating of these layers in the synoptic gospels depends on the knowledge that these gospels were composed in Greek within the Hellenistic Christian community, while Jesus and the oldest Christian group lived in Palestine and spoke Aramaic. Hence everything in the synoptics which for reasons of language or content can have originated only in Hellenistic Christianity must be excluded as a source for the teaching of Jesus. The critical analysis shows, however, that the essential content of these three gospels was taken over from the Aramaic tradition of the oldest Palestinian community. Within this Palestinian material again different layers can be distinguished, in which whatever betrays the specific interests of the church or reveals characteristics of later development must be rejected as secondary. By means of this critical analysis an oldest layer is determined, though it can be marked off with only relative exactness. Naturally we have no absolute assurance that the exact words of this oldest layer were really spoken by Jesus. There is a possibility that the contents of this oldest layer are also the result of a complicated historical process which we can no longer trace.

Of course the doubt as to whether Jesus really existed is unfounded and not worth refutation. No sane person can doubt that Jesus stands as founder behind the historical movement whose first distinct stage is represented by the oldest Palestinian community. But how far that community preserved an objectively true picture of him and his message is another question. For those whose interest is in the personality of Jesus, this situation is depressing or destructive; for our purpose it has no particular significance. It is precisely this complex of ideas in the oldest layer of the synoptic tradition which is the object of our consideration. It meets us as a fragment of tradition coming to us from the past, and in the examination of it we seek the encounter with history. By the tradition Jesus is named as bearer of the message; according to overwhelming probability he really was. Should it prove otherwise, that does not change in any way what is said in the record. I see then no objection to naming Jesus throughout as the speaker. Whoever prefers to put the name of "Jesus" always in quotation marks and let it stand as an abbreviation for the historical phenomenon with which we are concerned, is free to do so.

CHAPTER 25

Symbol, Event and Once-for-Allness

VAN A. HARVEY

Professor Harvey, chairman of the Graduate Program in Religion at Southern Methodist University, argues that the crucial element in Christianity is the "perspectival image" which emerged and the way it illumines human experience. Certainty about the historical Jesus, he argues, is relative and is not essential to the validity of this "perspectival image." It is no accident that Professor Harvey's book is dedicated to Professor Rudolf Bultmann.

IF one thinks of revelation as a paradigmatic event that casts up images that alter our interpretation of all events, this requires that we distinguish between two kinds of belief, and, accordingly, between two kinds of certitude: the belief that the actual Jesus was as the perspectival image pictures him, and the belief that the perspectival image does illumine our experience and our relationship to that upon which we are absolutely dependent. The former is a belief about a contingent fact remote from my own experience. Consequently, it can never have the immediacy of an event that impinges on my own life, although I may, of course, have a high level of certitude about it, depending on the data and warrants. The latter is also a belief, to be sure, but of a different order. In the first place, it is not a belief about a past event but a belief that an image cast up by a past event illumines some present experience. Consequently, this belief has to do with the present and can have an immediacy no remote event can acquire. In the second place, it is not a belief about one unique contingent event but has to do with the adequacy of an image for interpreting the structure and character of reality itself.

No remote historical event—especially if assertions about it can solicit only a tentative assent—can, as such, be the basis for a religious confidence about the present. Even if it were historically probable, say, that Jesus was a man who was completely open to transcendence, this belief in no way makes it any easier for someone two thousand years later to be so open—unless, of course, the silent presupposition is present that the object of faith is the same and can be trusted. But this silent presupposition is precisely what is at issue in the decision of faith, and no reference to a past event can establish that. Or even if we were to believe that the corpse of Jesus was resusciated, this fact could be the basis for a religious confidence only if that event were already interpreted as revelatory of the being with which one has to do in the present. But this, again, is precisely the affirmation of faith.

The difficulty with all the traditional orthodox attempts to ground the credibility of revelation in something objective like miracles or the fulfilment of prophecy is that they fail to see that there is no intrinsic connection between such external events and faith, *unless faith is already presupposed.* This, in turn, tells us something about the nature of faith. As Luther so clearly saw, history says nothing unless a "why" is discerned in it, unless it is "for us." This is why Luther's interpretation of miracles tends to relativize their importance. So, too, Herrmann and the dialectical theologians never wearied of repeating that faith is not believing things but the fundamental attitude one has toward the whole of existence. It is basically confidence in the nature of being itself.

This confidence must have some basis in one's present experience. No event or miracle that others tell us about can acquire the force of something we know for ourselves, and if one has the experience for himself, the appeal to a past fact is important largely because it provides us with an image to which we can return again and again and use in our present relationships with others. A fact cannot provide the ground or the object of faith when faith is properly understood, although it can awaken faith and provide the symbols that faith uses.

Actually, Christendom has always preserved some such insight as this, by distinguishing between the Christ after the flesh and the living Christ, or between Jesus Christ and the Holy Spirit. The doctrine of the Trinity, it could be argued, is a way of preserving the formative significance of a past event for interpreting a present and living reality. The Holy Spirit is the power that opens one's eyes to the Logos of all reality that was embodied in the man Jesus.

This argument should not be taken to mean that the image of Jesus has no correlation with the actual Jesus, since we have historical reasons for believing that it does. It means, rather, that this correlation is not itself an object of faith, that the truth of faith is not dependent upon such a correlation. Faith finds its certitude, its confirmation, in the viability of the image for relating one to present reality. In this sense, we could agree with Kähler and Tillich that it is the picture of Christ that has created and preserved the community of faith, were it not, as we have seen, that this terminology is systematically ambiguous. The power of the Christian message is mediated through the image of Jesus. It is this image which the Christian finds to be a reliable one for relating himself to the beings around him and to the power acting in and through all beings. Jesus Christ is the key image in a parable which the Christian uses to interpret the more inclusive reality with which all men are confronted and of which they try to make some sense.

The situation is not so much that the Christian has access to realities to which the non-Christian does not, or that the Christian believes that certain entities exist which the non-Christian finds doubtful. The situation is, rather, that both Christian and non-Christian are confronted with the same realities but interpret them differently. They regard them from different perspectives. If, for example, other men who do not call themselves Christian are struck, as we are told Ludwig Wittgenstein was often struck, by the feeling "How extraordinary that anything should exist?" and should testify it was always accompanied by the "experience of feeling absolutely safe,"[1] the Christian need not argue that this is an illusion or deprecate it because Wittgenstein did not believe in Jesus Christ. Rather, with the aid of the image of Jesus, the Christian will attempt to understand both his and Wittgenstein's common experience. Or, to use a slightly different example, if all men note that the rain falls equally on the lazy and diligent alike, and some men interpret this as a sign of cosmic indifference, there are others who may realize that they also are tempted so to interpret it but, with the aid of a suggestion out of their past, may see the same phenomenon in a different light, as the sign of a cosmic generosity. Or, if all men have

[1] Norman Malcolm, *Ludwig Wittgenstein, a Memoir* (London: Oxford University Press, 1958), p. 70, n. 1.

been terrified at times by the awesome creativity of being, some
have, with the aid of an image, been able to see this as the manifestation of an infinitely creative and boundless power that delights
in the sheer multiplicity and richness of life.

A perspective is a function of the weight and valence attached to
this or that experience and the way in which these, in turn, influence
the symbols and categories men use to relate themselves to other
experiences in the light of certain interests. There is clearly some
such logic as this illustrated in William James' reflections on the
difference between the inner life of the Greeks and Romans and
ourselves. The Greeks and Romans celebrated rectitude, virtue,
character, and self-sufficiency. Although they knew these were not
easily achieved, they nevertheless were not overly troubled by the
experience of hypocrisy and the corruption of virtue itself by self-
righteousness. It was Luther, James suggests, who broke through
this crust of naturalistic self-sufficiency, who saw that from one
standpoint, at least, all humanly accepted excellences and safe-
guards of character are childishness. And what was determinative
of this new self-understanding was another experience, an experience "of an unexpected life succeeding upon death. By this I don't
mean immortality, or the death of the body. I mean the deathlike
termination of certain mental processes within the individual's
experience, processes that run to failure, and in some individuals,
at least, eventuate in despair." [2] This experience of a new range of
life succeeding on our most despairing moments engenders (suggests) a still wider belief, of "a world in which all is well, in *spite*
of certain forms of death, indeed *because* of certain forms of death
—death of hope, death of strength . . . death of everything that
paganism, naturalism, and legalism pin their faith on and tie their
trust to." [3] And this belief James goes on, leads to another: the
"tenderer parts" of our personal lives are continuous "with a wider
self from which saving experiences flow in." [4]

Now these reflections of James hardly constitute an argument in
any strong sense of the word, but they do aid us in understanding
something of the structure of a perspective; and it is with structure
that I am primarily concerned here. An argument would necessarily

[2] William James, *Radical Empiricism and a Pluralistic Universe* (London:
Longmans, Green & Co., 1943), p. 303.
[3] *Ibid.*, pp. 305 f.
[4] *Ibid.*, p. 307.

take a quite different form. It would take the form of attempting to demonstrate that a given perspective has a viability, intelligibility, and comprehensiveness that the alternative perspectives do not, that it is less eccentric, better able to account for those experiences and structures to which the alternatives attach special weight, as well as for those elements the alternatives seem to ignore or take no notice of. Yet having said this, it is important to stress that the existential certitude of the believer lies in the brute givenness of these experiences, although, if he is not a "blind believer," he will seek to compare these experiences with those of other men and to test his interpretations in all of the ways that seem possible.

The basic objection to some such model as this, I am aware, is that it reduces Jesus to a symbol of some timeless truth. By resting all the weight on the illuminatory power of the event, on its content, I have interpreted Jesus, it may be alleged, as an occasion for faith in contrast to the object of faith. Or, as Kierkegaard put this objection approximately a century ago, I have treated Jesus like a Socratic teacher who, having once put the learner in mind of the truth, is no longer needed.[5]

This criticism itself, however, rests on certain questionable assumptions. In the first place, despite Kierkegaard's insistence on faith as a passion and his polemic against objectification and belief, his own view basically hangs on the identification of faith with propositional belief, although in this case the proposition is claimed to be an absurd one. But, it may be asked, what is saving about believing an absurdity? And if one tries, as Kierkegaard did, to argue that some absurdities are more relevant than others, does this not once more require him to make some appeal to our present and general experience? In the second place, this view, unless one is willing to take it to the lengths Kierkegaard did—he argued that it was sufficient for faith to believe only that God assumed human form and nothing more in the way of knowledge was required[6]— merely raises all the problems that are endemic to any position which insists that Christian faith is independent of all historical knowledge.

A third and more important difficulty with this kind of objection, however, is that it rests on the crude juxtaposition of symbol and

[5] Sören Kierkegaard, *Philosophical Fragments* (Princeton: Princeton Univ. Press, 1936).
[6] *Ibid.*, p. 87.

event that, in turn, rests on a quite unhistorical view of human nature. The distinction between timeless truths and events is simply too crude for theological or philosophical purposes. As our discussion of perspectives has attempted to show, the power of a paradigmatic event is precisely the fusion of universality and particularity. And once this principle is grasped, then symbol and history, as H. Richard Niebuhr has argued, are not opposites.

> For history may function as myth or as symbol when men use it (or are forced by processes in their history itself to employ it) for understanding their present and their future. When we grasp our present, not so much as a product of our past, but more as essentially revealed in that past, then the historical account is necessarily symbolic; it is not merely descriptive of what was once the case.[7]

The greatest difficulty with Kierkegaard's objection, however, is that it fails to appreciate the implications of the historicity of human existence for theology itself. Consequently, it prejudices the radicality and universality of God's grace. Kierkegaard's argument depends on the misleading analogy of religious truth with mathematical truth, an ironic error in one whom many regard as the first existentialist. The truth which Socrates taught to the slave boy had to do with geometry. There is a sense in which those truths could have been taught as well by another teacher, because the content of the knowledge is quite unrelated to the way it was mediated. But this analogy is singularly inappropriate with respect to self-knowledge. When it comes to this kind of knowledge, to the question of who I am, what I have learned is indissolubly connected with my teachers. I am this person with these images just because I have this historical past. In the realm of existential knowledge, teachers are not mere occasions. Their images stamp and condition the consciousness of those whom they have taught. The slave boy of the *Meno* could have been taught as well about the angles of a triangle by Alcibiades as by Socrates, but so far as the image of what it means to be a teacher who loves the truth and sacrifices everything to teach it, the content of that idea, as the history of the Western world indicates, cannot be abstracted from the picture of Socrates. Abraham Lincoln's conception of federal union might have been

[7] H. Richard Niebuhr, *The Responsible Self* (New York: Harper & Row, 1963), p. 156.

just as valid had it been held by Stanton, but this idea is indissoluble for most Americans from its embodiment in Lincoln. Human existence is historical existence. We are what we are, and our interpretations are what they are, because certain truths are indissolubly and powerfully wedded to certain persons in our historical past.

Having said this, however, it is important to realize that the confession that we have achieved such and such an understanding by means of this past is not to say that these realities can only be so apprehended. When we speak of revelation, we cannot mean that only in and through these particular events the divine has been disclosed. When we speak of revelation we cannot mean that God is making up for some previous lack of action or disclosure. Revelation, as John Oman once expressed it, can be better understood if it is regarded as God's way of

> dealing with the alienation which can see no gracious relation of God to us in any manifestation. In strict accuracy, we should speak of a historical reconciliation, rather than of a historical revelation, yet, seeing how God's manifestation is non-existent for us, or is even turned into sheer conflict and cause of distrust, till we are put into a position to interpret it aright, it is in effect a historical revelation. . . . Yet we should remember that it is revelation only as climbing an eminence affords us a prospect because the landscape is there already.[8]

We call Jesus the Christ because he discloses that reality encompassing every man but that not all acknowledge and interpret aright.

It is wrong to argue that this position is a new Gnosticism. It is but a modern restatement of an ancient theological alternative that goes back to the Logos theologians, that has emerged again and again in Christian history, and that has been reformulated more recently by such men as F. D. Maurice, H. Richard Niebuhr, and Karl Rahner. If one is searching for labels, then let it be called a radical historical confessionalism, for it is a position that tries to take with utmost seriousness both the Protestant principle of justification by faith and the historical character of human existence, of which the morality of historical knowledge is but a formalized constitutive part. The Christian community cannot disavow its own historical past, a past that constitutes the Christ event as the decisive

---

[8] John Oman, *Grace and Personality*, 2nd ed., rev. (Cambridge: Cambridge University Press, 1919), pp. 156 ff.

one for its self-understanding. Consequently, it has no other vocation than to represent the proclamation about Jesus again and again. On the other hand, the significance of Jesus lies precisely in the relevance of his image for understanding that final reality which confronts men in all events. Christians turn to Jesus not in order to rehabilitate any exclusive claim that a defensive Christianity wishes to make but because it understands that human beings only seem to decide concerning the truth about life in general when they are confronted by a life in particular. The Christian community confesses that this has happened to it and that this can happen again to those who would attend to this image. This is its historical destiny. It is most faithful to that destiny and the image of him who initiated it when it simply accepts and rejoices in that destiny and ceases to claim for this historical reality an exclusiveness that, when claimed, surrenders the very truth to which it witnesses.

CHAPTER 26

The Reality of the Christ

PAUL TILLICH

The late Professor Tillich of Union Theological Seminary, Harvard, and the University of Chicago, stressed the New Being manifest in Jesus as the Christ as the core of Christian reality. In the following passage he insists that there must have been an actual personal life in which "existential estrangement" was overcome since, otherwise, "the New Being would have remained a quest and an expectation and would not be a reality in time and space" as it actually is. But Tillich, like Bultmann and Harvey, does not regard the search for the historical Jesus as theologically crucial. Faith is not dependent on its results.

JESUS AS THE CHRIST

1. THE NAME "JESUS CHRIST"

CHRISTIANITY is what it is through the affirmation that Jesus of Nazareth, who has been called "the Christ," is actually the Christ, namely, he who brings the new state of things, the New Being. Wherever the assertion that Jesus is the Christ is maintained, there is the Christian message; wherever this assertion is denied, the Christian message is not affirmed. Christianity was born, not with the birth of the man who is called "Jesus," but in the moment in which one of his followers was driven to say to him, "Thou art the Christ." And Christianity will live as long as there are people who repeat this assertion. For the event on which Christianity is based has two sides: the fact which is called "Jesus of Nazareth" and the reception of this fact by those who received him as the

Christ. The first of those who received him as the Christ in the early
tradition was named Simon Peter. This event is reported in a story
in the center of the Gospel of Mark; it takes place in Caesarea
Philippi and marks the turning point in the narrative. The moment
of the disciples' acceptance of Jesus as the Christ is also the moment
of his rejection by the powers of history. This gives the story its
tremendous symbolic power. He who is the Christ has to die for his
acceptance of the title "Christ." And those who continue to call him
the Christ must assert the paradox that he who is supposed to overcome existential estrangement must participate in it and its self-
destructive consequences. This is the central story of the Gospel.
Reduced to its simplest form, it is the statement that the man Jesus
of Nazareth is the Christ.

The first step demanded of christological thought is an interpretation of the name "Jesus Christ," preferably in the light of the
Caesarea Philippi story. One must clearly see that Jesus Christ is
not an individual name, consisting of a first and a second name, but
that it is the combination of an individual name—the name of a
certain man who lived in Nazareth between the years 1 and 30—
with the title "the Christ," expressing in the mythological tradition
a special figure with a special function. The Messiah—in Greek,
Christos—is the "annointed one" who has received an unction from
God enabling him to establish the reign of God in Israel and in the
world. Therefore, the name Jesus Christ must be understood as
"Jesus who is called the Christ," or "Jesus who is the Christ," or
"Jesus as the Christ," or "Jesus the Christ." The context determines
which of these interpretive phrases should be used; but one of them
should be used in order to keep the original meaning of the name
"Jesus Christ" alive, not only in theological thought but also in
ecclesiastical practice. Christian preaching and teaching must continually re-emphasize the paradox that the man Jesus is called the
Christ—a paradox which is often drowned in the liturgical and
homiletic use of "Jesus Christ" as a proper name. "Jesus Christ"
means—originally, essentially, and permanently—"Jesus who is the
Christ."

2. EVENT, FACT, AND RECEPTION

Jesus as the Christ is both a historical fact and a subject of believing reception. One cannot speak the truth about the event on

which Christianity is based without asserting both sides. Many theological mistakes could have been avoided if these two sides of the "Christian event" had been emphasized with equal strength. And Christian theology as a whole is undercut if one of them is completely ignored. If theology ignores the fact to which the name of Jesus of Nazareth points, it ignores the basic Christian assertion that Essential God-Manhood has appeared within existence and subjected itself to the conditions of existence without being conquered by them. If there were no personal life in which existential estrangement had been overcome, the New Being would have remained a quest and an expectation and would not be a reality in time and space. Only if the existence is conquered in *one* point—a personal life, representing existence as a whole—is it conquered in principle, which means "in beginning and in power." This is the reason that Christian theology must insist on the actual fact to which the name Jesus of Nazareth refers. It is why the church prevailed against competing groups in the religious movements of the first centuries. This is the reason that the church had to fight a vehement struggle with the gnostic-docetic elements within itself—elements which entered Christianity as early as the New Testament. And this is the reason that anyone who takes seriously the historical approach to the New Testament and its critical methods becomes suspect of docetic ideas, however strongly he may emphasize the factual side of the message of Jesus the Christ.

Nevertheless, the other side, the believing reception of Jesus *as* the Christ, calls for equal emphasis. Without this reception the Christ would not have been the Christ, namely, the manifestation of the New Being in time and space. If Jesus had not imposed himself as the Christ on his disciples and through them upon all following generations, the man who is called Jesus of Nazareth would perhaps be remembered as a historically and religiously important person. As such, he would belong to the preliminary revelation, perhaps to the preparatory segment of the history of revelation. He could then have been a prophetic anticipation of the New Being, but not the final manifestation of the New Being itself. He would not have been the Christ even if he had claimed to be the Christ. The receptive side of the Christian event is as important as the factual side. And only their unity creates the event upon which Christianity is based. According to later symbolism, the Christ is the head of the church, which is his body. As such, they are necessarily interdependent.

4. THE RESEARCH FOR THE HISTORICAL JESUS
AND ITS FAILURE

From the moment that the scientific method of historical research
was applied to biblical literature, theological problems which were
never completely absent became intensified in a way unknown to
former periods of church history. The historical method unites
analytical-critical and constructive-conjectural elements. For the
average Christian consciousness shaped by the orthodox doctrine of
verbal inspiration, the first element was much more impressive than
the second. One felt only the negative element in the term "criticism" and called the whole enterprise "historical criticism" or
"higher criticism" or, with reference to a recent method, "form criticism." In itself, the term "historical criticism" means nothing more
than historical research. Every historical research criticizes its
sources, separating what has more probability from that which has
less or is altogether improbable. Nobody doubts the validity of this
method, since it is confirmed continuously by its success; and nobody
seriously protests if it destroys beautiful legends and deeply rooted
prejudices. But biblical research became suspect from its very beginning. It seemed to criticize not only the historical sources but
the revelation contained in these sources. Historical research and
rejection of biblical authority were identified. Revelation, it was
implied, covered not only the revelatory content but also the historical form in which it had appeared. This seemed to be especially
true of the facts concerning the "historical Jesus." Since the biblical
revelation is essentially historical, it appeared to be impossible to
separate the revelatory content from the historical reports as they
are given in the biblical records. Historical criticism seemed to
undercut faith itself.

But the critical part of historical research into biblical literature
is the less important part. More important is the constructive-
conjectural part, which was the driving force in the whole enterprise. The facts behind the records, especially the facts about Jesus,
were sought. There was an urgent desire to discover the reality of
this man, Jesus of Nazareth, behind the coloring and covering
traditions which are almost as old as the reality itself. So the research
for the so-called "historical Jesus" started. Its motives were religious
and scientific at the same time. The attempt was courageous, noble,
and extremely significant in many respects. Its theological conse-

quences are numerous and rather important. But, seen in the light of its basic intention, the attempt of historical criticism to find the empirical truth about Jesus of Nazareth was a failure. The historical Jesus, namely, the Jesus behind the symbols of his reception as the Christ, not only did not appear but receded farther and farther with every new step. The history of the attempts to write a "life of Jesus," elaborated by Albert Schweitzer in his early work, *The Quest of the Historical Jesus,* is still valid. His own constructive attempt has been corrected. Scholars, whether conservative or radical, have become more cautious, but the methodological situation has not changed. This became manifest when R. Bultmann's bold program of a "demythologization of the New Testament" aroused a storm in all theological camps and the slumber of Barthianism with respect to the historical problem was followed by an astonished awakening. But the result of the new (and very old) questioning is not a picture of the so-called historical Jesus but the insight that there is no picture behind the biblical one which could be made scientifically probable.

This situation is not a matter of a preliminary shortcoming of historical research which will some day be overcome. It is caused by the nature of the sources itself. The reports about Jesus of Nazareth are those of Jesus as the Christ, given by persons who had received him as the Christ. Therefore, if one tries to find the real Jesus behind the picture of Jesus as the Christ, it is necessary critically to separate the elements which belong to the factual side of the event from the elements which belong to the receiving side. In doing so, one sketches a "Life of Jesus"; and innumerable such sketches have been made. In many of them scientific honesty, loving devotion, and theological interest have worked together. In others critical detachment and even malevolent rejection are visible. But none can claim to be a probable picture which is the result of the tremendous scientific toil dedicated to this task for two hundred years. At best, they are more or less probable results, able to be the basis neither of an acceptance nor of a rejection of the Christian faith.

In view of this situation, there have been attempts to reduce the picture of the historical Jesus to the "essentials," to elaborate a *Gestalt* while leaving the particulars open to doubt. But this is not a way out. Historical research cannot paint an essential picture after all the particular traits have been eliminated because they are questionable. It remains dependent on the particulars. Consequently, the pictures of the historical Jesus in which the form of a "Life of Jesus" is wisely avoided still differ from one another as much as those in which such self-restriction is not applied.

The dependence of the *Gestalt* on the valuation of the particulars is evident in an example taken from the complex of what Jesus thought about himself. In order to elaborate this point, one must know, besides many other things, whether he applied the title "Son of Man" to himself and, if so, in what sense. Every answer given to this question is a more or less probable hypothesis, but the character of the "essential" picture of the historical Jesus depends decisively on this hypothesis. Such an example clearly shows the impossibility of replacing the attempt to portray a "Life of Jesus" by trying to paint the *"Gestalt* of Jesus."

At the same time, this example shows another important point. People who are not familiar with the methodological side of historical research and are afraid of its consequences for Christian doctrine like to attack historical research generally and the research in the biblical literature especially, as being theologically prejudiced. If they are consistent, they will not deny that their own interpretation is also prejudiced or, as they would say, dependent on the truth of their faith. But they deny that the historical method has objective scientific criteria. Such an assertion, however, cannot be maintained in view of the immense historical material which has been discovered and often empirically verified by a universally used method of research. It is characteristic of this method that it tries to maintain a permanent self-criticism in order to liberate itself from any conscious or unconscious prejudice. This is never completely successful, but it is a powerful weapon and necessary for achieving historical knowledge.

One of the examples often given in this context is the treatment of the New Testament miracles. The historical method approaches the miracle stories neither with the assumption that they have happened because they are attributed to him who is called the Christ nor with the assumption that they have not happened because such events would contradict the laws of nature. The historical method asks how trustworthy the records are in every particular case, how dependent they are on older sources, how much they might be influenced by the credulity of a period, how well confirmed they are by other independent sources, in what style they are written, and for what purpose they are used in the whole context. All these questions can be answered in an "objective" way without necessary interference of negative or positive prejudices. The historian never can reach certainty in this way, but he can reach high degrees of probability. It would, however, be a leap to another level if he transformed historical probability into positive or negative historical certainty by a judgment of faith (as will be shown at a later point). This clear distinction is often confused by the obvious fact that the understanding of the meaning of a text is partly dependent on the categories of understanding used in the encounter with texts and records. But it is not wholly dependent on them, since there are philological as well as other aspects which are open to an objective approach. Understanding demands one's participation in what one understands, and we can participate only in terms of what we are, including our own categories of understanding. But this "existential" understanding should never prejudice the judgment of the historian concerning facts and relations. The person whose ultimate concern is the content of the biblical message is in the same position as the one who is indifferent to it if such questions are discussed as the development of the Synoptic tradition, or the mythological and legendary elements of the New Testament. Both have the same criteria of historical probability and must use them with the same rigor, although doing so may affect their own religious or philosophical convictions or prejudices. In this process, it may happen that prejudices which close the eyes to particular facts open them to others. But this "opening of the eyes" is a personal experience which cannot be made into a methodological principle. There is only one methodological procedure, and that is to look at the subject matter and not at one's own looking at the subject matter. Actually, such looking is determined by many psychological, sociological, and historical factors. These aspects must be neglected intentionally by everyone who approaches a fact objectively. One must not formulate a judgment about the self-consciousness of Jesus from the fact that one is a Christian—or an anti-Christian. It must be derived from a degree of plausibility based on records and their probable historical validity. This, of course, presupposes that the content of the Christian faith is independent of this judgment.

The search for the historical Jesus was an attempt to discover a minimum of reliable facts about the man Jesus of Nazareth, in order to provide a safe foundation for the Christian faith. This attempt was a failure. Historical research provided probabilities about Jesus of a higher or lower degree. On the basis of these probabilities, it sketched "Lives of Jesus." But they were more like novels than biographies; they certainly could not provide a safe foundation for the Christian faith. Christianity is not based on the acceptance of a historical novel; it is based on the witness to the messianic character of Jesus by people who were not interested at all in a biography of the Messiah.

The insight into this situation induced some theologians to give up any attempt to construe a "life" or a *Gestalt* of the historical Jesus and to restrict themselves to an interpretation of the "words of Jesus." Most of these words (though not all of them) do not refer to himself and can be separated from any biographical context. Therefore, their meaning is independent of the fact that he may or may not have said them. On that basis the insoluble biographical problem has no bearing on the truth of the words rightly or wrongly recorded as the words of Jesus. That most of the words of Jesus have parallels in contemporaneous Jewish literature is not an argument against their validity. This is not even an argument against their uniqueness and power as they appear in collections like the Sermon on the Mount, the parables, and the discussions with foes and followers alike.[1]

A theology which tries to make the words of Jesus into the historical foundation of the Christian faith can do so in two ways. It can treat the words of Jesus as the "teachings of Jesus" or as the "message of Jesus." As the teachings of Jesus, they are understood as refined interpretations of the natural law or as original insights into the nature of man. They have no relation to the concrete situation in which they are spoken. As such, they belong to the law, prophecy, or Wisdom literature such as is found in the Old Testament. They may transcend all three categories in terms of depth and power; but they do not transcend them in terms of character. The retreat in historical research to the "teachings of Jesus" reduces Jesus to the level of the Old Testament and implicitly denies his claim to have overcome the Old Testament context.

The second way in which historical research restricts itself to the

---

[1] This refers also to the discovery of the Dead Sea Scrolls, which—in spite of much sensationalism in the publicity given to it—has opened the eyes of many people to the problem of biblical research but which has not changed the theological situation at all.

words of Jesus is more profound than the first. It denies that the words of Jesus are general rules of human behaviour, that they are rules to which one has to subject one's self, or that they are universal and can therefore be abstracted from the situation in which they were spoken. Instead, they emphasize Jesus' message that the Kingdom of God is "at hand" and that those who want to enter it must decide for or against the Kingdom of God. These words of Jesus are not general rules but concrete demands. This interpretation of the historical Jesus, suggested especially by Rudolf Bultmann, identifies the meaning of Jesus with that of his message. He calls for a decision, namely, the decision for God. And this decision includes the acceptance of the Cross, by his own acceptance of the Cross. The historically impossible, namely, to sketch a "life" or a *Gestalt* of Jesus, is ingeniously avoided by using the immediately given—namely, his message about the Kingdom of God and its conditions—and by keeping as nearly as possible to the "paradox of the Cross of the Christ." But even this method of restricted historical judgments cannot give a foundation to the Christian faith. It does not show how the requirement of deciding for the Kingdom of God can be fulfilled. The situation of having to decide remains one of being under the law. It does not transcend the Old Testament situation, the situation of the quest for the Christ. One could call this theology "existentialist liberalism" in contrast to the "legalist liberalism" of the first. But neither method can answer the question of wherein lies the power to obey the teachings of Jesus or to make the decision for the Kingdom of God. This these methods cannot do because the answer must come from a new reality, which, according to the Christian message, is the New Being in Jesus as the Christ. The Cross is the symbol of a gift before it is the symbol of a demand. But, if this is accepted, it is impossible to retreat from the being of the Christ to his words. The last avenue of the search for the historical Jesus is barred, and the failure of the attempt to give a foundation to the Christian faith through historical research becomes obvious.

This result would probably have been more easily acknowledged if it had not been for the semantic confusion about the meaning of the term "historical Jesus." The term was predominantly used for the results of historical research into the character and life of the person who stands behind the Gospel reports. Like all historical knowledge, our knowledge of this person is fragmentary and hypocritical. Historical research subjects this knowledge to method-ological skepticism and to continuous change in particulars as well as essentials. Its ideal is to reach a high degree of probability, but in many cases this is impossible.

The term "historical Jesus" is also used to mean that the event "Jesus as the Christ" has a factual element. The term in this sense raises the question of faith and not the question of historical re-search. If the factual element in the Christian event were denied, the foundation of Christianity would be denied. Methodological skepticism about the work of historical research does not deny this element. Faith cannot even guarantee the name "Jesus" in respect to him who was the Christ. It must leave that to the incertitudes of our historical knowledge. But faith does guarantee the factual trans-formation of reality in that personal life which the New Testament expresses in its picture of Jesus as the Christ. No fruitful and honest discussion is possible if these two meanings of the term "historical Jesus" are not clearly distinguished.

CHAPTER 27

The Good News of Jesus and the
Proclamation of the Early Church

JOACHIM JEREMIAS

Professor Jeremias of Goettingen asserts vigorously the
necessity of stressing the original historical event as an
essential part of the Gospel message. The historical event
is the "call" of God; the faith of the community is the
"response." But "the call, not the response, is the decisive
thing." Thus he rejects the tendency toward allowing the
kerygma or the community to become the final focus of the
message.

THIS brings us to one final query. If it is true that the good news
of Jesus in word and deed is the origin of Christianity, then it
may be asked: What is the relation between the good news of Jesus
and the early church's witness of faith? What is the relation between the pre-resurrection and the post-resurrection message,
between the gospel and the kerygma? With regard to these questions there are two things to be said.

(1) The good news of Jesus and the early church's witness of
faith are inseparable from one another. Neither of these may be
treated in isolation. For the gospel of Jesus remains dead history
without the witness of faith by the church, which continually re-
iterates, affirms, and attests this gospel afresh. Nor can the kerygma
be treated in isolation either. Apart from Jesus and his gospel the
kerygma is merely the proclamation of an idea or a theory. To

From Joachim Jeremias, *The Problem of the Historical Jesus*, 1964, pp. 22–24.
Reprinted by permission of Fortress Press, Philadelphia.

isolate the message of Jesus leads to Ebionitism; to isolate the kerygma of the early church leads to Docetism.[1]

(2) If, then, these two belong together, the gospel of Jesus and the early church's witness of faith, and if neither of these may be isolated, it is also of utmost importance to recognize—and this is decisive—that they are not both on the same level. The gospel of Jesus and the kerygma of the early church must not be placed on the same footing, but they are related to one another as call and response. The life, acts, and death of Jesus, the authoritative word of him who dared to say *abba*, the one who with divine authority invited sinners to his table, and as the servant of God went to the cross—all this is the call of God. The early church's witness of faith, the Spirit-led chorus of a thousand tongues, is the response to God's call. The ancient church liked to express this relationship in pictorial representations of the cosmic liturgy, in the midst of which is depicted a gigantic figure of the Crucified, toward whom, from the right and the left, there streams a countless throng on earth and in heaven. What such representations say is that Jesus of Nazareth is God's call to his creatures; confession of him is their response. This response always has a double aspect: it is praise and adoration of God, and witness to the world. It is inspired by the Spirit of God, but it does not take the place of the call. The call, not the response, is the decisive thing. The many-sided witness of the early church—of Paul, of John, of the Epistle to the Hebrews—must be judged in light of the message of Jesus.

Underlying our protest against the equating of the gospel and the kerygma is a concern for the concept of revelation. According to the witness of the New Testament, there is no other revelation of God but the incarnate Word. The preaching of the early church, on the other hand, is the divinely inspired witness *to* the revelation, but the church's preaching is not itself the revelation. To put it bluntly, revelation does not take place from eleven to twelve o'clock on Sunday morning. Golgotha is not everywhere; there is only *one*

---

[1] [Ebionitism was the variety of Jewish Christianity which separated from the church and became a sect emphasizing the necessity of the Law for salvation; it opposed Paul and presented only a minimal Christology, rejecting the Virgin Birth of Jesus and seeing in him only a man filled by the Spirit of God. For "Docetism," cf. note 17, above. Ebionitism severed its connection with the church of which Paul was an apostle; Docetism contested the connection of faith with the story of Jesus in all its stark reality.—EDITOR.]

Golgotha, and it lies just outside the walls of Jerusalem.[2] The doctrine of continuous revelation *(revelatio continua)* is a gnostic heresy. No, the church's proclamation is, from its earliest beginnings, not itself revelation, but it does guide toward the Revelation. This, at any rate, is the way Paul conceived of the task of the kerygma when he told the Galatians that the content of his preaching had been the depiction of Christ crucified before their eyes. (Gal. 3:1; cf. I Cor. 2:2).

Once more: according to the witness of the New Testament, the church's proclamation is not revelation, but it leads to the revelation. Jesus is the Lord. The Lord is above the one who proclaims the message. For faith, there is no other authority but the Lord. Hence, the historical Jesus and his message are not *one* presupposition among many for the kerygma, but the *sole* presupposition of the kerygma. Thus, indeed, the response presupposes the call, and the witness to the revelation presupposes the revelation. Only the Son of man and his word can give authority to the proclamation. No one else and nothing else.

[2] P. Althaus, *Das sogenannte Kerygma, op. cit.*, p. 34; Eng. trans. p. 58.

CHAPTER 28

The Church and the Reality of Christ

JOHN KNOX

Professor Knox, formerly of Union Theological Seminary and now at Episcopal Theological Seminary of the South-west, Austin, Texas, has sometimes seemed to belong in the same camp with Bultmann, Harvey, and Tillich quoted in sections 24–26. In the volume from which this selection is taken, however, he affirms: "It belongs to our existence as Christians to affirm the actuality of Jesus' experience—and not merely the bare fact of it, but something of the full, distinctive quality of it" (p. 21). In the chapter quoted below he argues that this affirmation is possible because of the link of the believing community to the historical Jesus through its living memory. This link does not provide de-tailed knowledge but, Professor Knox argues, it provides certain and definite knowledge of the real person behind the portrait.

For the purposes of this argument, the value of communal memories for scientific historiography does not need to be dem-onstrated, either as fact or as possibility. Our main point is, not that they are true, but that they exist—that is, exist as memories. Their content is for those who hold them a *remembered* content and therefore is *for them* not only true as facts are true, but real as actual life is real—the one, because the other. To share in a common memory is to participate in an experience of the meaning of a past event whose actuality can be as little doubted as the meaning itself.

If in this there be any truth at all, it cannot seem strange that one should speak of the Church's "memory" and more particularly of its memory of Jesus. Whatever else the Church is, it is a historical community, a cultural stream flowing without interruption from the first century into our own. Not merely its outward forms of belief and cult, but its inner substance has been largely transmitted from generation to generation in a continuous corporate life. Of this inner substance, as in all historical communities, shared memories form a large part; and that among these there should be some memory of Jesus himself ought not to seem incredible. So much can be said simply on the basis of the Church's nature as a historical community; but when one considers certain unique characteristics of the Church—features which distinguish it from other historical communities and make it the particular community it is—one finds that all we have observed about the reality and importance of common memory in the existence of historical communities acquires new point and force.

The first of these unique features appears when we remind ourselves of the singular significance which history has for the Church. Any work on modern historiography[1] is likely to note this fact and its importance. The Church has always been uniquely preoccupied with the idea of history, and it is hardly too much to say that it was in its life and thought that history first acquired full reality and universality. By "reality" I mean real movement in real time, from a beginning in the past to an end in the future—not the interminable cycle of nature, nor yet the mere successive bodying forth in transient forms of eternal and unchanging ideas. History involved real change; its events were not appearances only, "flowing, so to speak, over the surfaces of things," but were of the stuff and substance of existence. God was not aloof and inert; he was an actor, a doer. There was a *time* when he made the world out of nothing and there will be a *time* when he will bring it to an end. Meanwhile, he is working in it, creating and destroying, judging and healing.

This way of realizing the meaning of history had long been characteristic of Hebrew thought; but in being appropriated by the Church it was set free from nationalistic presuppositions which had limited and to a degree corrupted it. All mankind in the whole range of its history was now seen to constitute the field of God's creative work. The Church was no favored class or race, static and closed.

[1] As, e.g., that of R. G. Collingwood, *The Idea of History* (Oxford: Clarendon Press, 1946), pp. 46–52. The quoted phrase later in this paragraph is taken from this passage.

It was created to be the constantly enlarging sphere of God's healing, reconciling action for and among all men; and the center of
universal history was the moment when this "creation" took place,
this "action" began. Unless it be the Hebrew-Jewish people, no
historical community has ever been so fully engaged with history,
so deeply involved in it and so profoundly aware of its own involvement, as the Christian Church. And unless it be the Exodus from
Egypt, no historical event has ever been the object of such constant
recall and such sustained reflection as the Event in which the
Church had its rise. Would we not expect that in such a community memory would have an especially large place?

We must note, as a second feature, how completely dominated
the remembered Event is by the person of Jesus. I have referred to
the Event as the coming into existence of the Church. This, I have
argued in the preceding chapter, is the only accurate and adequate
way formally to define the Event, and most of this book will be devoted to showing the important implications of this formal definition.
But it says nothing about the actual content of the Event—persons,
circumstances, incidents—the "material," so to speak, to which the
Church's beginning gave unity, meaning, and identity. Now I should
say that all *evaluation* of the Event, all *theological interpretation*
of it, will have its ground, whether recognized or not, in one's
acceptance of the truth of the formal definition I have proposed.
But it is equally clear that whatever *memory* we may have of the
Event must be memory of its "content." One does not "remember"
ideas or concepts or generalizations or formal definitions, however
true they may be; one *remembers* only persons and things and happenings. And of this remembered content of the so-called Christ
Event, Jesus is the completely dominating center. Is there another
important event in human history consisting to so large an extent in
the simple existence of a single individual and the response which
he awakened? Surely we may say, then, that if in the Christian
community there has come down within and through the generations any authentic memory of its beginnings, that memory is a
memory of him.

We may observe, in passing, that this central and dominating
position of Jesus and his career within the content of the Event
makes somewhat difficult and strange for us the definition of its
essential character which I have been defending. I feel sure we find
it easier to agree with the definition of the American Revolution as

the coming into being of the United States of America than with the corresponding definition of the Event of Christ as the coming into being of the Church. And I suggest that the greater difficulty in the latter case is associated with the comparative simplicity of the content of the Event. When we consider the Revolution in its actual progress, we are concerned with declarations from many sources, battles won and lost by many warriors, decisions made and executed by many statesmen. In a word, we see a complicated interplay of persons and other factors; and, looking for unity, we are almost driven to recognize in the *issue* of the contest, in the emergence of the independent state, the only clue to its meaning and therefore to its being as the particular historical event it was. But although it is just as true that the Event of Christ has its reality as such in the emergence of the Church, this fact is more likely to be hidden from us because of the relative simplicity of what we actually see. Because Jesus is so incomparably important in the content of the Event, we find it easy to suppose that we do not need to look further than his career for its meaning. But this supposition is mistaken. Nothing could be more surely true than that the man Jesus —what he was heard to say and seen to do, what he was known to be, what was observed to happen to him—was the supremely important, almost the sole, content of the Event; for this reason we remember him. But it is not this remembered or recorded content which makes the Event the particular event it was, but rather the emerging community, where alone the memory had existence and Jesus himself historical importance.

A third feature of the Church which has the effect of establishing in a unique way the memory of Jesus within its life is its knowledge of the Resurrection. The meaning of this knowledge requires a chapter of its own, but its relation to the Church's memory must at least be noted now, although this aspect of the general theme will also belong within the later discussion. Not infrequently the "risen Christ" has been set rather sharply over against the "Jesus of history." If by the latter phrase one means the "Jesus" whose existence and character can be established by the methods of the historian, the separation is perhaps justified, for this "Jesus" may be found outside the Church, whereas the "risen Christ" can be known only within it. But if by the "Jesus of history" one means simply the man of Nazareth, the human Jesus, then the kind of separation we often make between the terms is not legitimate, for the particular knowledge of this Jesus which the Church has and treasures, quite as truly as its knowledge of the risen Lord, can be found only within it. He is *remembered* there; and the very meaning of the term "resurrection" requires the prior existence of this memory. The Church could not recognize one whom it did not remember. We cannot know again what we have not known before. The knowledge of Christ risen from the dead not only is inalienable, but also is near the center of the Church's existence. The meaning of that statement we shall consider more fully later. The point just now is that this knowledge inescapably and constantly implies the remembrance of Jesus, and that every recognition of Christ's reality and living presence in the worship of the Church is also an appeal to a memory of the human Jesus which belongs just as essentially to the Church's life.

This reference to worship suggests the last two items in this review of unique features of the Church. One of these is the customary reading from the New Testament, the collection of documents produced by the Church under the immediate impact of the Event and reflecting most vividly the primitive remembrance of Jesus. Here we are bound to think, first of all, of the Gospels, but the Epistles are almost as important, and sometimes even more important. For although the Epistles are less concerned with the facts of Jesus' career, they reflect, often more directly and immediately than the Gospels, the Church's remembrance of the man himself. The more precise relation of these early documents, especially the Gospels, to the Church's memory will be discussed a little later; but that the constant devotional use of them in private and corporate worship since very early times has had the effect of emphasizing within the life of the Church the importance of its memory of Jesus and of confirming the memory itself—this is so obvious as to need no discussion.

The final item, and certainly one of the most important, is the Lord's Supper. This rite has been the central act in the worship of the Church since the very beginning. It probably antedates both Scripture reading and preaching in Christian worship, although the associations of the three are very early and very close. The Supper has many meanings, symbolizing as it does the whole concrete reality of the Church's existence and of our actual, almost bodily, participation in it, and it will be referred to in other connections. Of particular relevance just now is the fact that the Supper has always been in a pre-eminent sense an occasion for recalling Jesus. It has always been "in remembrance of [him]." Long before the Gospels were written or before what Justin Martyr called "the memoirs of the apostles" could be read, Christians were asking, "Do you remember . . . ?" or were exhorting one another to "remember," as they met in their weekly or daily celebrations of God's creative, saving act in Christ—an act in the very substance of which they were being given to share. Ought it to be surprising that such a historical community, at the center of whose corporate life from its beginning had been such an act of remembrance, should have preserved some authentic memory of Jesus?

But whether deemed "authentic" or not by the disinterested observer, the memory is bound to seem so to one who shares in it; and this is the principal point I am seeking to make. The image the Church has of Jesus is such an image as belongs to memory. As such it is the Church's intimate and sure possession.

Thus far in this chapter we have dealt only with the question whether we can properly speak of the Church's "remembering" at all and, more particularly, of its "remembering" Jesus. We must now consider what this memory contains and how it is related to the Gospels, our only written records of Jesus' life. These two questions are closely related and can be best discussed together.

We may begin with a remark which applies not only to the Gospels, but also to the New Testament in all its parts. These documents are more valuable for the testimony they bear to the existence and nature of the early Church's memory of Jesus than for any statement of more "objective" fact they may make about him and his career. This is true because of both the greater certainty of this testimony and its greater relevance. As regards certainty, it is clear that the ancient documents put us directly and indubitably in touch with the memory, whereas we must establish the more objective facts by inference and argument. In many cases this can be done with the highest degree of probability; still, it remains true that any knowledge derived from the New Testament of what, precisely, Jesus said or did is, and must be, less certain than the knowledge of how he was remembered to have spoken and acted, and that any knowledge derived from this same source of what he was is really knowledge of what he was remembered as being. But the latter kind of knowledge has also the greater relevance. For Jesus of Nazareth, Jesus as a human being, insofar as he has any importance for Christian existence, is a memory of the Church. We will not say "only a memory," any more than a devoted family will say "only a memory" in referring to a deceased parent. In both cases the person in the past is very real and very important; but he exists as someone remembered, however significant the memory may be. One way of describing the Church is to say that it is the community which remembers Jesus; but one can equally truly define Jesus (in the only really significant meaning of that name for the Christian) as the one who is remembered. It is only as he is remembered that he has meaning for either Christian theology or Christian devotion. In a word, the human existence of Jesus, insofar as it has continuing being and importance, is a memory of the Church.

Although the reminder is probably not necessary, it will be safer to point out that we cannot think of the New Testament as providing us with an extra-ecclesiastical source for the "historical Jesus," or indeed for anything else. If the only surviving memory of Jesus is the Church's memory, the New Testament, which attempts (among other things) to record and convey that memory, is even more obviously the Church's book. Its several documents were written out of the Church's experience, and out of that experience alone. It does not provide us with a place to stand outside the Church; on the contrary, it draws us more deeply into the Church. It does not bring us what happened in some purely objective sense (as though that would be possible anyhow), but what was believed, and often remembered, to have happened by those among whom the event first occurred. To be sure, the New Testament does serve as a check upon, as well as a resource for, the life of the Church (including its memory) in every age, but this is because it speaks to us directly out of the life of the Church and the memory of the Church in its first, and in some ways most authentic, age—not because it has a position outside the Church or even alongside the Church in any sense or degree whatever. Its experience of Christ is in every respect the Church's experience; its memory of Jesus, the Church's memory.

When we ask more precisely how the memory of the Church is related to what the Gospels say, I believe one must answer that the Church remembers both more and less than the Gospels contain. It remembers *more* inasmuch as its image of Jesus himself, especially in his relation to his disciples, is not fully provided by the Gospels and could not be derived from them. It remembers *less* inasmuch as most of the factual content of such knowledge of Jesus as we have is provided by the Gospels alone. Since the second of these statements is likely to appear the more obviously true, we shall consider it first.

Here I must make clear that in affirming that a memory of Jesus exists in the Church, I am not suggesting that it contains a single specific datum concerning the circumstances or incidents of Jesus' career or a single sentence from his lips—that it contains anything at all which might in a specific way confirm, discredit, correct or supplement any item in the Gospels. For such facts of Jesus' career we are entirely dependent upon the written sources—and, one may add, upon these sources as understood by the critical historian. When I say, then, that the Church remembers Jesus, I do not mean that it remembers *facts about him*. Indeed, it is doubtful that we can ever properly be said to *remember* a fact about anything. Facts about things are abstractions; only the things themselves can in the strict sense be remembered. Although it would be rash indeed to say that many of the facts stated in the Gospels—that Jesus said or did this or that, that he went here or there, that this or that thing happened to him or in his presence—do not go back to a primitive memory of concrete events themselves, it would be much more rash to assert that there has persisted in the Church any independent remembrance of these same facts by which they can be tested. I certainly do not want to be understood as making such an assertion. The Gospels obviously tell us more about Jesus than any "memory" of the Church can be said to contain.

Moreover, they tell us a great deal. We have recognized the character of the Gospels as "Church books," reflecting in manifold ways the experiences and reflections of the churches in the final decades of the first century and adapted to meeting the felt needs of these primitive communities. But undoubtedly one of these felt needs was the need of authentic information about Jesus; and equally certainly the basic material in the composition of the Gospels was a tradition about him which went back to the earliest memories of the Church. Discrimination between this basic material and later accretions is exceedingly difficult and can never perhaps be at the same time both precise and sure. But I stand with those who believe that however critical our methods may be, we are left with a very substantial residuum of historically trustworthy fact about Jesus, his teaching and his life. It would fall outside the purpose of this book to try to indicate either the contents or the limits of this body of information;[2] but it is, without any question, considerable; and new studies in fresh areas (as, for example, in the Dead Sea Scrolls) are to a degree clarifying and confirming it. Although one could not truly say that the Church vitally requires this information—the Church really needs to know of Jesus only what it "remembers" of him—nevertheless, it is of great importance to the Church and we can be immensely grateful for it. My point at the moment, however, is simply that the Gospels undoubtedly tell us more about Jesus than any independent memory of the Church could conceivably provide.

But they also tell us less—and here a longer argument will be required. They tell us less because the image of Jesus himself which the Church carries in its heart cannot be derived simply and solely from the Gospels and has not in fact been derived from that source. It existed before the Gospels were written, and the Gospels, when they were written, did not displace it. The Gospels performed the immense service of putting into written form the words of Jesus and the stories about him with which the earliest shared memories of Jesus were associated. They do for us what the original materials of this kind, orally repeated in teaching and worship, did for the primitive Church. Not only would the remembrance of Jesus be immeasurably poorer without them; it is hard to see how, without them, it could ever have existed at all in any tangible or communicable form. But to say this is not to say that the memory itself was in early times nothing more than the aggregate of the scattered oral traditions and that now it is simply the Gospels which contain them. Such a statement is not true to the facts of the Church's life.

For the truth of the matter is that, whether the Church is deemed to have a right to this knowledge or not, it has always known more of Jesus than the Gospels tell us—not, I repeat, more facts about him or his life, but more of the man himself. Its picture of Jesus has not been derived solely from the Gospels. One can almost hear the obvious ironical retort: "Of course not! But how much better if it had been! Every generation and class of Christians has had its own picture. Each age has constructed 'Jesus' in its own image." The truth in this charge is not to be denied; the "peril of modernizing

[2] The recently translated book of G. Bornkamm, *Jesus of Nazareth* (New York: Harper & Brothers, 1961) is of great significance because of its success in doing this.

Jesus" is always present and is never entirely escaped. But having recognized this, we must not make the opposite error of assuming that all we truly know about the Jesus of the past is written in the Gospels and that therefore everything in the Church's image of Jesus which cannot be derived from a critical examination of the Gospels is an example of modernizing fancy. Such a conclusion denies the possibility that there has come down within the body of the Church—in, around, and underneath the Gospel materials and reflected more directly in certain statements in the Epistles— an authentic remembrance of Jesus. This a priori denial is arbitrary and ignores a basic element in the existence of all historical communities and of the Church in particular: the persistence of memory, the continuing presence, however muted, of what Papias centuries ago in this same connection called "the living and abiding voice." [3]

I venture to suggest two elements in this memory. One of them has to do with the personal moral stature of Jesus. This, I believe the Church knows, was greater than the Gospels alone would force us to conclude. Let it not be thought that I am in the slightest degree disparaging the greatness of the person who would emerge simply from the Gospels; I *am* saying that this person is not so great as the Church "remembers" Jesus to have been. The proof of this lies in the fact that critical studies of the "life" of Jesus, even when written by the ablest and most responsible historians on the basis of the most honest and careful examination of the Gospels, have never succeeded in satisfying the Church—that is, in seeming really adequate and true. I do not think that one can explain this fact by saying: "The historians have not been sufficiently gifted. They have lacked imagination and insight. The Gospels really say more about the 'historical Jesus' than historians have been able or have taken the trouble to hear." Such a statement would be unfair to scholars

[3] Quoted in Eusebius, *Church History*, III. 39. 4. This "memory" is obviously related to what the Church has called "tradition," but is not to be identified with it. The "memory," unlike "tradition," does not contain either factual data in the ordinary sense or doctrinal formulations. Its content is more concrete. So far as the original Event is concerned, it is only Jesus himself who is *remembered*. Still, it seems to me that a sound instinct has been at work among those who have insisted on the reality and importance of an extrascriptural source of knowledge of the Church's own intimate past. On this general subject see G. H. Tavard, *Holy Writ or Holy Church* (New York: Harper & Brothers, 1959), especially the discussion of John Eck on pp. 117 ff.

like Goguel and Guignebert, Case and Cadbury.[4] But neither can one explain the Church's dissatisfaction with such critical studies by saying: "The Church has in its mind the image of a divine being whom the historian cannot find in history simply because he was never there, and in the nature of the case, could never have been there. It has created out of its later experiences and reflection a purely illusory image of Jesus and can be content with nothing else." Such a statement does not do justice to the Church's concern for truth. Although both "explanations" are valid and relevant up to a certain point, they fall short of fully explaining the biographer's "failure." What must also be taken into account is the fact that we are dealing here, not with a historical figure known only through documentary sources, but with a beloved person the memory of whom has come down from generation to generation within the body of an organic human community. The fact that this process of transmission would probably have been quite impossible without the Gospels to guide and guard it must not blind us to the fact that it is something more and other than the Gospels. The Church has an impression of the moral greatness of Jesus which cannot have been derived simply from these books. Indeed, are we not constantly reading them, and sometimes even correcting them, under the influence of this prior impression? Here, as I have already hinted, the Epistles may often be more important than the Gospels because they reflect it more immediately.

The Christian cannot regard this impression as illusory, and one may offer strong arguments for its truth by appealing to the magnitude of the historical consequences which followed upon the brief career. But the Church's impression does not rest upon such arguments, nor can it be fully justified or sustained by them. One must simply say that the impression is there, that it belongs, and has always belonged, to the existence of the Church. It is a feature of what can only be called the Church's remembrance of Jesus. Others may doubt its truth; the Church is incapable of doing so.

---

[4] I have in mind such books as M. Goguel, *The Life of Jesus*, trans. O. Wyon (New York: The Macmillan Company, 1933); C. A. H. Guignebert, *Jesus*, trans. S. H. Hooke (London: Kegan Paul, Trench, Trubner & Co., 1935); S. J. Case, *Jesus; a New Biography* (Chicago: University of Chicago Press, 1927); H. J. Cadbury, *The Peril of Modernizing Jesus* (New York: The Macmillan Company, 1937); *Jesus: What Manner of Man?* (New York: The Macmillan Company, 1947).

Another element in the Church's image of Jesus which does not rest solely on what the Gospels say has to do with the relation in which he stood to his disciples and friends, and they to him. The relation was from the beginning remembered as one of love, that same kind or quality of love (agape) which the Church now knew as the bond of unity within its own life. It not only *knew* this love as a present continuing reality within the fellowship of the Church, but it also *remembered* it as already manifested in Jesus. Here again we touch on the meaning of the Resurrection, for the agape known in the Church, and known there as the Spirit of God, his very presence, could not have been recognized also as the Spirit of Christ if the same agape had not been remembered as the essential and distinctive quality of Jesus' own life.

I have said that the Church's knowledge of this quality goes beyond what the Gospels say. These are, generally speaking, strangely silent about Jesus' own inner attitudes, states of mind and heart. They tell us where he went, what he did or said, what happened to him, but rarely give us any hint of what he was feeling. One may infer from his teaching about God how he himself felt toward God, but we are not explicitly told. One may draw conclusions from his ethical teaching, not only as to how he *thought* about one's duty toward others, but also as to what his actual feelings toward others were; but these are never described and are seldom referred to. Sometimes, in his most passionate (and most characteristic) teachings, his inner feelings break through what may appear to be the determined objectivity of the Gospel record, and one seems for a moment to hear his very voice. But these occasions are rare indeed; and I wonder just what impression of the inner personal life of Jesus we should have if we needed to depend on the Gospels alone, or whether we should be able to hear his voice in his recorded words if we were not also hearing it in the common life of the Church.

My point, however, is somewhat different from this. I am referring primarily, not to the characteristic attitudes of Jesus toward God and toward men generally, but to his more intimate relation with those who responded to him and who formed the company of his disciples; and here, I believe it is true to say, the "memory" of the Church goes far beyond anything a critical reading of the Gospels would alone justify. Undoubtedly one reason the Church has always cherished the Fourth Gospel and has been unable to believe that it does not contain authentic historical truth about Jesus is that one can read there, and there only, such words as "Having loved his own . . . he loved them to the end" and "This is my commandment, that you love one another as I have loved you" (John 13:1; 15:12) —words which express a love of Jesus for his own which has a deep, sure place in the memory of the Church. Here again this memory is first reflected in the Epistles: when Paul speaks of "the love of Christ," he is "remembering" the love of Jesus for his disciples as well as recognizing the gracious presence of the risen Lord. But it is only *reflected* there. It existed already in the body of the Church and exists there still, deeply indebted to Gospels and Epistles, but not created by them, not exhausted by them, and never entirely to be displaced by them.

In all of this I have not been trying to establish data which the secular historian will find acceptable or usable in his attempt to construct "the historical Jesus." Indeed, I can readily believe that many a *Christian* historian will turn from this chapter, not only unconvinced that we can properly speak of the Church's memory of Jesus, but also persuaded that to do so is to be sentimental, if not dangerously obscurantist. To the latter I would only say: "Examine yourself. Is the image of the human Jesus which you possess as a Christian derived entirely from the facts established by the Gospels, and are you no more certain of it than this evidence justifies? Is not your image of Jesus both richer and surer than this? I believe it is. Either, then, you divide yourself: as a Christian affirming what as a historian you know you have no right to affirm; or you are mistaken in thinking that you do not share in, depend on, and trust as valid and true, the Church's memory of Jesus." This memory is one aspect of the existential reality of the Church. Whatever evaluation may be made of it by others, the Church's picture of Jesus has what seems to it to be the character of a remembrance—that is, it is the picture of someone known to have been real. And this remembrance is absolutely vital to its existence. It is this fact about the Church—or, better, it is this element in its nature—which makes impossible its accepting any denial of the existence of Jesus or any disparagement of his importance. What God did in bringing the new community into being was done, it knows, through him.

CHAPTER 29

The Christ of Faith

JAMES S. STEWART

Professor Stewart of Edinburgh University responds in this article to the general position of Bultmann and his "school." In the first half of the article he outlines the essential characteristics of Bultmann's *kerygma* theology. In the second half, which is quoted below, he restates these same points indicating his own negative response to the position thus described. The material excerpted provides insight into both Bultmann's views and those of a thoughtful critic.

THUS far I have been concerned to show that this very influential trend in contemporary theology has a positive contribution to make to an understanding of the relation between the Jesus of the Gospels and the Christ of the believer's faith. I have listed eight points at which, I believe, it represents insights of real cogency and value. But there is another side to it, and it seems to me that not a few of its underlying assumptions are ill-founded and insecure. Even at the points of strength there are basic weaknesses. It may help to make this clear if we review again the characteristic features already noted.

(i) *The emphasis on the kerygma.* It is true to say that the Church lived by proclamation. But clearly it recognized another obligation as well: to repeat and transmit the tradition of Jesus' words and deeds. It is true that Christ crucified and risen confronted men in the kerygma as present event. But clearly that confrontation owed its authoritative, decisive character precisely to its being rooted and founded on historical fact. It would be unrealistic to suppose that the men who in the Acts of the Apostles said 'Yes' to the kerygma were quite unconscious of the fact that He in whom they now be-

From James S. Stewart, *The New Testament in Historical and Contemporary Perspective*, 1965, pp. 268–280. Reprinted by permission of Basil Blackwell, Oxford.

lieved had walked the earth and suffered under Pontius Pilate. In other words, the alternative '*Either* faith-evoking proclamation *or* factual information' is a false alternative. It is suggesting that the two things are mutually exclusive when in point of fact they are nothing of the kind. Surely the contemporizing of the past in the kerygma does not involve a dehistoricizing of the gospel. If the placarding of the cross in the mission preaching involved a recapitulation of the crucifixion in the life of the believer, surely it did *not* involve a repetition of the atoning death of Jesus, that death of which St. Paul in Rom. vi says that it happened once, never again, once and for all, and of which the writer to the Hebrews declares that it was precisely this historical finality which, cutting through the endless repetitiveness of cultic sacrifice, gave Christ's death its saving efficacy and creative power. What does Bultmann mean by saying:

> The salvation-occurrence is nowhere present except in the proclaiming, accosting, demanding, and promising word of preaching (*Theology*, I, 302)?

Are we not to say that the essential 'salvation-occurrence' is Calvary itself? It is equally wide of the mark when he asserts that 'Paul was won to the Christian faith by the kerygma of the Hellenistic Church' (I, 187). Is that a recognizable description of what happened at Damascus?

There is, in fact, a way of overemphasizing the kerygma which virtually denies the creative significance of Jesus. 'The personality of Jesus,' claims Bultmann, 'has no importance for the kerygma either of Paul or of John or for the New Testament in general' (op. cit., I, 35).

> Jesus' manner of life, His ministry, His personality, His character play no role at all; neither does Jesus' message (op. cit., I, 294).

This is the kind of statement which a closer study of the New Testament epistles makes extremely precarious. 'The primitive tradition of Jesus is brimful of history' (Bornkamm, *Jesus of Nazareth*, 26). It just will not do to reduce the historical evidence of the Gospels to kerygmatized theology, the creation of the Christian community. T. W. Manson once suggested a simple test that could be applied in this connection. All the Pauline letters antedate the earliest Gospel. Now these letters abound in utterances which could readily be transferred to Jesus and presented to the faithful as oracles of the Lord. But how many are? It seems a little odd that if the story of Jesus was the creation of the Christian community, no use should have been made of the excellent material offered by one of the most able, active and influential members of the community *(The Background of the New Testament and its Eschatology,* 214–215).

This is an acute and valid observation. It may be questioned whether the kerygmatic Christology which disowns any interest in the earthly Jesus is taking with sufficient seriousness the statement of the New Testament that 'the word became flesh' (John i. 14), 'a human personal life, in whose features we should seek the features of the Father. In the *kerygma* theology,' says Paul Althaus bluntly, 'the Word has become—*kerygma!*' *(The So-called Kerygma and the Historical Jesus,* 46). So, too, Eduard Schweizer with justifiable impatience expresses himself thus in a recent article:

> If man were a computer, he would need nothing except the shortest and most theoretical kerygma, and even this in the form of some holes punched into cardboard. Since man is no computer, but a being of flesh and blood, he needs the manifestation of God's revelation in flesh and blood in order to continue believing, that is, following Jesus *(New Testament Studies,* July 1964, p. 432).

(ii) There is *the Easter emphasis* of this theology. This again is a valid insight. The living Christ was the focus of the Church's faith. No part of the Gospel narrative was written without the assurance that God had made this Jesus both Lord and Christ (Acts ii. 36). But surely the whole point of the resurrection appearances to the disciples is precisely that the One whom they there recognized was identical with the Master who had first called them to discipleship. Surely it is this continuity that is the sense of Paul's citation in 1 Corinthians of the earliest resurrection tradition: actual witnesses were available (cf. Althaus, op. cit., 28). Surely Peter's remark 'whom having not seen, ye love' should warn us against the view that the early Christians were uninterested in the life, ministry and personality of Jesus.

We should expect those men, believing what they did about Jesus, to be immensely interested in recalling anything that He

had said or done, simply because He had said or done it, however remote they might be from the modern 'biographical'
interest (D. M. Baillie, op. cit., 57).

T. W. Manson was making the same point when he wrote:

> It is at least conceivable that one of the chief motives for
> preserving the stories at all, and for selecting those that were
> embodies in the Gospels, was just plain admiration and love for
> their hero (op. cit., 214).

It seems to me that it would be flagrantly unrealistic not to recognize this. C. F. D. Moule has expressed it well:

> The real core of worship was the experience of the risen
> Christ within the Christian Church through participation in
> the Spirit. But Christians knew well that if they lost sight of
> the story behind that experience their worship would be like
> a house built on sand; and that if they preached salvation
> without the story of how it came they would be powerless as
> evangelists; and that if they could not explain how they came
> to stand where they did, they would be failing to give a reason
> for their hope. . . . The Christians knew the difference between
> the two—between the pre-resurrection situation and the post-
> resurrection situation—and their aim was to try to tell faith-
> fully the story of how the former led to the latter. And in actual
> fact, they succeeded better than is often allowed (*New Tes-
> tament Essays*, 173).

Of course, the real trouble with Bultmann's position is that for him
the Easter occurrence does not fall within the category of historical
event, but rather represents the victory of the cross as envisaged and
reinterpreted by the faith of the believing community: it is Calvary's
redemptive meaning mythologically expressed. That members of his
own school are now beginning to react against this radical dehistoricizing of the tradition is evidenced by these significant words
of G. Bornkamm:

> The Easter aspect in which the primitive Church views the
> history of Jesus must certainly not be forgotten for one mo-
> ment; but not less the fact that it is precisely the history of
> Jesus before Good Friday and Easter which is seen in this
> aspect. Were it otherwise, the Church would have been lost
> in a timeless myth, even if for some irrelevant reason or other

she had given the bearer of this myth the name of Jesus. . . .
Quite clearly what the Gospels report concerning the message,
the deeds and the history of Jesus is still distinguished by an
authenticity, a freshness, and a distinctiveness not in any way
effaced by the Church's Easter faith. These features point us
directly to the earthly figure of Jesus (op. cit., 23–4).

(iii) *The eschatological emphasis.* Here again is an essential element in the kerygma. In the word of the gospel the age to come,
the world beyond, stands at the door and knocks. But the community that heard that sound was not imagining or inventing it:
what it was hearing was an echo from a historic event, an echo that
penetrated through the tumult and the shouting of history till it
seemed to fill the universe. St. Luke knew perfectly well, when he
took up his pen to write, that it was nothing less than the in-breaking
of the Kingdom of God that was to be his theme; but in his opening
sentences, with their crucial emphasis on the personal testimony of
eyewitnesses, there is revealed the evangelist's true understanding
of the nexus between eschatology and history (Luke i. 1-4). Thus
J. M. Robinson can rightly say that

> in the message and action of Jesus is implicit an eschatological
> understanding of His person, which becomes explicit in the
> kerygma of the primitive Church (op. cit., 16)

I feel, however, that Robinson is on less sure ground when he says
later that the Gospel traditions

> retain a concrete story about Jesus, but expand its horizon until
> the universal saving significance of the heavenly Lord becomes
> visible in the earthly Jesus (ibid., 95).

This might seem to imply that the Christian community so manipu-
lated its traditions and stretched the facts as to elicit an eschatological significance which had not inhered in the story from the
first. It is surely due to the touch of Jesus Himself, and not to any
retroactive intention of the community, that the whole story is
vibrant with the message: 'The hour cometh, and now is.'

(iv) There is cogency in the claim that *it is impossible to write a
'Life of Jesus.'* It is not only that the materials for a biography in
any strict sense of the word are lacking; it is also that so many
reconstructions have been modernizing and subjective, reflecting the
theological preconceptions of their authors. The human Jesus, the

Jesus of history, has in fact been all too human. Unfortunately, what has happened in certain quarters is what might have been foreseen: the strength of the reaction has almost carried Christology right over into docetism. The features of the Man of Nazareth vanish, and only a mystical Christ-idea is left. Must we not assert against this that the *kenosis* of the incarnation and the humanity of Jesus mean that it is with history that faith must reckon? Paul Althaus rightly insists that to neglect the historical question of the authenticity of the apostolic preaching is tantamount to refusing to take the *kenosis* seriously (op. cit., 52–3). 'The *fides humana* can never create the *fides divina,* but the latter is never without the former' (ibid., 63). And William Manson has argued conclusively that what was present to the Church's mind was 'a tradition which was not of its own making but which was objectively given to it' *(Jesus the Messiah,* 29). 'Plainly, it was not a case of the Church being in absolute control of the tradition. At many points the tradition was in control of the Church' (ibid., 46). T. W. Manson's view agrees with this. 'There is a good deal to be said,' he wrote, 'for treating the Gospels as historical documents concerning Jesus of Nazareth rather than as psychological case-material concerning the early Christians' *(Background and Eschatology,* 215). 'Who shall forbid us,' demands Gerhard Ebeling, 'to ask the question concerning the historic Jesus? This defeatism has no justification' (quoted by Stephen Neill, *The Interpretation of the New Testament,* p. 271).

(v) There is the argument that *the measuring-line of history cannot validly be applied Christologically to the Father-Son relationship.* To this the answer is, Who ever claimed that it could? That in Christ God Himself is intervening for the saving of my life and the reconciling of the world is of course known only to faith. Nevertheless, saving faith in its innermost character is determined by the assurance that something quite decisive has happened in history, something as real, as factual as the nails that were driven into Christ's hands on Calvary. Faith would not be what it is if it knew nothing of a Jesus who ministered to the needy, sought the sinful, healed the sick, and died on Golgotha. Bornkamm indeed seems to regard it as suspicious that each of these little story scenes within the Gospels appears to contain 'the person and history of Jesus in their entirety,' and he concludes that this is indicative of 'a popular and unhistorical transmission' of the material in which 'mere history as such means very little' (op. cit., 25). I should prefer to look elsewhere for the explanation of this phenomenon. If each story stands independently as a microcosm of the gospel, a mirror of the total ministry, may the real reason be, not lack of historical perspective, but simply this—that every word, every parable of Jesus was crammed with heaven and every apparently common act afire with God? It is a strange thing perhaps to say, but again and again in reading Bultmann I have had the impression that his own Christian understanding and experience have been stamped, in ways which his theology would deny, with the seal and imprint of the person of Jesus and the events of the ministry. It is not these events which create faith—did not the apostle say that faith is the gift of God? Yet in His inscrutable will God has linked His gift to history; and if its roots in the earth are cut, faith inevitably withers away.

(vi) Arising out of the previous point, there is the claim that *historical criticism cannot mediate Gospel truth*. Again, of course, this must be admitted—in the sense that our basic Christian convictions are not blown about by every changing wind of historical research. But what I find distasteful here is the easy assumption that much of the historical concern in the earlier quest for the true portrait of Jesus was neither more nor less than a substitute—often deliberate, sometimes perhaps unconscious—but at any rate a substitute for existential encounter. Thus J. M. Robinson writes:

> Whereas the *kerygma* calls for existential commitment to the meaning of Jesus, the original quest was an attempt to avoid the risk of faith by supplying objectively verified proof for its 'faith' (*A New Quest of the Historical Jesus*, 44).

Is this not a serious charge to make—that those engaged in the quest were 'attempting to avoid the risk of faith'? Does this not seem to call in question the integrity of the writers of the 'Jesus of history' school?

> Sometimes, [continues Robinson] historical critical scholars absolutized their method of objectivity into a permanent avoidance of existential encounter with the history they were supposedly studying (ibid., 47).

Actually, the truth of the matter is quite different. The truth is that what these scholars were doing was to recognize, and indeed quite rightly, the revelatory importance of events located within world history. St. Luke was not substituting historicism for existential encounter when he began the main portion of his book with

the words—'Now in the fifteenth year of the reign of Tiberius
Caesar, Pontius Pilate being governor of Judaea, Annas and Caiaphas
being the high priests, came the word of God' (Luke iii. 1, 2). He
knew that God's saving act was mixed up with Jews and Romans,
Caiaphas and Herod and Pilate and Caesar; and that if we do not
meet Him there we might as well flee to the mad mythology of the
Gnostic mystics without delay.

I have quoted earlier Bultmann's dictum that it is

> forbidden to go behind the *kerygma,* using it as a source to
> reconstruct a historical Jesus. That would be precisely the
> χριστὸς κατὰ σάρκα who belongs to the past *(Glauben und Ver-
> stehen,* I, 208).

But now it has to be said that this is totally misleading. What Paul
is repudiating in the passage in 2 Cor. v. 16 is not a knowledge of
and an interest in the historical Jesus: it is the inadequacy of an
unenlightened Messianism. (So Baillie, op. cit., 45; Althaus, op. cit.,
35–6.) That nothing was further from the intention of the apostles
than to belittle the significance of the life and character and example
of Jesus could be shown from repeated passages in Paul, the writer
to the Hebrews, and the First Epistle of John. It is not only, as
D. M. Baillie remarks, that an 'important strain of New Testament
teaching sets Jesus before us as the prototype of the Christian character' (op. cit., 45). There is also this—that in the Jesus of Galilee,
ministering to the sick, seeking the sinful, and offering friendship
and hope to the disinherited outcasts of society, there is a revelation
of the character of God. Away back in 1929 Paul Althaus made
this prophecy:

> I believe that in the next years we shall have remorsefully to
> readmit much into Christology that it is fashionable now to
> despise under the title of 'the personality of Christ' (op. cit., 36).

Can we say, or can we not, of the Figure who confronts us in the
Gospels, 'He who has seen this has seen the Father'? This is not, as
Bultmann would suggest, a matter of indifference. It is an immensely
important question. This was well argued by the late Principal John
Baillie:

> Not just that a Saviour came, but the kind of Saviour He was
> —not just that God was incarnate in a man, but the kind of
> man in which He was incarnate, constitutes the essence of the

Good News. . . . If we ourselves were ignorant of the narrative of the four Gospels, we should have found it impossible to accept the theology and Christology of the Epistles (*The Sense of the Presence of God*, 210 f.).

It may be true that it is impossible now to write a 'Life of Jesus.' It may be true that much of the historical framework is uncertain and problematical. It may even be true, as Robinson says, that

a saying which Jesus never spoke may well reflect accurately His historical significance, and in this sense be more 'historical' than many irrelevant things Jesus actually said (op. cit., 99),

though I confess I find this slur on the irrelevancies of Jesus not a little disturbing. But in the last resort is there not a self-authenticating quality in the Gospel portrait, that transcends all difficulties, refusing to be categorized as community invention or a reflexion of the *Sitz im Leben* of the early Church, and making some at least of the disparaging of the historical look slightly absurd? The *Sitz im Leben* argument is, of course, valid up to a point. But as too often used today it simply illustrates the fallacy of arguing in a circle: for, as T. W. Manson pointed out,

the alleged modifications or inventions in the Gospels are used to define the positions of the early Church, and these positions are then used to account for the phenomena presented by the Gospels (*Background and Eschatology*, 214).

And what are we to make of the cognate argument that, because the story as we have it was written by believers, therefore the real Jesus, the bare fact in and for itself, must remain inaccessible to us? Who is this 'real Jesus'? What is this 'bare fact'? Would we encounter the historical actuality of Jesus more accurately through the detached report of an agnostic or an unbeliever? If we say 'yes' to that, we are simply betraying a defective understanding of history as personal relationship. The fact is, as Professor Herbert Farmer has put it,

if the Christian faith is valid and Christ does in fact have the transcendent significance claimed for Him, then only an account written from the angle of that faith could convey a historically trustworthy impression of Him (*Interpreter's Bible*, I, 19).

Another way of putting this would be to say that God's Holy Spirit, in creating life, does not work in a vacuum: He begins from a witnessed, recorded event. Revelation, ἀποκάλυψις, comes from God's Spirit only, as indeed it came to Simon Peter at Caesarea Philippi. 'Flesh and blood have not revealed it unto thee.' 'And yet,' as D. M. Baillie rightly remarks,

> it remains true that the revelation came to Peter as an inward witness to the Jesus whom he knew in the flesh, and it comes to us as a witness to the Jesus whom we know as an historical Personality through the Gospel story (op. cit., 51).

To sum up, then, this stage in our argument. History is admittedly not the final criterion of Gospel truth. But neither is there any Gospel truth in isolation from history. And this by the decree of God Himself.

(vii) *The nature of faith*, it is claimed, is something quite different from knowledge historically demonstrable—God's word requires no human legitimation. Only when all such fortuitous supports have been withdrawn can faith breathe freely. Once again, there is truth in the claim. There is a way of demanding proof which is essential scepticism. But there is another side to it. It is all very well to call faith 'a leap in the dark.' But surely the darkness was not unrelieved for the Church which knew that the Word had been made flesh. In this sense faith, as Bornkamm remarks, 'does not begin with itself but lives from past history' (op. cit., 23). Why did the early Church at its worship services, after the reading of the law and the prophets, rehearse the story of the deeds and passion of the Lord? Was it not because they 'recognized that their faith stood or fell with the sober facts of a story, and that it was vital to maintain the unbroken tradition of these facts'? (C. F. D. Moule, in *New Testament Essays*, 172). J. M. Robinson indeed asserts that 'to require an objective legitimization of the saving event prior to faith is to take offence at the offence of Christianity and to perpetuate the unbelieving flight to security, i.e. the reverse of faith' (op. cit., 44). But this misses the point that the real offence, the essential σκάνδαλον, of Christianity is precisely its historical particularity, and it is no 'unbelieving flight to security' that casts its anchor there. Paul Althaus is entirely justified in saying that 'the faith whose security has been removed in the manner that *kerygma* theology sets out to do, would be faith without foundations. But,' he asks, 'is a faith which in this sense is without foundations, still faith?' (op. cit., 54–5).

(viii) We look again at Bultmann's *existentialist emphasis*. Undeniably there is a valid insight here. No one is reading the New Testament aright until in every section of it, indeed at every sentence, he asks the questions—What is this saying to me about my own existence? What decision is it demanding of me now? For Christianity is not a message about 'religion': it is a message about life, or it is nothing. In this sense, 'all theological statements can be translated into terms of human concern' (Alasdair MacIntyre, *Encounter*, Sept. 1963). But while this is true, it seems to me that there are three points at which Bultmann's existentialist interpretation lies wide open to criticism: it is too abstract, too anthropocentric, too un-Christological.

Too abstract—for surely the quality of a decision must depend on the revealed character of the One for whom the decision is made. Surely Christian obedience, abstracted from the teaching and example of Jesus in his obedience to the Father, is something less than characteristically Christian. 'It is the earthly Jesus who manifests what the way of the believer looks like' (Eduard Schweizer, op. cit., 432).

Too anthropocentric—for the significance of a kerygmatic statement about Christ is not exhausted in the human response it elicits. Surely it is anthropomorphism run riot to suggest that the mysteries of the Church's creed are primarily guides for my self-understanding, pointers towards the implications of my existence. Of an earlier but similar theology James Denney once said:

> Instead of God being man's chief end, man is made God's chief end. God has no *raison d'être*, so to speak, but to look after us (*The Christian Doctrine of Reconciliation*, 236).

To declare with Bultmann that ultimately 'faith' and 'knowledge' are identical as a new understanding of oneself (*Theology* I, 318) is to make πίστις and γνῶσις pale shadows of what they represent in the Pauline and Johannine theologies. I have commented already on the modernizing peril, which sees in Jesus simply the too human reflection of a contemporary philosophy. These words of T. W. Manson express it well:

It is easy to laugh at those who, a couple of generations ago, saw in Jesus a good nineteenth-century liberal humanist with a simple faith in a paternal deity. It is less easy to see the joke when the Jesus of history is a twentieth-century existentialist, a kind of pre-existent Heidegger. But the Good News was not the clever anticipation by the carpenter of Nazareth of the most up-to-date philosophical ideas *(Background and Eschatology,* 220).

Hence follows the third criticism of this theology: it is *too un-Christological.* If it is a case of choosing between two interpretations of the Christ event, the one seeing in it the shattering and the re-making of history, the other regarding it as a mere act of the human consciousness, surely the whole New Testament demands the for-mer. When the New Testament speaks of the Sonship of Christ, is this merely a challenge to me to decide the question of my own sonship? When it speaks of His Messiahship, His Lordship over disease and demons and death, His Kingship over the Church and the universe, is this no more than a mythological picture of the need for self-understanding and the imperativeness of decision? Surely H. Reisenfeld is nearer the truth when he says that

> the way in which Jesus is described in the Gospels cannot be finally explained without assuming a Messianic conception in the mind of Jesus Himself *(Background and Eschatology,* 90).

The death and resurrection of Christ, as Paul indeed is never tired of insisting in Romans, Galatians and elsewhere, constitute God's su-preme summons to the believer to die with Christ and to rise with Him to newness of life: but is this *all* their meaning? In particular, can we here evade the basis in history? Professor David Cairns has cogently argued that

> what God intends to say to me through the cross should not be thrown into opposition to the historical grounds of the cross. Had Jesus been justly crucified as a zealot rebel, then neither Bultmann nor any other preacher would be happy proclaiming God's salvation through the cross *(A Gospel without Myth?,* 155).

'We love,' declared St. John, 'because He loved us first': to which we may now add that if we die with Him today, it is only because His dying for us in history was prior to any action of our own. Similarly with the Easter event. To interpret this, as Bultmann and others appear to do, primarily or merely in terms of the emergence of the Easter faith in the primitive community—

> the victory which Jesus wins when faith arises in man by the overcoming of the offence that Jesus is to him (Bultmann, *Theology*, II, 57)—

or to speak of Jesus spiritually risen today to help me towards a new self-understanding, is to do scant justice to the New Testament's constant insistence that something happened at Easter prior to and independent of the community's apprehension of it, and that before the God of the resurrection did anything for us He did something *for Christ*. This means that the cross and the resurrection have a meaning for us only because they have a prior meaning *within the being of God Himself*. It would be nonsense to attempt a purely existentialist interpretation of the work of reconciliation which the cross and the resurrection achieve: that would mean demythologizing the wrath of God in a way which would take the nerve out of the gospel. It is true that something has to happen in me before I can find peace with God, but, as Paul at any rate sees it, that is certainly not the heart of the situation. The heart of the matter, he declares, is what happened first in God. To quote James Denney again:

> Even if no man should ever say, 'Thou, O Christ, art all I want; more than all in Thee I find,' God says it. Christ and His work have this absolute value for the Father (op. cit., 235).

In the continuing debate on the Jesus of history and the Christ of faith, I have tried to show the position of a very influential modern school of theology, in its strength and in what I consider to be its weakness. My own view is that in its somewhat ostentatious indifference to the teaching and example of Jesus, and the facts of His earthly life and ministry, and in its reiterated assertion of the impossibility and indeed illegitimacy of the quest, it exhibits a quite arbitrary defeatism and a gratuitous historical pessimism. Whether such defeatism will turn out to be, as D. M. Baillie suggested, 'a transient nightmare of Gospel criticism' (op. cit., 58) remains to be seen. But at least there are welcome signs—not least in the writings of some of Bultmann's former pupils—that Christology is returning to fundamentals. It is realizing that to a faith which believes that 'the Word was made flesh,' what happened in the days of His flesh cannot but be of paramount importance. The life and witness of the Church are inalienably bound up with the ministry and mighty acts of Him whom now and for ever it hails as Lord.

CHAPTER 30

Out of Season Remarks on the "Historical Jesus" of the Bultmann School

OSCAR CULLMANN

> Dr. Cullmann is a Professor both at the University of
> Basel and at the École des Hautes-Études, Sorbonne, Paris.
> He stands against the existentialist interpretation of the Bult-
> mann school as the outstanding exponent of "salvation his-
> tory." Strictly speaking this article should perhaps have been
> included under "Part One: The Gospels as Sources" or
> under "Part Three: The Results of Research." It has seemed
> advisable, however, to place it here because of its implicit
> stress on the significance of the actual history underlying
> the Gospel tradition. See also Professor Cullman's *Salvation
> in History*, 1966.

I T is in itself a welcome development that precisely the students
of Bultmann[1] are re-opening the quest of the historical Jesus on

---

[1] There is a small parallel between the situation of the American reader of this
article and the position in which one finds himself when reading Irenaeus.
Professor Cullmann here offers a critique of perspectives expressed in essays
which are widely read in Europe, but unavailable in English and therefore
beyond the reach of most American readers. Two factors lessen the problem
somewhat. Unlike Irenaeus, Professor Cullmann belongs to the age of documentary footnotes which allow one's opponents to speak for themselves; some
of the material to which he refers is either available or summarized in English
(see particularly notes 4, 10, 20 and 21). Add to this Günther Bornkamm's
Jesus of Nazareth (New York: Harper, 1960), and no reader is relieved of the
responsibility to make his own decisions in connection with the debate. (Tr.)

Reprinted with permission from the *Union Seminary Quarterly Review*, Vol. 16,
No. 2, January, 1961, pp. 131–148.

the basis of form criticism. In the following remarks I want in no way to reject the task as they have formulated it, as though I considered it an impossible undertaking. Nor do I want to overlook the service which these theologians perform in searching for a new approach to this problem. I do want to examine whether it may not be the case that the result which they propose is endangered by principles evident in their work which are both foreign to form criticism and contrary to its original aim.

Form criticism as such consciously put the quest of the historical Jesus in the background, and we will see that in the first instance this procedure was methodologically correct. However, the results of form critical analysis justify and indeed call for an attempt to cast the old problem into new light and to risk new solutions. It has been correctly recognized that the gospels are by nature the church's witness to its faith and not historical reports, and this fact makes extraordinarily difficult the task of using the gospels as sources for the historical Jesus. However, this relieves neither the historian nor the theologian [1a] of the obligation to undertake this difficult task.[2]

[1a] With all due regard for the distinction between "geschichtlich" and "historisch" carried through by M. Kähler in his famous lecture, "Der sogennante historische Jesus und der geschichtliche biblische Christus" (1892) ("The so-called historische Jesus and the geschichtliche, Biblical Christ"), it is not permissible for the theologian securely to entrench himself in the safe territory of the primitive church's theology, unless he is willing to risk the danger of docetism. . . . It is, by the way, not the case that Kähler's essay found appropriate regard only since its new printing in 1928, as H. W. Bartsch (*Die christliche Botschaft und das Problem der Geschichte*, 1958) suggests. Everyone who experienced the rise of form criticism knows that a theological kinship between the position of form criticism and Kähler's distinction was recognized from the beginning.

[2] M. Goguel, who was inclined generally to dismiss the efforts of form criticism, raised an objection which was directed also against my essay on form criticism written more than 35 years ago (Les récentes études sur la formation de la tradition évangélique, RHPR, 1925, pp. 459 ff., 564 ff.): the fact, he said, that the gospels do not have it as their intention "to present" history may not prevent the historian from searching for history in them. At that time I was myself among those who emphasized the complete impossibility of recovering the historical Jesus. Today I would no longer write in this way, and together with K. L. Schmidt I have long tried to make use of form criticism not only negatively but also positively in order to render accessible the historical Jesus. Yet precisely today I maintain with the same vigor shown in that article what even then was important to me in form criticism: the effort at least to restrain arbitrariness in distinguishing churchly additions from historical elements.

The nature of the sources does exclude the composition of a biography of Jesus, but it does not make impossible the determination of essential historical elements concerning his life and teaching.[3]

However, the question regarding the church's witness to its faith should be placed first, before that of the historical Jesus. That is to say the content of the church's witness should first be presented according to motifs in the course of its development, rather than being immediately explained on the basis of a *preconceived* portrait of what Jesus said and did (regardless of whether the church's witness is seen as a break with this portrait or as its quintessence). If this rule is not observed, the return to the historical Jesus means not progress, but rather a step backwards to the situation before form criticism, even if one has learned from form criticism the basic questions to be asked. In that case the reticence which R. Bultmann has imposed upon himself with regard to the historical Jesus is decidedly preferable to the advance made by his pupils. With the rise of form criticism we felt delivered from all arbitrary distinctions between "genuine" and "non-genuine" words of Jesus, that is distinctions made on the basis of preconceived dogmatic or philosophical positions. But if the rule formulated above is not observed, our deliverance is only an illusion. Albert Schweitzer's *Quest of the Historical Jesus* was written in vain if the "liberal" portrait of Jesus, which corresponds to the idealistic philosophy of the nineteenth century, disappeared only in order to make room for the existentialist portrait which corresponds to the existentialist philosophy of the twentieth century.

OBJECTIVITY AND THE "HISTORICAL JESUS"
OF EXISTENTIALIST INTERPRETATION

In order to prevent misunderstanding regarding the extent of my judgment on the latest contributions of the Bultmann students to the problem of the historical Jesus,[4] I should like to accent the

---

[3] This is correctly emphasized by G. Bornkamm in the telling remarks in the introduction to his book on Jesus (1958). See also H. Conzelmann, "Zur Méthode der Leben-Jesu-Forschung," *ZTK*, 1959, p. 4.

[4] The reference is particularly to the various essays of E. Fuchs, G. Ebeling, and H. Conzelmann. In this regard see the research report of J. M. Robinson (*A New Quest of the Historical Jesus*, 1959), which in an attitude of complete agreement draws on writings of these men which were evoked primarily by Ernst Käsemann's article (*ZTK*, 1954). Since then the special issue of the

following point. Suppose I conclude that the danger of arbitrariness
in distinguishing between churchly additions and genuine historical
elements, indeed even the danger of being influenced by philosophical presuppositions, is no less in the work of these men than
in the portraits drawn by many scholars prior to form criticism. My
coming to this conclusion would not mean I somehow claim for my
own view a monopoly on objectivity. I am fully aware that all of
us who are not fundamentalists—and in the case of my own generation, all of us who are the children of liberalism—find ourselves
in great difficulty as soon as we re-open the question of the historical
Jesus. For we accept in principle the possibility of the whole spectrum: historically reliable elements, units of tradition only lightly
retouched by the church, and ones entirely composed by the church.
I do think, however, that much would already be accomplished if,
when one is determining the place of a given piece of tradition in
this wide spectrum, one renewed the *effort* at objectivity by relin-
quishing his own private way of formulating the questions. This
would certainly be preferable to rejecting this effort *a priori* as
prohibited and out of date on the basis of hermeneutical, existential
considerations, and replacing it by the "self-understanding of existence" as the principle of exegesis. I know quite well that an
exegesis completely free of presuppositions is impossible. I do consider it dangerous, however, when in connection with modern
philosophy and the needs of the preacher, a virtue is made of this
inevitable difficulty, and "self-understanding" is made the principle
of interpretation. In this respect too I emphasize that I do not consider my own exegesis to be free from all presuppositions. However,
a way of at least controlling arbitrariness seems to me to be available
in the conscious *effort* to respect the foreign character[5] of what is

------

ZTK has appeared, "Beiheft 1: Die Frage nach dem historischen Jesus," which
contains contributions by H. Conzelmann, G. Ebeling and E. Fuchs. See also
H. Conzelmann, "Die formgeschichtliche Methode," in *Schweiz. Theol. Ums-
chau*, 1959, pp. 54 ff.

When in the present essay I speak simply of the Bultmann school, that is
naturally a generalization which cannot be avoided here. It is not the case that
all of the characterizations in the following critical analysis apply to all representatives of this school. I emphasize this in order not to do an injustice to any
of them.

[5] This strangeness, for example the strangeness of the cross understood as
atoning death in the sense of an ontic happening (not as a means for understanding our existence), this strangeness is not considered by Bultmann. See
his article, "Das Befremdliche des christlichen Glaubens" (ZTK, 1958, pp. 185

affirmed in a text, so that I certainly do not reduce that affirmation (as happens in our time) until it "speaks to me" regarding my "understanding of existence;" as if it were only in this way that I could grasp with certainty the witness of those who preserved the gospel tradition, as if it were only thus that I could find a firm basis for my understanding of that witness. On the basis of such a reduction the Bultmann students confidently distinguish between material added by the church and an historical kernel. Such confidence really seems to me more dangerous than the caution which I require of myself in at least making the effort to approach the unattainable goal of objectivity. *Before* any final statement of faith, I try simply to listen to the strange affirmation of the text, to present them (for this *is* possible), and to reckon with the following proposition: the strange affirmations in the text can "speak to me" and become an object of faith even if I allow them to stand as testimonies to an ontic happening and not as subsequent objectifications of an affirmation concerning existence.[6] It is precisely when I do not *seek* the encounter by the reductionary method mentioned above that the encounter can occur, not, to be sure, in the only manner recognized today, but rather in the sense of my entry into the line of that foreign ontic occurrence.[7]

Such an effort will certainly not exclude our finding churchly additions as distinguished from an historical kernel, but we will find fewer of these additions than would be the case were we to follow the procedure influenced by existentialism. The possibility of freely discussing this matter would be greatly helped if the representatives of the Bultmann school would not conclude from this fact that a willful hesitancy to allot material to churchly additions rather than to the body of historically reliable data is inspired by an "uncritical" conservatism or even by the desire to find favor with modern church authorities.[8] I have at least made the attempt to

---

ff.). Where, to be sure, he accents particularly the historicity of the cross as it becomes an entity which addresses me.

[6] See G. Ebeling's observations on the "occurrence of the word" (Wortgeschehen).

[7] The way in which I understand this is to be more precisely detailed in my forthcoming book on eschatology and redemptive history.

[8] H. Conzelmann seems to insinuate this in his article, "Gegenwart und Zukunft in der synoptischen Tradition" (*ZTK*, 1957, p. 279), when he remarks with reference to my "redemptive history" solution to the eschatological problem, ". . . this latter is particularly acceptable to the church authorities"!

avoid being influenced in my exegesis by theological or philosophical schools. The labels "critical" and "uncritical" are greatly misused today, especially by the youngest followers of Bultmann. Harnack himself warned against judging the critical or uncritical attitude of an exegete by tallying his score with regard to genuine and non-genuine verdicts. Should not scientific "criticism" be exercised on the wholesale allotment of texts to churchly additions, as long as such allotment is not really justified by an objective necessity?

FORM CRITICISM AND EXISTENTIALIST INTERPRETATION

It was the desire to free exegesis from subjective arbitrariness in these decisions which caused many theologians of my generation, including myself, to welcome enthusiastically the rise of form criticism. Now this same desire causes me, in the name of the original aim of form criticism, to issue a warning against the alliance of form criticism with existentialist exegesis. For this alliance seems to me to endanger the advances made possible by form criticism, especially now when the quest of the historical Jesus is being re-opened. We shall see that the "historical" picture of Jesus which is coming to focus in the Bultmann school as a result of this alliance, owes more to existentialist exegesis than to its alleged basis, form criticism.

It is true that an interpretation of the gospels which has existential self-understanding as its goal *can* be combined with form criticism. R. Bultmann made this combination in his attempt to understand the witness which the church bore to its faith in its traditions. Hence his younger students have frequently made it a tacit prerequisite to being considered a form critic to make this same combination. Consequently they think they can deny the designation Form Critic to older representatives of this discipline who adopted it along with R. Bultmann years ago but decidedly reject his turning to existentialist exegesis.[9] Actually form criticism and existentialism have no more to do with one another than that one of the most significant New Testament scholars of our century is on the one hand one of the main founders of form criticism, and has on the other hand constructed a hermeneutic of the whole New Testament, in connection with the modern existentialist philosophy of Heideg-

[9] I am thinking here not only of myself, but also of K. L. Schmidt whose service in the emergence of form criticism ought to be generally recognized.

ger, which can but need not be brought into harmony with form criticism.[10]

I should like to show that it is not form criticism but rather its fusion with existentialism which leads to a portrait of Jesus that would probably have to fall under the judgment of Albert Schweitzer, if his *Quest of the Historical Jesus* were extended "from Wrede to the Bultmann School." The most recent works proceed by placing opposite one another 1) a portrait of Jesus as the primitive church saw him and 2) an historical kernel. But we must investigate the origin of that portrait and we must examine critically the basis of the historical kernel in form criticism. The latest work of the Bultmann students (Conzelmann, Ebeling, Fuchs) which appeared in the *Zeitschrift für Theologie und Kirche*, fails essentially to consider the question of how one arrives at the historical Jesus. Here the quest of the historical Jesus becomes rather the quest for the *connection* between two distinct entities: 1) the primitive church's portrait of Christ as the Bultmann students reconstruct it, and 2) the historical kernel as they establish it. What is this connection? Since Bultmann himself does not actually take up the quest of the historical Jesus as such, he only hints at the following answer: the connection lies in Jesus' calling his hearers to decision, for this call implies a christology. Bultmann's students, on the other hand, consciously take up "the quest," and while they do this with close reference to their teacher, they desire to go beyond him by greater precision. For them the connection between the church's portrait of Christ and the historical kernel lies in Jesus' "faith" (Ebeling) or in his "conduct" (E. Fuchs). Thus according to them there is a bridge between the Jesus who calls to decision, who has faith, who conducts himself in a definite way, and the quite different Christ *in* whom the church believes.

This may appear to be a satisfactory solution to the tension between the Jesus of history and the Christ of faith; is it really the result of applying the discipline of form criticism? Does it not to a much greater degree result from the existentialist posture which has basically affected the determination of both the community's portrait of Christ and the historical kernel? Has not this solution been outlined in advance, in a quite definite direction?

The fact that the picture of Jesus which has thus arisen answers

[10] See particularly "The Problem of Hermeneutics," pp. 234 ff. in Bultmann, *Essays*. (Tr.).

so thoroughly to the principles of existentialist philosophy leads us to suspect this latter to be the case. I do not want to base my judgment merely on this general observation. Still, we are witnessing once again the rise of a portrait of Jesus which is influenced by the philosophy of the time. Many people may rejoice to see this concord between the exegetes and the philosophers. Indeed one may entertain the possibility that a philosophy has finally emerged whose principles are fully suited to the interpretation of the Bible.[10a] But should not the result of Albert Schweitzer's *Quest of the Historical Jesus* cause us to pause and reflect, when it is precisely in the age of existentialism that research with respect to the historical Jesus is carried on in a way that corresponds to the new philosophical postulates regarding the encounter of "true existence," and what is more, when the historical Jesus is presented to us exclusively as the one whose person and work find their only meaning in this: that they call us to "decision" regarding our existence?[11]

I know that there is a fundamental distinction between the manner in which the 19th century portraits of Jesus emerged and the manner in which the existentialist historical Jesus of the Bultmann school is emerging. The former were unconsciously influenced by the ideals of 19th century philosophy, while the latter reflects consciously and as a hermeneutic principle the "self-understanding" of faith. But this hermeneutical principle of encounter is certainly an essential element in contemporary philosophy. Now it may be necessary for the theologian to enter into occasional conversation with the philosophers of his time and to learn from them. But the possibility that the philosophers may influence the *exegete* has always represented a danger from the time of early gnosticism. Is our time a happy exception to this rule? Hardly! The manner in which the Bultmann school distinguishes between churchly additions and historical elements proves that the use of existentialist principles offers no protection against the danger of making these distinctions

---

[10a] See Bultmann's initial essay in H. W. Bartsch, *Kerygma and Myth*, especially the comment on p. 25, "some critics have objected that I am borrowing Heidegger's categories and forcing them upon the New Testament. I am afraid this only shows that they are blinding their eyes to the real problem, which is that the philosophers are saying the same thing as the New Testament and saying it quite independently." (Tr.).

[11] One could be tempted to see a parallel between the "faith" or "conduct" of Jesus, which is spoken of today, and the "inner life" of Jesus which Wilhelm Hermann saw as the link between the historical Jesus and the Christ of faith.

on the basis of presuppositions which are in fact foreign to the subject matter.

We have seen that the latest contributions to our problem seek to present the primitive community's traditional witness in terms of the motifs and content which characterized it in the course of its development, then to establish from that basis an historically authentic kernel different from the church's witness, and finally to show the link which connects the two in spite of their divergence. This procedure is thoroughly appropriate to the subject matter and corresponds to the requirements of form criticism. If, in spite of this, we cannot escape the impression of a certain arbitrary fixing of the boundaries and the connection between churchly additions and the historical kernel in the work of the Bultmann students, indeed an arbitrariness which exceeds the unavoidable, then this results not from their employment of form criticism but rather from their violation of it. Such a violation of form criticism seems to me to be present both in their comprehension of the church's witness and in their establishment of the authentic historical kernel. Therefore we want now to examine in order: 1. how the Bultmann school goes about presenting the church's witness; 2. how it determines the historical kernel.

THE CHURCH'S WITNESS TO THE CHRIST

As for the first: According to its original intention, form criticism is concerned with disclosing the formal laws and faith motifs which shaped the tradition. Therefore as a discipline, form criticism should put aside the question of what really happened in the life of Jesus and what he really taught. It should stop when it has reached the earliest form in which the *primitive community* handed down a narrative or a saying, and that means it should part with the convenient and naive method of designating as later churchly addition everything which does not fit into a preconceived ideal picture of the historical Jesus. The material with which form criticism works is precisely the *Church's construction* as such, inasmuch as this encompasses the *whole* gospel tradition. If the gospels were really considered only from the viewpoint of tradition, a distinction between material added by the church and material not added by the church would have no meaning, since from this point of view the gospel tradition as a whole is naturally a "church construction."

The latter may consist of historical elements equally as well as un-historical. For in principle the historical deeds and words of Jesus may have corresponded just as adequately to the tendencies of the tradition-making, believing church as did the church's own remould-ing and creation of new material. Therefore one endeavors to refrain not only from all positive declarations in favor of the historicity of an event or the genuineness of a saying, but also from negative verdicts to the opposite effect. One identifies developments which took place in the formation of the tradition, but one refrains from going back behind the church's tradition to the historical Jesus himself.

It was a violation of the principle of neutrality when Bultmann, in connection with W. Wrede's theory about the "messianic secret," declared as non-genuine all words of Jesus expressing in any way a "messianic self-consciousness" by the use of Jewish titles of honor like "Son of Man," "Servant of God," "Son of God" etc. Reference to Wrede's Messianic Secret has since become dogma in the Bult-mann school.

Even before the quest of the historical Jesus began to be renewed, the Bultmann students went further than their teacher in violating the original neutrality. Originally *two* possibilities were necessarily left open with regard to a given unit of tradition: the possibility that the tradition-making church had handed on without em-broidery naked facts from the life and sayings of Jesus, because these facts *themselves* already mirrored a tendency of the primitive community; on the other hand the possibility that the church trans-formed the facts or even created "idealized" scenes or words. Today, however, form criticism is defined precisely as "thinking based on the disjuncture" between the historical Jesus and the community.[12] This is not in accord with the original intention of form criticism.[13]

We shall see, to be sure, that even the Bultmann students reckon with an authentic historical kernel, and thus accept in practice the

[12] See H. Conzelmann, "Gegenwart und Zukunft in der synoptischen Tradition" (note 8 above): "We who are assembled here have a certain handicap. We are accustomed to thinking on the basis of the *disjuncture* (Conzelmann's italics) between the historical Jesus and the church. . . . But obvious as this *starting point* (my italics) may appear to us, we must realize that beyond a few Middle-Europeans it is apparent to only a small number. The majority of the British do not respond to form criticism. . . ."
[13] On the other hand it was also not intended that one should employ form criticism in order to rescue the historicity of the whole tradition.

possibility of materials not refashioned by the tradition. But according to them the historical kernel should be disclosed only on the basis of a prior determination of elements within the tradition which contradict the content and development of the church's witness. In order to discover such elements it would be necessary first to present objectively the content and development of this witness with regard both to its forms and to its faith motifs rather than taking an assumed *kerygma* preached by Jesus as a measure of the disjuncture.

Here one sees the result of that mixing of form criticism with existentialist exegesis which we mentioned above. Those who proceed in this way do not begin by simply presenting the faith-witness of the tradition-making church. At the very outset they *interpret* that witness by the existentialist methods of interpretation, and that means that everything which does not address me in my self-understanding, which does not become kerygma, is evaluated as an "objectifying" expression in which certain tendencies of the primitive church are expressed, namely tendencies which by "objectification" into an ontic occurrence or by periodization into a Redemptive History *(Heilsgeschichte)* distort that essential kerygma which critically examines my existence. In this procedure, however, there is a tacit identification between that which is kerygma for the self-understanding and the kerygma proclaimed by the historical Jesus.

To be sure, one does not find in these contributions by the Bultmann students the statement: it is settled that that which addresses me in the witness of the gospels as kerygma is the kerygma proclaimed by the historical Jesus. Actually, however, we have now shown that in the background behind their judgments regarding the church theology in the synoptics stands precisely this presupposition, which is therefore *a presupposition regarding the historical Jesus.* Thus, in their analysis of the eschatological tendencies in the synoptics it is made a point of departure that the primitive church distorted Jesus' quite simple "punctiliar" eschatology which envisaged the immediate nearness of the Kingdom of God and that Kingdom's call to decision. In contending with the problem of the delay of the parousia the church is said to have distorted Jesus' simple eschatology by constructing a redemptive history made up of a series of periods. In the works of the Bultmann students this introduction of *Jesus'* eschatology does not follow on the heels of an analysis of elements in the tradition which stand in tension with the witness of the church, elements which thus constitute a historical kernel. Rather, Jesus' eschatology is introduced already at the beginning of the analysis, at the stage when one is establishing the church's witness.[14] One may appeal to the inevitability of a circle. The fact remains, however, that the distinction between the church's theologizing and Jesus' message is here being made once again on the basis of a postulate regarding Jesus' kerygma.

It has been shown that in Luke we find a redemptive history worked out in a fully developed form,[15] and this conclusion is in itself correct and valuable. It is, however, too quickly connected with the questionable assumption that Jesus' call to decision is "punctiliar" and that this call cannot be reconciled with the idea of a redemptive history. Actually the growth of the gospel tradition which can be traced by form criticism allows us to speak only of a progressive *development* of redemptive history, connected, to be sure, with the church's experiencing the passing of extended time. It does not allow us without further ado to explain this redemptive history as a break away from Jesus' eschatological thought. Behind this explanation stands that existentialist reduction of the synoptic eschatology which is based on a definite conception of the quintessence of Jesus' kerygma. I do not here discuss the question whether a series of events bound together in the manner of a redemptive history may be kerygma in the sense of our entry into the line of an ontic occurrence.[16] I want rather to show how the above mentioned analyses of the church's witness in the gospel tradition, instead of remaining within the framework of form criticism, are burdened from the start by a reduced and quite definite picture of Jesus.

Now we grasp why it is that as soon as form criticism is linked with the existentialist reduction of the synoptic witness, it must be

---

[14] This is not always so clearly evident as it is in E. Grässer's *Das Problem der Parusie—verzögerung in den synoptischen Evangelien und in der Apostelgeschichte* (1957), which openly admits the procedure tacitly followed by almost all representatives of the Bultmann school. He speaks of a necessary working hypothesis. But a working hypothesis would have to contain as few hypothetical elements as possible. Yet here it is settled in advance that Jesus' eschatological proclamation is limited to the statement: the Kingdom of God stands immediately at hand.

[15] It is the lasting service of H. Conzelmann to have shown this (*Die Mitte der Zeit*, 1954).

[16] In my forthcoming book, *Eschatologie und Heilsgeschichte*, I hope to discuss this in greater detail.

understood as "thinking based on the disjuncture." Every so-called "objectifying" or "historicizing" statement in the synoptic tradition which is not kerygma in a definite sense must be regarded as a distortion, a "disjuncture."

Because of its being linked with this interpretation, the church's witness in the synoptic tradition appears already in a quite definite perspective. If it is on this basis that the quest of the historical Jesus is being renewed in our time, then that has important consequences. Form criticism had put the quest aside. Representatives of the Bultmann school are no doubt right in saying it cannot be left at that indefinitely. But precisely when the quest is being renewed, we should hold fast to those valuable elements which grew out of the healthy reaction of form criticism against all arbitrariness in distinguishing between "churchly additions" and "historical parts." And to follow this course would make it mandatory that the quest not be prematurely joined to the problem of discovering the kerygma, joined, that is, right at the outset of one's investigation of this latter problem.

Furthermore, in the analysis of the gospel tradition, its laws and motifs, mere constructions should not play too great a role. Instead, one should reckon with definite motifs of later churchly development only in those places in the text where a comparison between the three synoptics or the presence of various layers of tradition really exhibits such motifs. Where such is not the case, one must at least exercise care. A certain reticence is called for when a given tendency which is believed to be seen in the development of the gospel tradition finds no confirmation by the direct testimony of the New Testament letters. I am thinking in this connection of the role which is said to have been played in the formation of the gospel tradition by the so-called "painful" problem of the delay of the parousia. The Bultmann school took over from the "thorough-going eschatology" of Albert Schweitzer and his followers the idea that this problem and the search for its solution dominated the entire thought of the primitive church.[17] To be sure, we notice in the letters something of a positive experiencing of an extension of the present period of time, but we do not find any real "problem" connected with it. Such a problem does not appear at all until the latest New Testament writing, II Peter (chapter 3), and perhaps in

[17] See O. Cullmann, "Parusieverzögerung und Urchristentum. Der gegenwärtige Stand der Diskussion," *TLZ*, 1958, pp. 1 ff.

the appendix chapter of John's Gospel (21:23). This observation does not exclude the presence of the problem in the tradition-making church, but it is a warning against introducing it as a motif of "churchly addition" in passages where there is not the least necessity for it.

In addition, in analyzing the synoptic deposit of the church's witness, its motifs and the laws according to which it developed, one should bear in mind above all, that besides remoulding and creating factors there were also purely conserving factors at work. Precisely if one takes form criticism seriously one should not silently pass over or dispatch with a few critical words [18] Riesenfeld's remarks concerning the parallels with the manner in which the words of a rabbi were handed down.[19]

In passing on the gospel tradition, the church or the Evangelists were sometimes led by the tendencies of the community's theology to make selections from among the historical elements. Above all, one must realize that they made these selections so as to incorporate as many elements as possible *which in themselves already corresponded to these tendencies without re-working or modification.*

This leads us directly to the second methodological question which we have raised. If we want to find the historical Jesus, next in importance to the analysis of the church's witness is the determination of the *certain historical kernel.*

THE HISTORICAL KERNEL

As it is distinguished from churchly additions, how is this kernel established according to the procedure in the Bultmann school? We can reduce this procedure to two propositions: 1) Everything in the gospels which stands in tension with the tendencies of the tradition-making primitive church can be traced back to Jesus. This first proposition is entirely acceptable, if one can assume that the scholar's delineation of these tendencies is not influenced by a picture of Jesus which the scholar has already in mind. Here we are indeed on solid ground, and yet an important restriction must be observed. It is an authentic historical kernel which we seek in a given unit of tradition. This *kernel,* however, cannot be subsequently used as

[18] See J. M. Robinson, *A New Quest of the Historical Jesus,* p. 64, note 1.
[19] H. Riesenfeld, "The Gospel Tradition and its Beginnings. A Study in the Limits of 'Formgeschichte'" (opening paper at the Congress on "The Four Gospels" held in Oxford, 1957).

a reliable *criterion* on the basis of which we may determine in other less certain pieces of tradition what is churchly addition and what is not. For the basis of those passages, fortuitously preserved for us, which stand in tension with the church's theology is *much too narrow* to allow this reliable kernel to serve as a criterion for its own further precision or extension, or for the gaining of a *total picture* of the historical Jesus. If this restriction is not taken seriously, a picture with a foreshortened perspective must necessarily result. The work of the Bultmann students is unusually exposed to this danger because existentialist interpretation has a natural tendency to reduction.

More ponderous is the second proposition, which stands in the background rather than being expressly stated: Material in the gospels which corresponds to a tendency of the primitive church is usually to be regarded as churchly addition in the sense of the disjuncture (remoulded or newly created material); for disclosing the historical Jesus such material may according to the Bultmann school at most be used subsequently, on the basis of a kerygmatic encounter accomplished by means of a reduction undertaken by existentialist interpretation. In this proposition, which is not justified by form criticism as such, there lies a further source of the one-sidedness with which churchly additions are distinguished from historical elements. On what basis do we know that a theological concern of the primitive church cannot have been *in the same form* a basic motif in the thought of Jesus? It is true that from among the passages which display a tendency of the church, one must choose those which contain an historical kernel without alteration; and regarding the remaining passages, one must make a judgment as to the extent of the alteration. Judgment in this matter is difficult and cannot be made with the same degree of certainty which is possible in connection with the first proposition stated above. However, this uncertainty may not be understood, as the Bultmann school often understands it, as an occasion for extending the existentialist reduction to such great lengths that the whole of this very *extensive material* is either allowed no role in solving the problem of the historical Jesus, or is traced back to an already established kerygma.

There is, to be sure, an element of truth in this second proposition if we tie it to the following criteria: Let us take the example of a story about Jesus which is differently reported, either in the same gospel or in the synoptic parallels, so that one report excludes the other while only one corresponds to an intrusive tendency of the primitive church. In such instances, the form of the story corresponding to the church's tendency must be considered a non-historical element; and the same holds for sayings which are contradictory, if one of them corresponds to a tendency of the church. Also, wherever a report or a saying is found which both reflects a tendency of the church and is incompatible with the contemporary *environment* of the historical Jesus, one may conclude that he is dealing with a churchly addition (in the sense that it lacks historicity) or with an alteration. Finally, wherever a generally valid law of legendary development is visible in a tendency of the church, historicity is to be questioned—with caution, of course. Otherwise, the rule should hold that *so long* as no such necessity is present, an effort should be made to let narratives and sayings stand (in the form given) as reports and words of the historical Jesus, even when they correspond to tendencies of the early church. This procedure does not rest on "conservatism," but on the justified scientific concern not to fall into boundless arbitrariness. In this regard the Bultmann students also seek a criterion. But the quest for existential self-understanding in which they believe to have found it, does not offer us a criterion. And the historical "remaining fragment," established according to their first proposition stated above, is, as we have said, too narrow a basis to serve as a legitimate criterion, since it must in this case lead to a one-sided foreshortening.

We could show by many examples how it is that tacitly to proceed on the assumed probability that the tendency of the earliest church was different in principle from that of Jesus leads to arbitrary judgments on the basis of which the portrait of Jesus is narrowed and simplified. I will mention only a few points. It is said for example, that the demand to "watch!" corresponds to a concern of the earliest church in connection with the problem of the delayed parousia. The church wanted, so this argument runs, to help its members in this connection by issuing the warning that the Kingdom of God had not yet arrived. Accordingly the words: "Watch, for you do not know. . . .," which we find in many variant forms in the synoptics, are said to have been composed by the church and placed in Jesus' mouth. Now that argument is correct to this extent, that it was *also* a tendency of the early church to exhort

Christians to "watch!," and we have direct evidence proving this. The only immediate conclusion from this is that the church was interested in handing down such sayings. But why should one draw the further conclusion that this demand was not a concern of Jesus himself?

The extremely important question of Jesus' "self-consciousness" basically determines our comprehension of his work and teaching. In the contributions of the Bultmann students this important question is extensively answered on the basis of the sort of short cuts which simplify the picture of Jesus in a one-sided way corresponding to the existentialist tendency to reduction. Where truly literary and form-critical reasons are given for denying to Jesus himself a particular saying regarding his atoning death, one may justly conclude that one is dealing with a churchly addition. On the other hand, the mere fact, in itself certainly correct, that the earliest church was christologically interested in interpreting Jesus' death as an atoning death, can in no way lead to the conclusion that Jesus could not have regarded himself as the Ebed Yahweh (Servant of the Lord). How does one know that the church's tendency on this point introduced an idea foreign to Jesus himself? In the area of Christology many similar questions force themselves upon us. I ask only this further one: even if the emphasis on the Messianic Secret is as important for Mark as Wrede showed it to be, to what extent have we the right to draw from this that well-known and far-reaching negative conclusion regarding Jesus' messianic self-consciousness which has been elevated to a scientific dogma?[20] In answering this question one must bear in mind something which can be deduced from many sayings: when one keeps in mind the problem of the Zealots which was so important for Jesus, the Messianic Secret may be completely explained by the specially conditioned self-consciousness of Jesus which excluded his being misunderstood as the political messiah.[21]

In the last analysis what really lies behind the elimination of all christological connections between synoptic sayings of Jesus and Jewish messianic titles is often (though not always) the forced reduction to a kerygma which concerns "self-understanding." That is

[20] See Bultmann, *Theology of the New Testament*, vol. 1, pp. 26 f. (Tr.).
[21] See O. Cullmann, *The State in the New Testament* (1956), pp. 12 ff.; *The Christology of the New Testament* (1959), pp. 117 ff.

why, in the view of the Bultmann school, it is only the authority (exousía) of the Jesus who calls one to decision which can stand as a christological point of departure.

CONCLUSION: THE BRIDGE FROM THE CHRIST OF
FAITH TO HISTORICAL JESUS PREDETERMINED
BY EXISTENTIALIST PHILOSOPHY

Since the Bultmann students' delineation of the witness borne by the tradition-making church as well as their fixing of the historical kernel is in the final analysis already governed by the existentialist posture, one can hardly be surprised that the way in which they bring these two entities together can only confirm the existentially foreshortened picture of Jesus. They have outlined in advance the bridge which leads from the Jesus who calls to decision to the Christ who is the object of faith according to the church's kerygma (a kerygma which stands behind the objectifying assertions of the church's theology).

Once more I emphasize that even if we leave aside the quest for the self-understanding of existence, the use of form criticism cannot offer a guarantee of absolute "objectivity" in our quest for the historical Jesus. However, we must proceed from it alone and not from the existentialist interpretation if we want at least to near the goal. Only in this way can we ourselves hope correctly to evaluate that role which expressly secondary additions of the church can play in limiting *and* extending the portrait of the historical Jesus (secondary additions which the Bultmann students also allow to play a supplementary role in the positive delineation of the historical Jesus).

The Bultmann school consciously chooses to give up the attempt at objectivity in the usual sense of the term, that is it surrenders for the sake of an existentialist interpretation the attempt to exclude one's own attitude. However, to do this does not eliminate the severe difficulty in which the exegete stands who takes it as his task to distinguish the historical Jesus from the Christ of faith. On the contrary, to travel this road intensifies that difficulty and threatens to throw us back into those arbitrary distinctions from which form criticism should have delivered us. In stating this concluding judgment I do not want to undervalue the service of the Bultmann students in their attempt to find on the basis of form criticism a new solution to the quest of the historical Jesus. I do want, however, to indicate the danger which lies in combining form criticism with the existentialist method of exegesis. We are all indebted for at least some important contributions by authors who either belong to the Bultmann school or stand near it.[22] In such cases, however, one finds only the application of form criticism and not its combination with existentialist exegesis.

[22] I have in mind G. Bornkamm's in many respects excellent book on Jesus (1958), although I cannot agree, to be sure, with his statements on the self-consciousness of Jesus, which express the viewpoint of the whole Bultmann school.

BIBLIOGRAPHY

BIBLIOGRAPHY

A. Materials Used in the Anthology

Barrett, Charles K., *The Gospel According to St. John* (London: S.P.C.K., 1955).

Bornkamm, Guenther, *Jesus of Nazareth,* tr. by Irene and Fraser McLuskey with James M. Robinson (New York: Harper and Brothers, 1960).

Brown, Raymond E., *The Gospel According to John, I–XII,* Vol. 29, *The Anchor Bible* (Garden City, N.Y.: Doubleday & Company, Inc., 1966).

Bultmann, Rudolf, *Jesus and the Word,* tr. by Louise Pettibone Smith and Erminie Huntress Lantero (New York and London: Charles Scribner's Sons, 1934).

———, "The Primitive Christian Kerygma and the Historical Jesus" in *The Historical Jesus and the Kerygmatic Christ,* ed. by Carl E. Braaten and Roy A. Harrisville (New York: Abingdon Press, 1964).

Cullmann, Oscar, "Out of Season Remarks on the 'Historical Jesus' of the Bultmann School" in *Union Seminary Quarterly Review,* Vol. 16. (Jan. 1961), pp. 131–148.

Dahl, N. A., "The Problem of the Historical Jesus" in *Kerygma and History,* ed. by Carl E. Braaten and Roy A. Harrisville (New York: Abingdon Press, 1962).

Dodd, C. H., *The Interpretation of the Fourth Gospel* (Cambridge: Cambridge University Press, 1953).

———, *New Testament Studies* (Manchester: Manchester University Press, 1953).

Fuller, Reginald H., *The New Testament in Current Study* (New York: Charles Scribner's Sons, 1962).

Gerhardsson, Birger, *Memory and Manuscript: Oral Tradition and Written Transmission in Rabbinic Judaism and Early Christianity,* Vol. XXII *Acta Seminarii Neotestamentici Upsaliensis* (Copenhagen: Ejnar Munksgaard, 1961).

Harvey, Van A., *The Historian and the Believer* (New York: The Macmillan Company, 1966).

Jeremias, Joachim, *The Problem of the Historical Jesus,* No. 13, Facet Books, Biblical Series, tr. by Norman Perrin (Philadelphia: The Fortress Press, 1964).

Knox, John, *The Church and the Reality of Christ* (New York: Harper and Row, 1962).

Leon-Dufour, X., "The Synoptic Gospels" in *Introduction to the New Testament,* by A. Feuillet and A. Robert, tr. by Patrick W. Skehan and others (New York: Desclee, 1965).

Manson, Thomas W., *Studies in the Gospels and Epistles,* ed. by M. Black (Manchester: Manchester University Press, 1962).

McArthur, Harvey K., "Basic Issues: A Survey of Recent Gospel Research" in *Interpretation,* Vol. XVIII (Jan. 1964), Union Theological Seminary in Virginia. Reprinted in *New Theology No. 2,* ed. by Martin E. Marty and Dean G. Peerman (New York: The Macmillan Company, 1965).

Robinson, James M., *A New Quest of the Historical Jesus* (London: S.C.M. Press, 1959).

Sandmel, Samuel, *We Jews and Jesus* (New York: Oxford University Press, 1965).

Stauffer, Ethelbert, *Jesus and His Story,* tr. by Richard and Clara Winton (New York: Alfred A. Knopf, 1960).

Stewart, James S., "The Christ of Faith" in *The New Testament in Historical and Contemporary Perspective,* essays in memory of G. H. C. Macgregor, ed. by Hugh Anderson and William Barclay (Oxford: B. Blackwell, 1965).

Taylor, Vincent, *The Life and Ministry of Jesus* (New York: Abingdon Press, 1955).

Tillich, Paul, *Systematic Theology,* Vol. II (Chicago: University of Chicago Press, 1957).

Wikenhauser, Alfred, *New Testament Introduction,* tr. by Joseph Cunningham (New York: Herder and Herder, 1958).

B. *Additional Recent Full Scale Studies of Jesus*

Anderson, Hugh, *Jesus*, (Englewood, N. J.: Prentice-Hall, Inc.).

Anderson, Hugh, *Jesus and Christian Origins* (New York: Oxford University Press, 1964).

Barrett, C. K. *Jesus and the Gospel Tradition*, (Philadelphia: Fortress Press, 1968).

Beck, Dwight M., *Through the Gospels to Jesus* (New York: Harper and Brothers, 1954).

Betz, O., *What Do We Know About Jesus?* (London: SCM Press, 1968).

Bruckberger, R. L., *The History of Jesus Christ*, tr. by Denver Lindley (New York: The Viking Press, 1965).

Bundy, Walter E., *Jesus and the First Three Gospels* (Cambridge: Harvard University Press, 1955).

Colwell, Ernest C., *Jesus and the Gospel* (New York: Oxford University Press, 1963).

Connick, C. Milo, *Jesus, the Man, the Mission and the Message* (Englewood Cliffs, N.J.: Prentice-Hall, Inc., 1963).

Dibelius, Martin, *Jesus*, tr. by C. Baker and F. C. Grant (Philadelphia: The Westminster Press, 1949).

Enslin, Morton Scott, *The Prophet from Nazareth* (New York: McGraw-Hill, 1961).

Gilmour, Samuel M., *The Gospel Jesus Preached* (Philadelphia: The Westminster Press, 1957).

Goguel, Maurice, *The Life of Jesus*, tr. by O. Wyon (London: Allen and Unwin, Ltd., 1933).

Goodspeed, E. J., *The Life of Jesus* (New York: Harper and Brothers, 1950).

Grandmaison, Léonce de, *Jesus Christ, His Person, His Message, His Credentials*, tr. by Basil Whelan (London: Sheed and Ward, 1930–1934), 3 Vols.

Guignebert, Charles, *Jesus*, tr. by S. H. Hooke (London: Kegan Paul, Trench, Trubner and Company, 1935).

Hunter, A. M., *The Work and Words of Jesus* (Philadelphia: The Westminster Press, 1950).

Klausner, Joseph, *Jesus of Nazareth*, tr. by H. Danby (New York: Macmillan Company, 1925).

Lagrange, Marie Joseph, *The Gospel of Jesus Christ*, tr. by Luke Walker and Reginald Ginns (Westminster, Md.: Newmann Bookshop, 1938).

Lebreton, Jules, *The Life and Teaching of Jesus Christ*, tr. by Francis Day (New York: The Macmillan Company, 1950), 2 Vols.

Manson, T. W., *The Teaching of Jesus* (Cambridge: Cambridge University Press, 1935), 2nd ed.

McCasland, S. Vernon, *The Pioneer of Our Faith* (New York: McGraw-Hill Book Company, 1964).

Neil, William, *The Life and Teaching of Jesus* (Philadelphia: J. B. Lippincott Company, 1965).

Perrin, Norman, *Rediscovering the Teaching of Jesus* (New York: Harper and Row, 1967).

Prat, Ferdinand, *Jesus Christ: His Life, His Teaching, and His Work*, tr. by John J. Keenan (Milwaukee: Bruce Publishing Co., 1950).

Rollins, W. E. and M. B., *Jesus and His Ministry* (Greenwich, Conn.: Seabury Press, 1954).

Steinmann, Jean, *The Life of Jesus*, tr. by Peter Green (Boston: Little, Brown and Company, 1963).

Zahrnt, Heinz, *The Historical Jesus*, tr. by J. S. Bowden (New York: Harper and Row, 1963).